The L. L. Bean Guide to the Outdoors

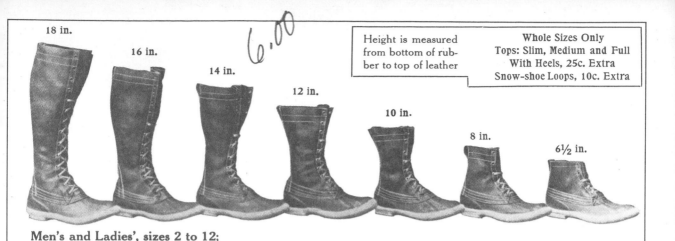

6.00

18 in. 16 in. 14 in. 12 in. 10 in. 8 in. 6½ in.

Height is measured from bottom of rubber to top of leather

Whole Sizes Only
Tops: Slim, Medium and Full
With Heels, 25c. Extra
Snow-shoe Loops, 10c. Extra

Men's and Ladies', sizes 2 to 12;						
$13.75	$11.75	$10.25	$8.75	$7.25	$5.85	$4.50
Boys', sizes 2 to 4;	-	-	6.00	4.75	3.75	3.15
Misses' and Youths', sizes 8 to 1;			-	4.00	3.00	2.25

Showing our different width Hunting Shoes

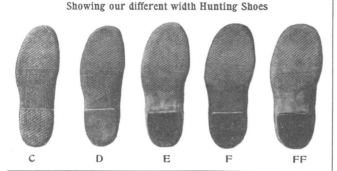

C   D   E   F   FF

15¢ can free with each pair of Hunting Shoes

15¢   25¢   45¢   75¢

This dressing is put up especially for leather-top rubbers, but there is no dressing made that is better for moccasins, heavy work shoes, leather gloves, mittens and harnesses.

FREE
MAINE HUNTING SHOE REPAIR OUTFIT

Consists of can of Water-proof Dressing and Rubber Repair Patches, with cement for applying same.

This Envelope Contains Rubber Repair Patches, Tube of Cement and Emery Paper

DIRECTIONS
Clean parts to be cemented thoroughly with emery paper. Apply the cement to these surfaces and allow to dry two minutes, then press firmly together.
Extra repair outfits, 20¢ each

L. L. BEAN   FREEPORT, MAINE

LADIES' SPORT MOCCASIN

Price $8.75 Delivered free

This shoe is the result of long, careful study to take care of the increasing demand for a practical outing shoe for ladies. It is eleven inches high, water-proof sole and soft, handsome, brown moccasin leather upper. Especially designed for tramping and early fall hunting. It comes in all sizes from 2½ to 8 and in three widths, D, E and EE. It is nearly water proof and a very practical all-around shoe. See guarantee tag on page 3 that is attached to every pair. With every pair we give a can of Bean's Water-proof Dressing. Send for free sample of leather.

L. L. BEAN, FREEPORT, MAINE

The L. L. Bean Guide to the Outdoors

Bill Riviere with the staff of L. L. Bean

Research by Bruce Willard   Illustrated by J. Nicoletti

 Random House   New York

Library of Congress Cataloging in Publication Data
Riviere, William A.
The L. L. Bean guide to the outdoors.
Includes index.
1. Camping—Equipment and supplies. 2. Outdoor recreation—Equipment and supplies. I. Bean (L.L.), Inc. II. Title.
GV191.76.R58   796.54   80-6009
ISBN 0-394-51928-0

Manufactured in the United States of America
98765432
First Edition

Design by Anne Lian

Dedicated to the memory of
Leon Leonwood Bean
1872–1967

Contents

Introduction

My grandfather, Leon L. Bean, was the most enthusiastic outdoorsman I've ever known. I remember fishing with him when I was a little boy and how excited he'd get when I hooked a fish. "L.L." had caught countless trout and salmon in his lifetime, but he'd shout and carry on as if this were the first fish he'd ever seen. Hunting was an equal passion of his. A guide he once had on a caribou hunt on the Gaspé Peninsula of Quebec was asked what kind of a hunter L.L. was. "Fine," he replied. "Only trouble is, you have to keep up with him."

L.L. grew up in the hill country of western Maine during the late nineteenth century. Orphaned at the age of twelve, he had to make his own way working on the farms of friends and relatives. I think he was a natural-born optimist, but this experience fully developed his country boy confidence and genuine affection for people. There are many stories told of his youthful Yankee ingenuity and their common theme is that he made the most of every moment. He particularly enjoyed the time spent hunting and fishing and his early love for the woods and waters of Maine were to last his lifetime.

L.L.'s passion for the outdoors and his ingenuity came together in 1912 when he decided to market his leather-top/rubber-bottom boot. He'd been fooling around with the design for several years and it had kept his feet comfortable and dry on a variety of trips in the back country. He liked his new boots a lot and, being L.L., saw no reason why everyone else who enjoyed the outdoors shouldn't like them as well. Supremely confident, he published his first mail-order booklet, loudly proclaiming the virtues of L. L. Bean's "Maine Hunting Shoe." The public couldn't resist the common-sense logic and undisguised enthusiasm of his appeal. His business was solidly begun.

Business and pleasure became one and the same for my grandfather. His schedule was based on whatever was in season—bird, deer and duck hunting in the fall and winter, and salmon and trout fishing in the spring and summer. His catalogs followed the seasons. L.L. always kept a diary, recording information for future trips and keeping notes on product ideas he liked. These ideas invariably showed up in his catalogs and by the mid-1920s he was offering a complete line of personally tested hunting, fishing and camping equipment.

"No doubt a chief reason for the success of the business," he later wrote, "is the fact that I tried on the trail practically every article I handle. If I tell you a knife is good for cleaning trout, it is because I found it so. If I tell you a wading boot is worth having, very likely you might have seen me testing it out at my Lane's Island duck blind." His convictions, and his uniquely personal and direct way of expressing them, were the genius of his catalog.

In addition, L.L. couldn't do enough to please people. To hear that one of his products failed in the field was a shock to his system. He'd charge around the factory bellowing at anyone in earshot, trying to find an explanation. Then he'd write the customer, return his money, enclose a gift or invite him fishing. That customer was a real person to L.L. and he'd put his trust in the catalog. If he was upset, so was L.L. and, in turn, everyone else in the company until that customer was satisfied.

Anyone who'd ever worked for him could not help being permanently influenced by L.L.'s strong personality, fundamental honesty and compulsive desire to please people. I was no different, being lucky enough to have worked with him for seven years. The important things I've learned about business are based on that experience with L.L.: on his deep-rooted belief in testing products to determine their practical worth, and on his absolute fairness in dealing with people.

Our company is larger now, but we all continue to be active in camping, backpacking, canoeing, hunting, fishing, cross-country skiing and snowshoeing, and outdoor living in general. We want the same emotional commitment to our products that L.L. had and that can only come from actually using them. We won't sell anything that we wouldn't use ourselves. Our people believe in L.L.'s tradition of individual customer service; we are individuals too. Each of us also shares his feeling that the outdoors is the best place to be.

L.L. once said, "To my mind, hunting and fishing is the big lure that takes us into the great open spaces and teaches us to forget the mean and petty things of life." Our sporting activities are the means to that end, our incentive to get back to a more natural environment. A lot has been written on the physical and spiritual rewards of the outdoor life and in more poetic language than L.L. or I could ever achieve. But whatever the language, we feel good when we come upon a wild pitch of white water, the serenity of a winter snowfall, the sparkle of a sunlit morning trail or the flash of a whitetail deer. The wilderness inspires and renews us.

It also needs to be said that the availability of truly natural environments with plenty of fresh air, wildlife and clean water is of critical importance to us all. Their value is profound, obvious in many physical ways, but beyond human comprehension in most. Anyone who has spent much time outdoors knows this. There's no better place to be and we need to keep the natural environments that we have. At a time when the abundance of wildlife was taken for granted and creel or bag limits were not, L.L. once stated, "I am a firm believer in the conservation of all fish and game and the strict enforcement of all game laws." The L. L. Bean Company continues to be deeply committed to maintaining our wildlife populations and our natural environments. All of us who enjoy the outdoors share this responsibility to maintain its natural vitality. In Appendix IV you will find many conservation groups listed, all worthy of your support.

When L.L. wasn't hunting or fishing, he always found time to talk about it. He'd lean back in his chair, put his feet on his desk and swap stories with visiting sportsmen. His advice on equipment and its usage was eagerly sought and he'd just as excitedly give it.

Well-known Maine writers such as Kenneth Roberts, Ben Ames Williams and John Gould were involved in these discussions. They encouraged L.L. to write his own book.

This he did in 1942, "with the sole object not to bore my readers with personal yarns and experiences, but to give definite information in the fewest words possible on how to hunt, fish and camp." True to his word, L.L.'s book was tightly written in 104 pages including lots of pictures. He conservatively claimed it could be read in eighty-five minutes. Over the years L.L.'s *Hunting—Fishing and Camping* sold 200,000 copies at a dollar a copy and he never ceased to brag, "That wan't bad for a boy who never got through the eighth grade."

It wasn't either, though I wish he'd put in more of his personal yarns and experiences. The information, however, was good, simple and direct and that was L.L.'s style. He'd never use a compass, for instance, that "was all cluttered up with figures, lines and ornaments. Who could be bothered with all those other little marks?" His whole approach was to simplify techniques and the paraphernalia that went along with them, so that they didn't get in the way of his enjoyment of the outdoors.

In the forty years that have passed since L.L.'s book was published, many more people have become attracted to the outdoor life. Trip planning has become increasingly important in finding wilderness experiences away from other people. Where this is not possible, outdoors "etiquette" is required to make sure that everyone can enjoy our finite natural environments. In addition, the fragility of our wilderness sites has become clear and conscious attention to maintaining their natural integrity is essential. "Take only photographs and leave only footprints," was recently the motto. Now even footprints are a problem on eroding trails. These issues are fully discussed in several sources mentioned in our appendixes and they deserve your attention.

The theme of this book is that quality outdoors experiences demand quality equipment. It's obviously difficult to enjoy a scenic hike if your feet are wet and blistered. The spontaneity and excitement of a river trip can be greatly hampered if you are constantly patching your canoe. Even your personal safety can be at stake if your equipment fails. You also need to know the types of apparel, equipment and footwear that are appropriate to your activity.

Since L.L.'s time, new designs and technological advances in materials have occurred at an accelerating rate in all categories of outdoor equipment, to meet the demands of today's sophisticated customers. The trends have all been toward gear that is lighter, stronger, more easily maintained and more functional. There has never been a greater assortment of high performance and reliable equipment. At the same time, there has never been a greater assortment of poorly designed and generally inappropriate products.

It's been a challenge at L. L. Bean to convey in our catalogs the background information behind our product selections, to explain why we think, as L.L. did, that our products are the best for the use intended. There's simply not been enough space to describe all the field testing we've done, to discuss the equipment we've rejected and to give the technical perspective within which we make our recommendations.

So we decided it was time to write another book, a book that would guide the outdoors enthusiast through the vast array of equipment and simplify the selection process. Together with our good friend and fellow Maine native, Bill Riviere, we set out several years ago to put this guide together. Bill is a long-time Maine guide and professional outdoorsman. He's spent most of his life in a canoe, on snowshoes, fishing and hunting in Maine, or tramping trails to the north, south and west. Bill knows his equipment. He also knows how to write outdoor books and several of them are listed in our appendix.

Our staff provided Bill with all the information on outdoor equipment and its uses that we've accumulated over the years. This comes from our own experiences in the woods and on the streams of Maine and elsewhere, as well as from the experiences collected from our customers throughout the country. In addition, we solicited and received a lot of technical information and advice from our many excellent suppliers. The initial result was enough material to have brought L.L. to the balls of his feet with a fist-pounding roar.

With the unspoken but quite tangible admonition to be simple and direct, we proceeded to cut and cull as much as we could, consistent with the amount of information we needed to convey. "Personal yarns and experiences" were again minimized. We decided not to discuss technique in any detail because of the many excellent books already written on various outdoor activities. We concentrated on the essentials of design, construction and materials that went into the equipment within our range of knowledge—and on how to use it to best advantage. It's still taken 294 pages "to give definite information in the fewest words possible." Consequently, I'd suggest you not attempt to read our book from cover to cover, but start with the section that interests you most. Then you may want to branch out as your needs and curiosities arise. I think you'll find the chapters give you sufficient information to make informed and intelligent choices of equipment from today's wide assortment. We've used examples of our own products in most cases. Our intent is not commercial, though we obviously think that the products we sell are the best in their categories or we wouldn't carry them. We present them as models for discussion and comparison with others.

Equipment choices should also be more than a comparison of specifications and prices. Once you've determined your specific functional needs, take a look at secondary design and aesthetic features that strike your fancy. Most outdoorspeople take pride in their equipment and develop a style of dress to suit their personalities. This can make the choices fun as well as practical, and add a little bit more to your pleasure outdoors. Always, however, try to obtain the best you can afford. Your time is too valuable to waste on faulty gear.

A further purpose of this book is to encourage you to be selective in what you carry on your trips. Bill Riviere appropriately quotes Henry David Thoreau on several occasions. While L.L. never read *Walden,* he would certainly have agreed that "our life is frittered away by detail . . . simplify, simplify." Simplicity, however, can begin only by knowing what you can do with or without. Our guide may appear to be overly complicated. It actually contains the minimum background knowledge we feel essential in selecting equipment for adequate preparedness and safety margins. Once you gain experience in the outdoors (and begin keeping your own lists), you'll learn how to get the most from your equipment and what details you can do without. With your duffel loaded with only the bare essentials, you are free to enjoy your outdoor adventures.

Preparedness also means staying in reasonably good physical shape. You can cover a lot more ground and put up with more extreme conditions if you've got strong legs and healthy lungs. Many of us at L. L. Bean jog, skip rope, ride bicycles or play racket sports to stay active when we're not outdoors. L.L. used to walk briskly back and forth to work in order to "exercise his legs." Fitness adds to your outdoors experiences just as both add to your life. L.L. lived to be ninety-four, sound of mind and body, and enjoyed every minute of it.

"One thing I learned throughout my lifetime," he wrote in 1960, "is the fact that outdoor recreation, such as hunting, fishing and camping, has added years to my life span, also to the lives of my two companions. For the last sixty years our only hobby has been outdoor recreation. Our ages range from 87 to 88, and all are in good physical condition, and alert. We still enjoy the same sports. The other members of my family, not lovers of the great outdoors, have passed away at an early age. My father and mother both died, a few days apart, at the ages of 43 and 41. These facts prove to me that outdoor life adds years to your life."

LEON A. GORMAN

Foreword

It is one of the major regrets of my life that I never knew Leon Leonwood Bean. Although L.L.—everyone called him that—remained active in the business until his death at age ninety-four in February 1967, my visits to his Freeport, Maine, showroom always managed to coincide with those occasions when he was away, fishing or hunting or rooting for the Red Sox at Fenway Park.

Not that he neglected his business. One reason L. L. Bean, Inc., flourished was because he staffed it with personnel who not only knew outdoors equipment, but also how to use it. You could get pretty solid advice at Freeport even when L.L. was at Merrymeeting Bay duck hunting, in the Maine woods after deer, at Moosehead Lake for trout, or in New Brunswick fishing for Atlantic salmon. You had only to visit the showroom to see that the company was (and still is) in good hands.

This freed him to spend much time afield. Even then, he never really stopped working. He tried out new products constantly and tested the latest in outdoor clothing. Whatever proved its worth went into the catalog; whatever failed he discarded. He often suggested modifications to manufacturers to bring a product up to his standard.

It was this refusal to accept mediocrity that led L.L. to start his business back in 1912. Returning home from the woods one day, he cursed the heavy boots that tortured his feet. Rubber overshoes and wool socks, which he then tried, were not much better. So he enlisted a local cobbler to sew leather uppers to a pair of rubbers, and inserted innersoles with a steel arch-support. His design proved light, waterproof and comfortable. What's more, it provided leg protection against brush and brambles. L.L. had invented the Maine Hunting Shoe®.

With $400 borrowed from his brother Guy, L.L. began turning out the boots in a modest basement "factory," selling them through the mail; his only sales tool was a simple, one-page flyer sent to holders of Maine hunting licenses. The boots were hardly an instant success, however. Of the first hundred pairs sold, ninety were returned. The rubber was too light and tore away from the uppers. L.L. made good on the faulty pairs and turned to perfecting the boot through the use of heavier rubber bottoms. Improvements have continued to this day; L. L. Bean, Inc., now produces more than 100,000 pairs annually, and to date has sold a total exceeding 2 million.

No boots last forever, of course. With characteristic thrift, L.L. advertised that "throw-ing away the good leather uppers of the Maine Hunting Shoe® is like throwing away a five-dollar bill." He urged his customers to return their old boots for new bottoms and for the reconditioning of the uppers. Today the repair room is busier than ever. Close to seven thousand pairs of Maine Hunting Shoes® are rebuilt each year.

Business grew. L.L. added "outdoor specialties"—tents, sleeping bags, camp cutlery, cook kits, fishing tackle, snowshoes and clothing—until his catalog offered just about everything to equip either a single sportsman or an entire expedition. Boot and shoe sales soared, too, with the addition of dozens of styles, all manufactured at L.L.'s rapidly expanding Freeport factory.

The catalogs (early editions are now collector's items) became noted for their terse, straightforward descriptions. L.L. came up with a no-questions-asked guarantee and a quick-refund policy. His philosophy was startlingly simple and successful: "Provide good merchandise at a reasonable price and treat the customer like a human being." No high-sounding phraseology, no glowing adjectives, no rhyming or alliterative catch phrases.

When the showroom opened in 1940, customers were intrigued with the simple wooden showcases, the pipe racks, the mounted fish on the walls, the casually hung antique snowshoes and the sales personnel who wore checkered shirts and moccasins. "We'll stop at Bean's" became a byword among vacationers headed for Maine. They make it an annual pilgrimage, a sort of ritual renewal of the soul with the Great Outdoors. To them, going to Maine without visiting L. L. Bean's is like going to Buffalo without seeing Niagara Falls. Since 1954, the showroom has been open twenty-four hours a day, 365 days a year, and it's not unusual to see the parking lot crowded in the middle of the night.

Not all the mail brought orders for clothing or equipment. L.L. began to receive requests for information and advice on hunting, fishing, camping and canoe trips. L. L. Bean, Inc., began to resemble a branch office of the Maine Publicity Bureau. This kindled a new idea in L.L.'s mind. He became a writer, publishing *Hunting—Fishing and Camping* in 1942. The text was down-to-earth, and the book was, in its time, probably the most concise outdoor manual ever written. It sold close to 200,000 copies before going out of print in 1967. It, too, is now a collector's item.

Over the years, I had reread L.L.'s little book several times, marveling at how much of the woodsmanship described remained valid—even if some of the equipment suggestions were out-of-date. A few years ago, I suggested to Leon Gorman (L.L.'s grandson, who is now president of the company) that I update the book. The idea, he agreed, had possibili-ties.

Meanwhile, in New York, Jason Epstein, a vice-president at Random House, and Angus Cameron, a senior editor at Alfred A. Knopf and a dedicated outdoorsman, had conceived the idea of an *L. L. Bean Guide to the Outdoors*. They put the proposal to Leon Gorman, who liked it. Recalling my proposal to update his grandfather's book, Leon suggested that I write the new version.

Cooperation by the L. L. Bean staff smoothed the way for what was a monumental task. I was given free access to L. L. Bean facilities. I got an outsider's inside view. Whenever I expressed doubt concerning a particular piece of equipment or clothing, it was provided to me for my own evaluation. I sat in with L. L. Bean buyers as they listened to salespeople who wanted to have their products represented in the L. L. Bean catalog. When an item was accepted, it was usually on the condition that it be modified to meet L. L. Bean standards.

I had always considered company "field-testing trips" as little more than vacation junkets for executives, and tax-deductible ones at that. I learned otherwise when I was included on a week-long L. L. Bean product evaluation excursion in the Maine wilds, one of several that run each year. True, some of the best campfire cooking I had ever eaten, two days of running white water, and some pretty fair fishing can be likened to "vacation" activities. You actually hunt, fish, camp, canoe, chop wood or tinker with camp stoves. Nothing about the Bean testing trips smacks of the laboratory. Equipment and clothing are subject to the same use, and abuse, as they are when an L. L. Bean customer takes to the woods with them.

My own experience was a revelation. I learned that my canoe, which I'd considered the finest trip craft available, was decidedly inferior to the new L. L. Bean design. My tent leaked; the Bean tents did not. We saw one tarpaulin shredded by high winds and another that withstood the blow without damage. My "canoe shoes," actually a modern version of old-time Larrigans, bound my feet painfully in the canoe and made toting over the portages torture. I wished I had worn my "Bean boots," as the others in the party had. As for clothing, we were each issued a variety of garments—shirts, trousers, underwear and jackets—only a few of which have since made it to the catalog.

The L. L. Bean Guide to the Outdoors was never a one-man project. Thus the first-person pronoun "I" or "me" appears only in this author's foreword, not in the text that follows. True, my views are reflected throughout, but so is the labor of many others on the Bean staff who answered my seemingly endless questions, researched the technical data, corrected my errors, suggested additions or deletions and frequently accepted my suggestions gracefully. There were numberless conferences at Freeport, and Bean staff members came to my home to assist me.

Some are due special thanks. Leon Gorman, for instance. A man overseeing a $100 million corporation has little time for swapping woods yarns, but he always found time for my visits. Whatever I needed, I got. Leon saw to it.

Then there was Bill End, L. L. Bean's vice-president, an avid hunter, fisherman and canoeist. He generously devoted many hours to consultations and came up with excellent suggestions regarding the organization of the text.

A great debt is owed to Bruce Willard, L. L. Bean's assistant product manager, who was especially helpful with the clothing and footwear chapters, providing me with a detailed outline that incorporated much information only an expert could supply. If these chapters reflect some degree of expertise, it is due primarily to Bruce's input. His efforts went beyond this, however. While continuing his regular duties, Bruce conducted extensive research on products about which I had doubts. He also supervised the production of the illustrations, working on his own time with Joe Nicoletti, the artist, thus assuring the technical accuracy of the drawings. Without Bruce's unstinting efforts, the production of this book would certainly have faltered.

Also, there was Angus Cameron. His phone bill must have been astronomical. His calls were frequent and lengthy, not aimed at driving me to greater production but rather toward guiding me with the general tone of the book. His assistance was invaluable.

Special thanks are due Rob Cowley, my editor at Random House. Throughout page after page of the manuscript, he made repairs where I and my typewriter had run roughshod over the rules of English grammar and punctuation. He rounded up hyphens I had scattered and he mended numerous infinitives I had splintered. Where the text reads smoothly, Rob is due credit for it.

I am most indebted, however, to my wife Eleanor. She, too, proofread and corrected the manuscript and the subsequent galley proofs. More important, though, as the work progressed over the months, and the years, it was with patience, understanding and encouragement that she so often intervened when I was ready to chuck it all. Without her support, I would surely have bogged down.

I have long believed that when the time comes, any person appearing at the Pearly Gates should be given an alternative destination—the state of Maine. What's more, those who have led exemplary lives should also be awarded an eternal, automatically renewable, unlimited L. L. Bean gift certificate.

BILL RIVIERE
January 1981

The L. L. Bean
Guide to the
Outdoors

Chapter 1

Into the Backcountry: You and the Weather

Most of us enjoy the outdoors, but usually for different reasons. To some, it represents the challenge of running a wild pitch of white water, or scaling a mountain peak under a winter sky. Others take a more leisurely approach. For them, the outdoors offers a chance to return to simplicity—to pitch a tent in a lakeshore pine grove, to savor the aroma of a campfire's woodsmoke at evening, to taste meals cooked in blackened pots.

To still others, the outdoors brings to mind winding woods trails where red-cap moss clings to decaying logs, partridge berries hide under leaves that glisten in the mottled sunlight, and a pink lady's slipper hangs its head in the shade.

A fisherman's favorite vision of the outdoors is a fat trout rolling in a foam-flecked pool; the hunter's, a ten-point buck bounding away with its white flag at full mast. A cross-country skier conjures up pristine snow, the silence broken only by the muffled swish of skis as the landscape slips by. No matter what your approach, the rewards are, in a sense, custom-made. Whatever you seek—adventure, serenity, respite—the outdoors will provide it.

Of course, this doesn't just happen. Planning is required. Variations in weather and terrain will govern your activities and dictate your choice of clothing and equipment. In rugged mountains, the light footwear so well adapted to canoeing won't do. You'll need trail boots for traction and support. Clothing must be adaptable: it may be 85 degrees along the approach trail, but once above the tree line, chilling winds and moist clouds sweep the barren ledges. And you'll need a lightweight tent that will withstand high winds, and a compact sleeping bag.

By way of contrast, a July canoe trip along a placid river with no portages en route places only limited restrictions on you. Footwear is not critical, and clothing (except for rainwear) need not be specialized; you can even include a few luxuries forbidden to the mountain backpacker. However, if you're in parts of Canada or the northeastern states, you'd better take along a mosquito-proof tent.

Weather is the governing factor for all outdoor activities. When it's stable, contending with it is easy. However, weather is rarely stable. Conditions may change daily, even hourly, and certainly seasonally. To assume that the sun will shine and that only gentle breezes will blow throughout your trip is asking for trouble. Learn to expect the unexpected.

PLANNING AHEAD FOR WEATHER

Even in the relatively small northeastern states, climatic conditions can vary tremendously on any given day. Most New Hampshire residents know, for example, that while they are basking in mild weather in the Merrimack River Valley, the summit of 6,280-foot Mount Washington may witness severe winds and temperatures as low as the record of 8 degrees in June. Manhattan's residents live in a climate quite unlike that of Mount Whiteface in the Adirondacks. In the larger states and the Canadian provinces, the variations are even more pronounced. Toronto's climate can be likened to that of the American Midwest while James Bay, several hundred miles north, is a subarctic environment.

You can safely conclude, then, that the farther you travel from home, the more likely you are to encounter weather conditions quite unlike those to which you are accustomed. The change may not be adverse, of course. If you're a Pennsylvanian who wants to explore Okefenokee Swamp in February, the southern climate will no doubt delight you. But it will be a change. And you'll want to plan for it with regard to your clothing and equipment.

For any extended outing, obtain accurate advance information about the area you plan to visit, particularly about its weather and terrain. Chamber of Commerce booklets are rarely of help, since they are mainly devoted to describing the "bounteous beauties and unlimited recreational opportunities" of their respective areas. Publications issued by state and provincial fish and game departments are likely to be much more helpful. But there is probably no better source of information than an experienced outdoorsman living in the region you plan to visit. Guides and outfitters, too, will supply accurate and relevant advice.

Government weather services in both the United States and Canada publish, on a regional basis, records of mean/maximum-minimum rainfalls, snowfalls and wind velocities, as well as of temperatures. Booklets outlining the special climatic features and topography of each area are also available. (See the Appendix.) These reports can be extremely helpful. None will guarantee you a sunny sky on August 21 of any given year on the arctic coast of the Northwest Territories, but they can warn you that snow squalls are a possibility and that temperatures of 80 degrees can occur. Thus, no matter where you plan to travel in the United States or Canada, you can be well posted in advance of the weather prospects.

Remember that while such climatic reports are helpful in planning a trip, they can't tell what the weather will be once you arrive. Nor should you depend entirely on a portable radio. The weather forecasts usually cover too wide an area, sometimes several states. Weather systems are often erratic. A storm may dump two inches of rain on part of the forecast area, yet a few miles away it may cause only a drizzle or a heavy overcast. On the other hand, a forecast of "cloudiness" may fail to mention the possibility of a blizzard in the mountains.

Weather, good or bad, rarely approaches without some warning signs, such as wind shifts and cloud formations. And there are dozens of other natural signs that you can monitor to predict weather in a specific area for twelve to twenty-four hours to come.

PREDICTING WEATHER

It stands to reason that men who live close to the weather understand it best—seamen, farmers, trappers and loggers, whose work is subject to its whims. Long before the advent of government forecasting services, it was they who observed the natural signs—and they who composed some of the early weather rhymes which, while not infallible, are remarkably accurate. Early sportsmen, too, took to rhyming their forecasts. Wind was of special significance to the seventeenth-century naturalist Izaak Walton, and the following couplets are attributed to him:

> When the wind is in the North
> The skillful fisherman goes not forth;
>
> When the wind is in the East
> 'Tis good for neither man nor beast;
>
> When the wind is in the South
> It blows the flies in the fish's mouth;
>
> When the wind is in the West
> There it is the very best.

While this three-hundred-year-old rhyme may be lacking in literary finesse, many fishermen adhere to its advice. A blow out of the north, they know, is generally brisk, blustery and cool, often too much so for comfort, especially in a small boat. A south wind often precedes rain in the summer and will start fish feeding, especially trout and salmon. When such a wind arises, guides will head for the north side of a lake and troll close to shore for some lively fishing. In the winter, the south wind may result in a cold rain or perhaps a January thaw. As a storm progresses, circulating winds may shift into the east and northeast, culminating in heavy rain or snow and increased velocities. This is the "nor'easter," rarely a gentle storm.

One thing is certain: the weather will not change until there is a shift in the wind. Don't look for a nor'easter to abate so long as the wind howls out of the northeast, not even if it drops somewhat. Only when the wind shifts toward the west will the storm end. Wind, while a prime indicator of weather, is most reliable when used in conjunction with a barometer.

Early seafarers were among the first to understand this and to adopt the barometer aboard ship. This instrument consisted of a mercury-filled tube, gimbal-mounted to compensate for the ship's rolling and pitching. Atmospheric pressure caused the mercury to rise or fall within the thirty-two-inch tube that was marked in increments of one tenth of an inch.

The mercurial barometer has been largely replaced by the aneroid type, which is more compact, less expensive and equally accurate. Activated by a flexible vacuum chamber and a springlike device, the needle moves "up" or "down" on a circular scale which, like the old-time seaman's barometer, is graduated into tenths, or sometimes hundreths, of an inch. Combination barometer/altimeters small enough to fit into a jacket pocket are now available. While not all outdoorsmen carry one, it's a worthwhile instrument if you're serious about knowing what tomorrow's weather will be in the backcountry. In a woods cabin, a wall barometer will help you plan the next day's activities.

Barometric pressure is greatest at sea level because air, which has weight, is densest there. As a reference point, barometric pressure has been established at sea level at a mean 29.92 inches. As you move to higher ground, the air becomes thinner and lighter; hence, the pressure drops. (This is the reason pocket barometers can be used as altimeters.) When you first buy the barometer, though, adjust it for your altitude by raising its reading one tenth of an inch for each ninety-two feet of elevation, or roughly one inch per one thousand feet. Most aneroid barometers have an adjustment screw on the back for this purpose.

Pocket Barometer/Altimeter

Why, then, does barometric pressure vary even when the instrument is not moved? Simply because atmospheric pressure is not consistent. There are "highs" and "lows." Any reading below 29.92 inches is considered a low, generally indicating the proximity of a storm. A reading above this point is a high, usually signaling fair weather.

To visualize a high, try to imagine a huge dome, perhaps one thousand miles across and rising thousands of feet, with winds circulating in a clockwise direction, thrusting outward from the center. The air is dry and clouds are few, or are clearing.

By way of contrast, a low is a depression, an inverted dome into which clouds, rain or snow funnel. Humidity is high and the winds circulate in a counterclockwise direction. This is a storm system, and the lower the pressure the greater the storm's intensity.

Both high and low systems generally move in a northeasterly direction across the country, although they may occasionally slip directly eastward or even somewhat to the southeast.

A rising barometer with the wind shifting into the west is a sure sign of immediate good weather. In contrast, a falling barometer and an easterly wind portend no good. However, forecasts with a barometer and wind directions are not always this cut and dried. There are variations between the two extremes. The U.S. Coast Guard has compiled a Wind-Barometer Chart covering these variations. If you have a backwoods cabin, copy the chart and post it on the wall next to your barometer, or if you carry a pocket barometer on your trips, keep a copy of the chart in your outfit. You'll never again be surprised by a "sudden" storm.

Wind-Barometer Chart

Wind Shift	*Barometer Reading*	*Coming Weather*
SW to NW	30.10 to 30.20 and steady	Fair with slight temperature changes in one or two days
SW to NW	30.10 to 30.20 and rising rapidly	Fair, followed within two days by rain
SW to NW	30.20 and above and stationary	Continued fair with no decided temperature change
SW to NW	30.20 and above and falling slowly	Slowly rising temperature and fair for two days
S to SE	30.10 to 30.20 and falling slowly	Rain within twenty-four hours

S to SE	30.10 to 30.20 and falling rapidly	Wind increasing, rain within twelve to twenty-four hours
SE to NE	30.10 to 30.20 and falling slowly	Rain in twelve to twenty-four hours
SE to NE	30.10 to 30.20 and falling rapidly	Increasing winds, rain within twelve hours
E to NE	30.10 and above and falling slowly	In summer, with light winds, rain may not fall for several days; in winter, rain or snow in twenty-four hours
E to NE	30.10 and above and falling fast	In summer, rain probably within twelve hours; in winter, rain or snow with increasing winds
SE to NE	30.00 or below and falling slowly	Rain will continue one to two days
SE to NE	30.00 or below and falling rapidly	Rain with high wind followed within thirty-six hours by clearing, and in winter, cold
S to SW	30.00 or below and rising slowly	Clearing in a few hours, fair for several days
S to E	29.80 or below and falling rapidly	Severe storm imminent, followed in twenty-four hours by clearing, and in winter, cold
E to NE	29.80 or below and falling rapidly	Severe NE gale and heavy rain; in winter heavy snow and cold wave
Shifting to W	29.80 or below and rising rapidly	Clearing and colder

Note: All readings are at sea level. Add one tenth of an inch for every ninety-two feet at your location.

Homespun Weather Forecasting

It's interesting to note that old-time seamen, who had no such chart to guide them, understood the implications of wind/pressure combinations. Referring to their barometer as "the glass," they devised this rhyme:

When the glass falls low, prepare for a blow;
When it rises high, let all your kites* fly.

And the rate of barometric change was noted, too:

Long falling, long last;
Short notice, soon past.

While wind and atmospheric pressure are vital elements of weather forecasting, other natural signs are tip-offs. The color of the rising sun is a perfect example. From this came one of the best-known of weather rhymes:

Red sky at morning, sailors take warning;
Red sky at night, sailors' delight.

The "red sky at morning" refers to sunrise colors, with the sun a dull maroon sphere, usually rising among gray clouds. You can bet on rain or snow before the day is out. "Red sky at night" applies to sunsets. During a heat wave, the sun may set as a huge red ball, its brilliance dulled by haze, a sure indication that the heat wave will continue. In the fall, a clear western sky may be colored brilliantly by the setting sun, a sign of more good weather.

Even rainbows augur localized changes in weather, usually during periods of showers. There are ancient rhymes for these, too—one version for landsmen, another for seafarers:

Rainbow in the morning, shepherds take warning;
Rainbow at night, shepherds' delight.

Rainbow to windward, foul fall the day;
Rainbow to leeward, damp runs away.

Since storms move from west to east, a "rainbow in the morning" is created by the sun shining through rain clouds in the west. These are headed toward you. A "rainbow at night"—actually late in the afternoon—results from sunlight shining through showers in the east. These have already passed.

A favorite nocturnal sign, the "ring around the moon," is created by moonlight shining through the ice crystals that make up high cirrus clouds. Since these are often the forerunners of rain or snow, the ring is simply corroboration. Folklore has it that the larger the ring, the sooner the storm; that the number of stars visible within the ring indicates the number of days before the storm's arrival or the number of days it will last. All are old wives' tales.

---

* "Kites" were the topsails of sailing vessels.

Clouds

Clouds are eloquent messengers. Their relative elevation, shape, size and even color have long been recognized as indicators of developing weather patterns. At least one early weather rhyme covered the subject:

> Mackerel scales and mares' tails
> Make lofty ships carry low sails.

The "mackerel scales" are cirrocumulus clouds arrayed in a mottled pattern resembling fish scales. High above these there may appear "mares' tails"—wispy, elongated, white cirrus clouds, their ends swept upward, and flying at great speeds (although due to the great altitude, often 20,000 feet or more, this is not readily apparent). When you see these clouds in combination with the "mackerel scales," check your barometer. Chances are it's falling, or it will soon, with rain or snow to follow within twenty-four to forty-eight hours.

Recognizing the various cloud formations is not difficult, nor should their Latin names deter you from becoming your own weather forecaster. Basically, there are only three types: cumulus—white, fluffy puffballs, typical of a fair summer day; stratus—elongated layers, sometimes in a series of rolls, and usually dark gray; and cirrus—ice crystals at high altitude. All other clouds are combinations or variations of these, which can be further divided into: high (20,000 feet or more); middle (6,500 to 20,000 feet); and low (under 6,500 feet).

The high clouds are:

Cirrus: detached wisps, hairlike or fibrous, formed of delicate filaments—the mares' tails. When distributed widely in scattered patches, they usually portend fair weather. When thick, you can expect rain within twenty-four hours.

Cirrus

Cirrostratus: transparent, whitish voile of fibrous or smooth appearance, covering all or part of the sky, and producing a halo phenomenon popularly known as "sun dog." When followed by an approaching bank of altostratus, a warm front is on its way.

Cirrostratus

Cirrocumulus: thin, white, grainy and rippled patches, sheets or layers, showing slight vertical development in the form of turrets and towers. These clouds often increase in size throughout the day and disperse at night. They are generally a sign of fair weather, although in the summer they may develop vertically during the afternoon, indicating a brief shower or thunderstorm.

Cirrocumulus

Among the middle clouds, there are only two:

Altostratus: a grayish layer of uniform, striated fibrous appearance, they cover all or part of the sky, and are composed of water droplets, ice crystals, snowflakes. They are thin enough in parts to reveal the sun vaguely as through ground glass—hence the layman's term, "ground-glass sky." Precipitation is likely within twelve hours.

Altostratus

Altocumulus: most often seen as an extensive sheet of regularly arranged cloudlets, white and gray, and somewhat rounded. Sometimes they appear in parallel rolls separated by lanes, and, rarely, in a honeycomb pattern, in which ragged holes alternate with cloudlets. Ice crystals form at low temperatures. These clouds are often a sign of unsettled weather or an approaching front.

Altocumulus

And finally, the three low clouds:

Stratus: a low-lying gray layer with a rather uniform base, often opaque enough to mask the sun; they produce drizzle, ice prisms or snow grains. Stratus clouds are sometimes formed by lifting fog. These are the clouds, gray and ominous, which obliterate hilltops and which seem to hover only a few feet above a lake or the sea.

Stratus

Nimbostratus: a dark gray cloud layer, thick enough to blot out the sun. It brings continuous rain or snow. Nimbostratus clouds often result from a flow of warm air from the south into a northern region of cold air. They usually portend longer periods of inclement weather, particularly when seen in conjunction with east or southeast winds.

Nimbostratus

Stratocumulus: gray and whitish, non-fibrous, they are like altocumulus but lower; in cold weather they contain a larger element of water droplets. This formation threatens an almost immediate storm, and if it is part of an approaching cold front, it produces gusty winds and possibly a thunderstorm.

Stratocumulus

Even a cloudless day is a weather sign. A clear sky with only a light breeze and mild temperatures is known among old hands in the outdoors as a "weather breeder." Actually, it results from unstable air that has cleared away haze, dust and pollution, and is quite likely to be followed by rain. Occasionally, however, a "weather breeder" may persist for a number of days.

Fog

Probably more rhymes have been written about fog than about any other aspect of weather, two of the most descriptive being:

> Evening fog will not burn soon;
> Morning fog will burn 'fore noon.
>
> Fog that starts before night,
> Will last beyond the morning light.

Fog is simply a stratus cloud lying close to the ground. Following a warm day, it is the result of rapid cooling of land and water surfaces. Fog generated at night bodes fair weather. But if it forms during the day, a storm system is en route. Early morning fog is common in the North, particularly in September and early October as warm waters of lakes and rivers are cooled by the chilly night air. This fog will burn off as the sun rises higher or " 'fore noon."

Dew

Dew, or lack of it, is a good weather indicator. It's simply the condensation of moisture in the air when the relative humidity close to the ground reaches 100 percent. During an overnight canoe trip, feel your overturned craft after you get up in the morning. If it is wet, plan on a good day. This is dew and there will be no rain. However, if it's dry, keep your raingear handy. The same is true at night. A dry canoe means rain before daylight.

Smoke and Sounds

You may hesitate to place complete confidence in any one natural weather sign but, when a number of them are observed, they frequently corroborate each other. Some seemingly minor indications are helpful in this respect. Take the behavior of smoke. When smoke rises into the sky and is quickly dissipated, it's under the influence of a high-pressure system which, in turn, portends good weather. However, when campfire smoke settles downward, seeping into low places, it is because of the prevalence of a low-pressure system; bad weather on the way.

An old English weather rhyme combines smoke's behavior and wind as an indicator:

> When smoke goes west, gude weather is past;
> When smoke goes east, gude weather is neist.

Despite the quaint spelling, the message is clear. Smoke going west is borne on an east wind, the forerunner of foul weather; smoke going east is carried by a fair-weather westerly wind.

Sounds also contribute to forecasting. Under a lowering canopy of clouds on a calm day, sounds carry great distances, frequently with a hollow ring. Decreasing atmospheric pressure gives sound waves increased range, hence a distant train whistle or the shouting of children across a lake can be clearly audible. Rain or snow often follows within twelve hours.

No rhymes seem to have been devised with regard to odors but experienced woodsmen and farmers have long supported the notion that you can "smell" rain coming. Lowering pressures release swamp and marsh gases, cooking smells travel farther, a skunk's presence is more perceptible and even hunting dogs work more efficiently.

With today's use of computers and satellites in weather forecasting, citing the behavior of animals, birds and insects may bring sneers. Yet early farmers, woodsmen and seamen swore by it, not as an infallible sign, but as corroborative evidence. Some of these signs include the following:

- Deer and elk head for low country as a storm approaches.
- When birds of long flight hang about home, expect a storm.
- Bats flying late in the evening indicate fair weather. Bats that "speak" while flying tell of rain tomorrow.
- Milkweed closing at night indicates rain. The pitcher plant "opens its mouth" before a rain.

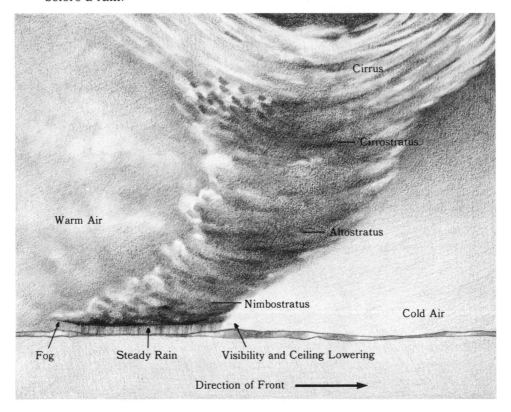

A warm front moving over a land mass. Note the progression of clouds as the warm air and rain approach. Unlike a cold front, warm fronts generally develop slowly, the actual progression of clouds taking up to twenty-four hours.

Homespun weather forecasting is often likened to folklore. It is no such thing. Folklore usually involves superstition. Early weather lore was not based on this but, rather, on a close and perceptive observation.

Thunderstorms

At any given moment some 1,800 thunderstorms are in progress somewhere on earth. Despite this, the odds that you will escape being struck by lightning are overwhelmingly in your favor—providing that you take common-sense precautions. No other natural phenomenon gives clearer warnings. Don't disregard them.

Thunderstorms approach from the west or northwest; their courses are usually easterly or southeasterly. When you observe one to the north, south or east of your position, that thunderstorm will do little more than graze you. A storm to the east

Cumulonimbus

has gone by, and contrary to some beliefs, it cannot turn around and come back.

It may seem strange that the violence of thunderstorms evolves from friendly cumulus clouds on a pleasant summer day. But when the temperature and humidity are high, the puffball cumulus clouds begin to tower, developing vertically. As this process goes on, the clouds attain a cumulonimbus status—the undersides darken and the tops soar up to 25,000 feet to form an "anvil top."

The cause is humid air, heated at the earth's surface, rising until it reaches altitudes cool enough to condense its moisture into cumulus clouds. The earth's warming effect varies from area to area so that the air rises unevenly. Also, it is unstable. Its condensation rate varies. Tremendous winds are created by air being sucked into the base of the rising air mass. These winds can attain hurricane force.

Another type of thunderstorm is the frontal variety, which can occur at any time of day or night, even in winter; it is created by a cold front moving into a region of warm air. The cold atmosphere lifts the warm air by sliding under it, forcing it to cooling altitudes, there to condense and form cumulonimbus clouds. This process may form a series of thunderstorms moving abreast along a line several hundred miles long. Such storms, however, are less common than the localized ones oc-curring on hot, humid summer days.

Thunderstorms present a double-barreled threat: high winds and lightning. Lightning carries currents that may peak at 200,000 amperes, and is capable of totally disintegrating nonconductors and semiconductors such as wood or brick. Prominent objects in exposed areas, such as a small boat or canoe in the middle of a lake, are prime targets. If you're caught out as a storm approaches, it's safest to flee northward or southward, to one side of the storm's path. Running before it should be your last resort. Even then, unless you have a good head start, the storm could well overtake you.

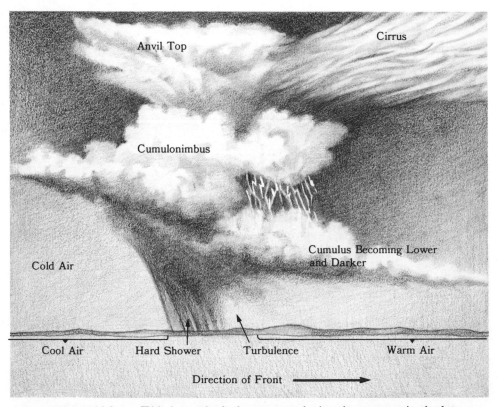

Approaching cold front. This is particularly common during the summer in the late afternoon. Note darkening cumulus clouds and vertical development into cumulonimbus.

Other danger spots are mountainous barrens above timberline or large clearings at lower elevations. Fire lookout towers and peaks should be avoided. A slope between two peaks, while not ideal is preferable. A gully or stream bed can be dangerous since they may serve as pathways for electrical currents that travel through the ground. Shallow caves, seemingly a logical haven, are also hazardous because currents can jump from the roof to the floor. In a pinch, with no safe shelter at hand, discard your metal packframe if you're carrying one and leave it at some distance—at least a few hundred feet. Don your raingear and crouch down.

In the woods, seek the shelter of a stand of even-growth timber, even scrub brush, but never close to, or under, a dominant tree. If you want to play the odds, it's been determined that oaks are struck most frequently, followed by elm, poplar, pine, ash and maple, in that order. Folklore has it that the American beech is rarely, if ever, struck. Don't bank on it!

On-the-Trail Forecasting

While natural signs and early weather rhymes can be remarkably accurate, relying on them calls for close observation and correct interpretation. With practice, you can develop this skill. However, for those who spend only an occasional weekend outdoors, "mare's tails and mackerel scales" may prove difficult to identify and interpret.

Portable weather instruments such as a compass (to establish wind directions and shifts) and a pocket barometer/altimeter can be helpful, especially when used with the chart on pages 7–8. However, you can develop skill as a weather forecaster simply by noting natural signs about you. Ask yourself the following questions:

- From which direction is the wind coming? Has it switched within the last six hours?
- Have there been any marked changes in barometric pressure? Are they gradual or rapid?
- What types of clouds can you see? Have they appeared in any particular sequence, such as high clouds followed by middle clouds that would indicate an approaching front? Are they developing vertically, the sign of an afternoon shower or thunderstorm?
- Is it humid or dry? Remember the significance of dew.

A number of portable weather computers, developed recently, are valuable in areas where local weather patterns are unfamiliar. Among them are the Sager Weathercaster®, Pocket Weather Trends® and Taylor's Weather Forecast Computer®. Each translates your observations into a six-to-twelve-hour forecast for your immediate area, a thirty-to-fifty-mile radius. They vary slightly in size and most require the use of a pocket barometer.

WEATHERING THE OUTDOORS

The body's normal core temperature is 98.6 degrees Fahrenheit (37 Celsius). Whenever that temperature strays above or below this point, hyperthermia (over-heating) or hypothermia (excessive cooling) can result. As long as the weather is mild and dry, the body can easily maintain its normal temperature. However, once the thermometer registers above or below the benign 70 to 80 degree range, the body must either speed up the cooling process or conserve or add heat to maintain comfort.

While the body absorbs heat from external sources such as the sun or a brisk campfire, metabolism—the burning and converting of food to energy—is its main source of heat. Activity such as chopping wood or packing up a steep slope can increase the metabolism rate and boost heat productivity by as much as 750 percent.

The body also loses heat in four ways: through convection, conduction, radiation and evaporation.

Convective heat loss results from the flow of air next to your skin. Since this air is usually colder than your skin temperature, it draws heat and whisks it away. Clothing, which reduces the flow of air over your skin, holds down convective heat loss.

Conduction, as the word implies, means simply that heat is conducted from the body to another element upon contact. When a deer hunter sits on the ground, or when a canoeist perches himself on the seat of an aluminum canoe, body heat is carried off by conduction. Clothing, foam pads under sleeping bags, and sheepskin innersoles help minimize such loss.

To understand loss by radiation, think of your body as a room radiator. It radiates warmth in the same manner. The rate of heat loss depends on the differ-ence between the body's temperature and that of the surrounding atmosphere. As this difference increases, proportionately more heat is lost. Radiation accounts for up to 50 percent of your total heat loss, much of it through the head. When your head is protected by some sort of hat, the body will direct its heat elsewhere, to the hands and feet, for example. Hence the adage, "If your feet are cold, put on a hat."

Evaporational heat loss comes from sweating and the involuntary process known as insensible perspiration. Even when we are inactive, the body passes off about one-and-a-half pints of moisture a day. This moisture is a natural by-product of metabolism. Heat, of course, is lost with the moisture. Some is dispelled through exhaling warm air, but a greater percentage is lost through the continu-ous drying of the skin.

Sweating, not to be confused with insensible perspiration, occurs when the body generates more heat than it can dispel through the normal processes of convection, conduction and radiation. In warm weather, sweating is beneficial in that it helps the dispersal of excess heat. In cold weather, sweating is detrimental to comfort and is usually the result of wearing improper clothing. Heat loss then becomes difficult to control.

Normally, when ambient temperatures are not severe, the body can balance heat gain and loss, the heart pumping blood and warmth throughout the body, each part getting its share. However, when heat loss begins to exceed heat production, the core temperature—that of the torso and head—is in danger of dropping. This triggers vasoconstriction, the constricting of blood vessels that carry heat to the arms, hands, legs and feet. This reduces the amount of warmth delivered to these extremities, conserving it for the torso and head.

On the other hand, when heat production exceeds loss, vasodilatation takes over. The blood vessels become slightly dilatated, thus encouraging the delivery of heat to the extremities. Sweating accompanies the process.

But you can't rely entirely on the process of vasoconstriction and vasodilatation. It's up to you to balance the comfort equation. In cold weather, increase heat production and slow heat loss; in warm weather, accelerate that loss.

Wind and Water

Wind greatly accelerates convective heat loss. For example, at 40 degrees Fahrenheit with a fifteen-mile-per-hour wind blowing, the effect on the body equals that of a 25 degree temperature. This has come to be known as the wind-chill factor, often mentioned by TV weathermen during wintertime forecasts. The following chart illustrates the effective temperature resulting from combinations of actual temperatures and wind speeds. The chart is helpful for determining the amount of protection needed for exposed flesh—the face and hands, for example. The danger of frostbite—freezing of the flesh—indicated in the chart can be eliminated or at least minimized by wearing facemasks, heavy mittens and proper footwear.

Just as wind accelerates heat loss through convection, so does moisture through conduction. Water not only nullifies the insulation value of most clothing but it also readily conducts heat away from the skin, causing further chilling through convection and evaporation. This is why a wet T-shirt feels so cold on a windy day, even when the temperature is 70. The rate of heat loss through wet clothing can be 240 times that lost while wearing dry clothing. Wet clothing, therefore, can be termed one of the most frequent causes of hypothermia.

Some years ago, a young rock climber became stranded on a ledge on New Hampshire's Cannon Mountain. His partner, unable to extricate him, went for help. By the time rescuers were alerted, it was almost dark. In the meantime, the stranded climber huddled in light clothing as rain began to fall and the temperature dropped into the upper forties. When help finally arrived the next morning, he was dead. The press reported that he had died of "exposure", which was certainly true. More correctly, however, his killer had been hypothermia.

Wind Chill Table

Thermometer Reading (°F)

MPH	Wind speed	50	40	30	20	10	0	−10	−20	−30	−40	−50
0	no movement			wind chill equals thermometer reading								
10	feel breeze on face	40	28	16	4	−9	−21	−33	−46	−58	−70	−83
15	moderate breeze	36	22	9	−5	−18	−36	−45	−58	−72	−85	−99
20	small branches move	32	18	4	−10	−25	−39	−53	−67	−82	−96	−110
25	strong breeze	30	16	0	−15	−29	−44	−59	−74	−88	−104	−118
30	large branches move	28	13	−2	−18	−33	−48	−63	−79	−94	−109	−125
40	gale	26	10	−6	−21	−37	−53	−69	−85	−100	−116	−132

little danger if   danger to   frostbite danger—use
clothed properly   exposed flesh   extreme caution

Hypothermia results from the lowering of the body's inner-core temperature. The greater the drop in the body's temperature, the more severe the effects. The initial symptom is shivering, one of the body's ways of producing warmth. Unless steps are taken to warm the victim, the shivering accelerates, speech becomes slurred and muscles stiffen. This is followed by impairment of judgment; shivering ceases, unconsciousness follows. Death occurs when the core temperature drops to approximately 80 degrees.

Death by hypothermia is often associated with mountaineering or arctic exploration. However, it is most common in boating accidents. In the North, during the weeks following ice-out when water temperatures may be under 40 degrees, a person may die within fifteen minutes. Even if rescued from the cold water immediately, the victim's condition may continue to deteriorate unless he is warmed without delay. Nor do you need to fall overboard to become a candidate for hypothermia. Excessive sweating that wets your clothing may produce the same effects, particularly if you are physically weary and you have no dry clothing into which to change. And this can happen even when temperatures are in the fifties.

Obviously, the most effective way to avoid hypothermia is to remain dry. Carry suitable outerwear when there is even the remotest chance that you might be caught in a rainstorm on an exposed mountain ridge. And, when canoeing or kayaking during the spring run-off, wear a wet suit and take along a change of dry clothing.

Chapter 2

Clothing: Comfort Through Thick and Thin

It's second nature to adjust your clothes when you feel a chill or when you begin to overheat. You unbutton your collar or roll up your sleeves to cool off, or snug up your jacket to ward off the cold. But beyond these obvious fine tunings, you need a system of dress that allows you to adapt to the weather and to your level of exertion. The most effective method is known as "layering."

Layering involves wearing a number of complementary lightweight garments rather than one or two bulky ones. Comfort—a reasonable balance between heat loss and gain—is achieved by removing or adding layers as required; the system is equally effective in warm or cold weather.

To remain reasonably cool while climbing a wooded trail on a hot July day, peel down—remove your shirt and perhaps your undershirt. Then, at midafternoon, the trail emerges above the tree line onto a barren ridge; the wind out of the northwest is brisk and cold. Put your undershirt and shirt back on, and add a light wool sweater. You might top them off with a windproof nylon shell. That's layering.

Skiing cross-country over varied terrain, it's easy to work up a sweat. It may be bitterly cold, but fishnet underwear and a light wool shirt are probably adequate protection as long as you're active. However, perspiration may be building up, so you ventilate, opening your collar and cuffs. You even remove your hat. The miles slip by. Come noon, it's time for a trailside lunch. You feel the cold for the first time since you started out. Button up and put your hat back on. If that's not enough, reach into your pack for a poplin pullover and flip up the hood. The chill is gone. That's layering.

Each layer must provide warmth and ventilation without hindering mobility, all the while adding as little weight as possible. Of course, with a twenty-ounce wool stag shirt and a sweater, plus a down parka, you might withstand an icy blast all the way from Hudson Bay. You'll be warm, but it will be difficult to adjust your dress if you become overheated. What's more, the bulk will hinder your move-

The Layering System

ments. A better combination might include fishnet underwear, a light wool shirt, a thin wool sweater and a windproof shell. These will give you comparable warmth and allow you to move about more freely. Remember that fit will affect the efficiency of layering. Clothing worn closest to the body should conform well to body contours without binding. Outer garments may be looser.

There's nothing new about the layering concept. More than forty years ago, when L.L. used to disappear for the better part of the hunting season, he called it "onionization." It was his claim that onionization not only kept him comfortable but helped to get him home each night. In the morning, before he left the hunting camp he called the Dew Drop Inn, he'd layer up with as many as six or seven lightweight wool shirts and sweaters. As the sun warmed the woods, he would peel off a layer and hang it on a tree limb. By midafternoon, when it started to turn chilly, he would be down to two layers. The time had come to head back, and he would follow his trail of shirts and sweaters, putting on one after another until he was fully dressed and back in camp.

FIBERS AND FABRICS

Although layering provides a way to adapt to variations in weather and activity, the effectiveness of the system depends as much on the properties of the fibers/

fabrics that make up each layer. These fibers/fabrics not only determine how well each layer deals with the four major types of weather—cold/dry, cold/wet, warm/dry and warm/wet—but they also influence breathability, water and wind resistance, and washability of the garments.

In the layers closest to the body, breathability and absorption are key considerations. The fibers/fabrics next to the skin must allow excess heat to be released and perspiration to be absorbed or wicked to outer layers of clothing. Absorption is generally governed by the type of fibers in a fabric. Natural fibers tend to absorb and hold moisture, while synthetics transfer (wick) it away from the skin to the outer layers. Breathability is governed by a fabric's construction. Open weave and knit fabrics allow the freest passage of moisture; tightly woven fabrics do not generally breathe as well.

Among secondary layers such as shirts, trousers, sweaters and vests, warmth, strength and, to a lesser degree, weight are the key considerations. Warmth is determined by the volume of dead air trapped around the body. In any piece of clothing, that volume is largely governed by fabric thickness. There is no hard and fast rule for determining the thickness required: too many variables exist, such as your metabolism rate and the fit of the clothing. However, the following chart, devised by the U.S. Army Corps of Engineers, translates temperatures into suggested thicknesses of insulation for various activities. The figures do not take into account the cooling effect of wind and they should be considered merely as guidelines:

	Insulation Required for Comfort (inches)		
Temperature (F)	*Sleeping*	*Light Work*	*Heavy Work*
40°	1.5	.8	.20
20°	2.0	1.0	.27
0°	2.5	1.3	.35
−20°	3.0	1.6	.40
−40°	3.5	1.9	.48

Strength determines how well a fiber/fabric wears (its abrasion resistance) and how it launders. On the whole, synthetics are superior to natural fibers/fabrics, although fabric construction has some influence.

Weight designations are useful when evaluating two or more similar types of fabric. Heavier-weight fabrics tend to be a bit stronger and warmer than lighter varieties. Since lighter fabrics are often preferable for layering, a compromise between weight and efficiency is called for.

The following charts indicate the range of woven fabric weights used in outdoor shirts and pants. Weights for cotton, cotton-blend and synthetic fabrics are calculated in ounces per square yard; wool fabrics, in ounces per linear yard.

Common Cotton, Cotton-Blend and Synthetic Fabric Weights (ounces)

	Lightweight	Medium Weight	Heavyweight
Shirts	3–4	5–6	7–10
Pants	7–8	8–11	12–15

Common Wool Fabric Weights (ounces)

	Lightweight	Medium Weight	Heavyweight
Shirts	6–9	10–15	16–20
Pants	8–10	11–17	18–32

In addition to being breathable, warm and strong, fibers/fabrics used in outer layers of clothing must be wind and water resistant. A wind-resistant shell fabric best reduces convective heat loss. Without an outer layer capable of turning the wind, any combination of shirts and sweaters is relatively inefficient.

Wind resistance is governed solely by fabric construction—the size of the fibers/yarns and how tightly they are woven or knit. Thread count—the number of yarns per square inch—indicates how tightly, or loosely, a fabric has been woven. Among nylon materials, a thread count of 160 by 90 is considered highly wind resistant. In heavier, blended fabrics, thread counts of 115 by 70 and 184 by 64 are usually an indication of wind resistance.

Fabrics must also contend with moisture, whether it comes from your own body in the form of perspiration or from rain, snow and sleet. Inner layers of breathable and absorbent fabrics minimize the first threat; water-resistant and waterproof outerwear eliminate the second.

Water-resistant fabrics are not waterproof. They will turn a light rain for only a brief period. Water resistance depends either on the fabric's ability to swell when wet and close up the holes between the yarns, or on chemical additives such as Zepel® or Scotchguard®. Waterproof fabrics, on the other hand, have chemical, plastic or rubber-based coatings, and water cannot penetrate them. But these coatings seal the fabric so effectively that it is not breathable.

No one fiber/fabric fulfills all the requirements for outdoor garments. However, there are two determining criteria you should consider: first, the characteristics of the fiber(s) and second, the manner in which the fiber(s) is made into fabrics.

NATURAL FIBERS

Cotton

There are numerous types and grades of cotton, ranging from coarse, heavy fibers to the better pima, supima, Sea Island and Egyptian varieties. The latter grades are stronger because the fibers are longer. All cotton is carded to remove impurities before being spun into yarns. The best cotton materials, however, are woven of cotton that has been both carded and combed, the latter process to eliminate short fibers.

Cotton is a highly absorbent and comfortable fabric next to the skin. Its "quick-cooling" effect is refreshing on a hot day when you've paused, your shirt soaked, at the end of a steep section of trail. In cold weather, cotton garments are a poor choice. Their absorbency, so desirable in warm weather, causes them to collapse against the skin, drawing heat away from the body. Cotton also mildews if not dried thoroughly.

Wool

Wool is probably the most versatile of all fibers. In his book, *Hunting—Fishing and Camping*, L.L. wrote:

> As I have been quite a successful deer hunter for the past thirty-one years (shooting 32 deer), I am taking the liberty of recommending just what I wear: Two pairs knee-length heavy woolen and two pairs light woolen stockings: two union suits same as worn at home; one pair medium-weight all-wool pants; two medium-weight all-wool shirts and a medium-weight all-wool coat.

Most of us associate wool with cold weather, but a wool shirt comes in handy at any time of the year. The insulation value of wool can be a godsend when an unexpected chill arises.

Because of their scaly nature, wool fibers trap dead air space, and provide insulation. Even when they are thoroughly wet, the insulation value is only slightly diminished. Wet wool is warm. It absorbs and disperses moisture slowly, drying without the characteristic quick-cooling effect of wet cotton. Wool drapes well and its natural elasticity allows it to "give and take" with body movements. However, it is not especially wind resistant, it is susceptible to abrasion and its strength is relatively low. To offset the latter two shortcomings, most of the wool fibers that go into outdoor garments are blended with nylon, usually 85 percent wool, 15 percent nylon. This detracts little, if any, from wool's ability to insulate.

To appreciate wool, it helps to understand the properties of the two yarns: woolens and worsteds. "Woolens" are bulky, "fuzzy" yarns. In fabric form they are thick and warm, though not as wind resistant as worsteds.

Worsteds are woven with yarns spun from the longer, finer fibers of sheep shearings, resulting in a fabric that is firmer, smoother in finish, more abrasion resistant and generally longer wearing, though not quite as warm as woolens.

Wool fabrics come in varying grades. "Virgin wool" indicates a fabric whose yarns have never before been used. "Recycled" wool is made from scraps and waste cuttings or wool that has been spun, woven or knit from used garments.

Since quality can vary greatly, the layman's best recourse is to check the labels of the garments, as required by the Wool Products Labeling Act.

Silk

Silk is a medium- to high-strength fiber produced by silk worms. The thinnest and one of the most absorbent of all natural fibers, it drapes well and is pleasant to the touch. Its use in outdoor clothing is limited primarily to liners for gloves, and in socks and underwear. Here it is particularly effective as an insulator because of its hollow fibers. High cost and marginal durability are its major drawbacks.

SYNTHETICS

With the exception of nylon-shell fabrics and polyester insulations, synthetics are used in outdoor clothing primarily to enhance natural fibers. They are blended to achieve greater strength and stability, and to reduce weight. Synthetics are not only durable, but also easy to wash and quick drying.

The most commonly used synthetics are nylon and polyester, followed by acrylic, olefin, rayon and spandex.

Nylon

Nylon is exceptionally strong, lightweight and abrasion resistant. Like most synthetic fibers, it is also relatively nonabsorbent. In outerwear shell fabrics nylon turns water and dries quickly; and in socks and glove liners it wicks moisture from the skin. However, the same lack of absorbency causes it to feel cool against the skin in cold weather and hot on warm days.

Nylon has a low melting point and can be readily damaged by a hot flatiron, campfire sparks or even cigarette or cigar ashes. It is subject to static and tends to turn yellowish with age. And, when brushed against tree limbs, nylon is noisy. Any hunter wearing a nylon jacket as he stealthily stalks his prey might just as well wear a cowbell around his neck.

Polyester

Polyester is a smooth, stiff fiber of medium to high strength, with excellent resiliency. It is frequently blended with natural fibers. It dries quickly and resists wrinkling. Polyester fibers are also texturized and/or crimped for use as insulation in sleeping bags, as well as clothing. Like nylon, it has a low melting point. The higher the percentage of polyester in a fabric, the more it is subject to static and pilling, and the harder stains and odors are to remove.

Other Synthetics

Rayon, acrylic, olefin and spandex are used much less extensively than nylon and polyester. Rayon is a medium-weight fiber of moderate durability with characteristics akin to cotton, and is commonly used for lining wool garments. Acrylic is a lightweight, resilient fiber of average strength with a wool-like feel. It is not particularly durable or absorbent, but is used to produce bulky garments such as sweaters, caps and socks. It does not irritate or cause itching when worn next to the body.

Olefin is the lightest of all fibers—nonabsorbent to the degree that it floats; and durable enough to be used for indoor-outdoor carpeting. Two different types are manufactured—polypropylene and polyethylene—but only polypropylene is used in clothing—primarily in socks and underwear where it encourages the escape of moisture from the skin. Because of its low moisture absorbency, static and pilling are common problems.

Spandex is a lightweight, extremely elastic and durable fiber, used mostly in socks and underwear to enhance fit. Spandex is also blended with cotton, wool, polyester or nylon to create stretch fabrics for jeans and hiking trousers.

Chart of Fiber Characteristics

	Cotton	*Wool*	*Silk*	*Nylon*	*Polyester*	*Rayon*	*Acrylic*	*Olefin*	*Spandex*
Absorbency	excellent	excellent	excellent	fair	poor	good	poor	poor	poor
Strength—dry	excellent	good	good	excellent	excellent	fair	fair	good	poor*
Strength—wet	excellent	fair	fair	good	good	poor	poor	good	poor*
Resiliency	poor	good	fair	good	excellent	poor	good	excellent	excellent
Abrasion Resistance	good	fair	fair	excellent	good	fair	fair	excellent	good

* Compensated for by its elasticity

Blends

Fibers are frequently blended to combine the advantageous characteristics of different fibers and to reduce or offset their respective weaknesses. In outdoor apparel a natural fiber such as wool or cotton is usually blended with nylon or polyester. The absorbent natural fibers enhance comfort and warmth, while synthetics add strength, light weight and durability, and make for easy care.

Blending is most often done in a textile plant at the spinning stage by mixing natural and synthetic fibers to form the blended yarn used in weaving or knitting. Less frequently, blending is accomplished during the weaving process itself by using a natural fiber yarn in the "warp" (the yarns that run lengthwise in a fabric) and synthetic yarns in the "fill" (those that run crosswise).

The four most common blends are wool/nylon, wool/cotton, cotton/polyester, and cotton/nylon. In the case of wool/nylon, 15 percent nylon (by weight) is introduced into the wool fabric to increase strength and abrasion resistance, and also to help the wool hold its shape. Such a blend does not seriously affect wool's warmth nor its absorbency. Wool/cotton blends, usually in a 50/50 proportion, combine the comfort and washability of cotton with the warmth of wool.

Cotton/polyester blends are probably the most common. They combine the strength, durability, quickness to dry and easy care of polyester with the comfort and absorbency of cotton. There are numerous combinations ranging from 83 percent polyester—17 percent cotton (in outerwear) to 65 percent cotton—35 percent polyester (in shirts). Proportions vary according to the fabric's intended use. Cotton/nylon is a less-common blend but the characteristics are similar. It is most commonly found in a 60/40 nylon combination for use in outerwear where durability, breathability and the fabric's ability to absorb a water-repellent finish are important.

FABRICS—WOVEN AND KNIT

Fabric construction, whether woven or knit, begins with yarns. These are fibers that have been spun or twisted together to form continuous strands. Fibers may be all of one kind, or as cited earlier, different types may be blended. Loosely spun fibers create bulky yarns, which in turn are woven or knit into thick fabric for warm garments; or the fibers may be spun tightly to create smoother, stronger and abrasion-resistant yarns. Further, yarns may be doubled, or "plied," for extra strength.

In the weaving process, fill yarns are pulled over one warp yarn, then under the next. Endlessly different patterns or weaves can be created by varying the number of warp yarns interlaced with each fill yarn.

There are three basic weaves, the simplest being the plain weave. Here, each fill yarn is pulled over one warp yarn and then under the next. Plain weaves are generally tight and moderately strong. The most common use for them in outdoor clothing is in nylon taffeta, which is noted for its wind resistance. By running reinforcing yarns throughout the fabric at evenly spaced intervals the "rip-stop" effect is achieved and the fabric's resistance to tearing is increased.

Unbalanced plain-weave fabrics are those that have more warp yarns than fill yarns per square inch. They are the basis for broadcloth and poplin. These fabrics are tightly woven, too, yet they drape better and are a bit stronger than plain weaves. They are commonly used in shells, shirts and lightweight trousers.

The second broad category of weaves is twill. These are recognizable by the diagonal rib or twill line that appears on the fabric's face. Twills—such as denim, chino, tweed, whipcord, flannel, gabardine and serge—tend to be stronger, heavier and more abrasion resistant than plain-weave fabrics.

The last of the three major weaves, the satin weave, is not widely used in outdoor apparel. It produces luxurious fabrics with smooth surfaces, but they are subject to abrasion because of the wide spacing of the yarns. Abrasion resistance and strength can be increased significantly by tightly packing the yarns—as was done for a number of older military flight jackets—but the process is very costly.

Knit fabrics are produced by interlooping yarns. As loops are drawn through previous loops, stitches are formed. Vertical columns of stitches are called "wales"; horizontal rows, "courses." Because of their loop construction, knits are more elastic than woven fabrics and they tend to be bulkier, and more effective in trapping pockets of air. However, their looser construction makes knit fabrics less wind resistant and subject to snagging.

While there are numerous knits used in outdoor clothing, only two need to be mentioned—"weft" and "warp" knits. Weft knits are made by looping a yarn into a previously knit edge. The yarns are stitched horizontally to create a series of courses across the fabric. Weft-knit fabrics can be flat or circular knit. Flat knitting, such as common hand knitting, produces a flat or open piece of fabric. Circular knitting is done in a tubular fashion to produce seamless garments such as socks, stockings, sweaters and hats. Jersey knits, double knits and pile knits (including terry cloth and velour) are specialized types of weft knitting.

The yarns in warp-knit fabrics run the length of the fabric rather than across it; they zigzag and intermesh with other loops to create courses. Tricot, raschel, simplex and milanese are warp-knit fabrics. Because of their generally more open construction, they are not widely used in outdoor apparel but they see some use in thermal underwear and in the linings of certain laminated rainwear.

INSULATIONS

Clothing, no matter how thin, traps a layer of air, reducing the amount of heat that can escape from the body. However, the insulation values of different fibers and fabrics are clearly not equal. Certain woven and knit fabrics, particularly those made with wool, trap a large volume of air; but in thicknesses sufficient to keep you warm, they're also heavy and bulky. The best insulations are those with the greatest "thermal efficiency"—warmth to weight ratio.

The most thermally efficient of all insulations is down—the breast undercoating of waterfowl—fluffy filaments, clusters, fibers and tiny feathers. Incidentally, the demand for down doesn't endanger wild fowl. Down comes from Eastern Europe and the Far East where ducks and geese are raised for the table.

When used in garments (and in sleeping bags—see Chapter 4), down is blown into tubes where the particles cling together loosely to form minute dead-air pockets. These inhibit heat transfer yet allow body moisture to escape. Down-filled garments, highly compressible and resilient, are 20 to 30 percent less bulky than comparable polyester-filled apparel, and conform better to body contours.

Fill power—the volume filled by one ounce of down when it is fully lofted—is the best indication of quality. While some grades of down are capable of lofting to 800 cubic inches, they are likely to be blended with grades of lesser loft to create mid-range mixtures of 500 to 550 cubic inches. This is more than adequate. Down quality varies, of course. The best grades, containing the largest percentage of down clusters, as opposed to fiber, feathers and landfowl residue, will generally provide the highest fill-power rating and will produce the warmest garments and sleeping bags.

As for goose down being superior to duck, the evidence is not conclusive. Geese were once slaughtered for the table when full grown, and, naturally, their down clusters were larger than those of ducks. But because geese are now killed for the food market at a younger age, the down clusters obtained more closely match those secured from the processing of mature ducks. In downs of equal loft, whether it be goose or duck, thermal efficiency is the same.

While the qualities of down are admirable, it has certain shortcomings, not the least of which is its expense. When wet or damp, its loft breaks down into soggy mats which provide little or no insulation. In cold weather it may even freeze. Some sort of waterproof shell is needed to protect down garments against moisture. Down dries very slowly, a serious handicap in camp.

The numerous designs and constructions of down garments affect weight, loft and warmth. In fact, the quality of the down is but one factor to consider. Equally important is the quilting method used in manufacturing.

The simplest and perhaps the most common construction, sewn-through quilting, produces the lightest, least expensive and least bulky apparel, adequate for cold, though not arctic weather. Its main shortcoming is that body warmth escapes through the seams where the filling is compressed. However, when it's worn with a windproof outer shell, it will provide adequate protection under most conditions.

Sewn-Through Construction

The double-offset quilting system, found in some sleeping bags, is superior, but it's rarely used in clothing due to added weight and cost. Here, a fully lofted compartment in one layer is positioned over the seam of another. In this way, each seam is backed up by a fully lofted compartment. This adds bulk and some weight, but keeps heat from leaking through the seams.

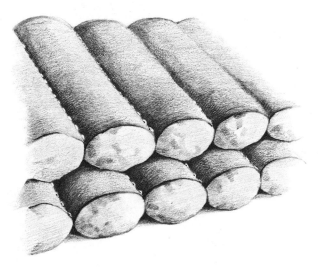

Double-Offset Quilt Construction

Triple-layer construction is a good compromise between the relative inefficiency of sewn-through quilting and the bulk of the double-offset method. This design incorporates a free-floating fabric over the sewn-through tubes, reducing heat loss and increasing wind resistance.

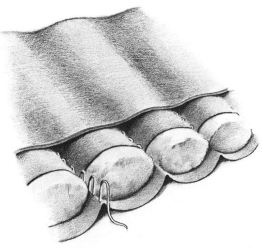

Triple-Layer Construction

Baffle construction, also incorporated into sleeping bags, is used almost exclu-sively for expedition-weight down parkas. Baffles—walls of mesh fabric—are in-serted between the inner lining and the outer shell to form compartments or tubes into which the down is blown. These baffles are sewn at an angle, to form square-, triangular- or parallelogram-shaped tubes that allow the down to loft fully. Since down is not compressed between the inner and outer fabrics, heat loss is min-imized. Such parkas are usually lighter, more compressible and, of course, more expensive than the double-layer quilted models. Comfort in the arctic doesn't come cheap.

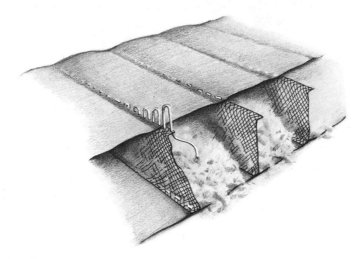

Baffle Construction

Polyester fill is the synthetic counterpart of down. It is made up into batts, or sheets of matted fibers, which, like down, create tiny dead-air pockets to trap body warmth. The three types most commonly used in outdoor apparel are Du Pont's Hollofil II®, Celanese's Polar Guard®, and microfiber polyester and polyes-ter/olefin insulations such as the 3M Company's Thinsulate®.

Hollofil II® consists of short hollow fibers (treated with silicone to prevent their matting), which are assembled in batt form to make them easier to handle. Polar-Guard® batts are made of continuous filament fibers. They are not silicone-treated, but, like Hollofil II®, the batts are resin-coated. As for thermal efficiency, there is little difference between the two, though PolarGuard® is sometimes pre-ferred because it requires less quilting. Hollofil II® on the other hand, compresses more readily and produces better garment drape.

Insulations such as Thinsulate® are also produced in batt form. Since these insulations are made from microfibers, it is possible to trap the same volume of dead air as is trapped in traditional polyester insulations, while using less loft space. Thus, the batts are thinner and denser and provide the warmth of polyester batts or down filling of approximately twice their thickness. However, because most microfiber batts are a bit stiff, it's imperative that the manufacturer design garments with a close fit in order to achieve the greatest warmth.

Polyester fills have marked advantages over down. They absorb less than 1 percent of their weight in water and maintain close to 85 percent of their loft when wet. Thoroughly soaked, a jacket can be wrung out and worn immediately with little loss in comfort. It will dry quickly, too. As a welcome bonus, polyester is easy to care for and it is priced considerably lower than down.

On the whole, however, polyester fill is not quite as thermally efficient as down. Given the same loft, polyester will be somewhat heavier. Nor does it compress as well. Even under the best care, polyester fills will not maintain their original loft for more than three years.

THE INNER LAYER—UNDERWEAR

In the layering process, the correct choice of underwear is critical. After all, this is the layer closest to your body and it will remain in contact with it all day long. And, of course, underwear is the "foundation" for the layering process.

For warm weather, cotton T-shirts and shorts are ideal. Easy to wash, they're a blessing in camp or on the trail. They don't chafe, they're light and unrestricting, and comfortable next to the skin. Men have a choice of boxer shorts or briefs, and it's mainly a matter of personal preference. Boxer shorts provide somewhat better

ventilation; briefs conform to the body and offer a little more support. Women's underwear is often made of some type of synthetic—usually nylon. In warm weather synthetics tend to become clammy and may chafe. Whenever possible, select cotton underwear. As for undershirts, the sleeveless type may prove uncomfortable under a heavy pack because its straps press against the shoulders. T-shirts are a better choice for backpacking.

Cotton, so pleasant in warm weather, is a poor choice for winter wear. One big-game outfitter in the Northwest refuses to take out clients who show up with long cotton underwear—and for good reason. Big-game hunting is strenuous and it's not difficult to work up a sweat. Perspiration-soaked cotton underwear becomes a serious liability when chilling winds rise and temperatures drop. Cotton longs are sold in both the common thermal ("waffle-knit") variety and in regular flat-knit fabrics. Stay away from both types for active outdoor wear.

Perhaps the most versatile underwear is fishnet, available in cotton and cotton blends for summer wear and in polypropylene and wool/polyester blends for cold weather. In the summer it's cool; in winter, it ventilates moisture while retaining body warmth. The fabric stretches well yet reshapes without hampering movement. For optimum ventilation and warmth, choose fishnet underwear having four to six holes per square inch. Fishnet is not inherently a warm fabric; it is effective only when a shirt or pair of trousers is worn over it. It traps pockets of heat next to the body, allowing excess heat in the form of moisture to escape easily.

Fishnet has one drawback. It occurs when you sit for some time in a pair of fishnet longs or when you carry a pack over a fishnet shirt. The coarse mesh, pressured into the skin, leaves an irritating imprint—affectionately known as "waffle-butt." This can be avoided by selecting fishnet underwear with solid-fabric shoulders, seats and knees.

With suitable outer layers, fishnet can be adequate for the coldest weather. There'll be times, however, when you'll want to keep bulky outer garments to a minimum—in a duck blind, for instance. Too many layers of clothing make swinging a shotgun difficult. In such a case, wear conventional two-layer wool/cotton long underwear over the fishnet. This combination, and a minimum of outer layers, will give you complete freedom of movement.

For maximum warmth, select wool. No other type of underwear can match its warmth and breathability. A couple of 100 percent wool types are available but most are blended with 15 percent nylon. Merino and Angora wools are particularly comfortable against the skin.

Wool, however, can cause itching, and two-layer underwear is an alternative. The inner layer is cotton, the outer a wool blend, with thin dead-air space separating the two. During strenuous activity, such underwear (like most wool types) may be too hot. Two-layer underwear is also bulkier than fishnet and slow to dry, and thus is not suitable for cross-country skiers and backpackers. Nevertheless, during moderate activity—ice fishing or deer hunting, for example—or during extremely cold weather, it is a good choice. When buying it, select one size too large—it shrinks.

One of the newer innovations is polypropylene underwear, which is well adapted to year-round, cool-weather wear. The fabric, light and elastic, conforms well to the body, and does not absorb water. Rather, it rapidly wicks away moisture. For this reason, polypropylene is fast becoming the favorite of skiers, bicyclists, runners and even white-water canoeists—nearly everyone who's active in cool weather. Like other synthetics, it dries quickly.

Insulated underwear—whether the filling is down, polyester or pile—has a place in arcticlike cold when activity is limited. Its warmth is supreme but it's far too bulky for general wear and does not breathe well.

The fit of underwear, especially for cold weather, should be somewhat snug yet should not hamper movement. Too loose a fit may cause chafing. Turtlenecks give extra warmth but they also hamper ventilation—and in this respect, zipper-, button- or crew-necks are preferable. Most people prefer two-piece long underwear. Just be sure that the top is long enough to tuck firmly into the lower half. As for that old standby, the one-piece "long john," or union suit, Horace Kephart had some pithy comments in his 1917 classic, *Camping and Woodcraft:*

> Union suits are not practical in the wilds. If you wade a stream, or get your legs soaked from wet brush or snow, you can easily take off a pair of drawers to dry them, but if wearing a union suit you must strip from head to foot. Moreover, a union suit is hard to wash, and it is a perfect haven for fleas and ticks—you can't get rid of the brutes without stripping to the buff.

The right choice of underwear is especially important in cold weather. It's not likely that you will change it during the day. A common mistake is to put on long johns far too heavy for the day's intended activity. It's wiser, when you plan to be active, to go light with undergarments. Depend on easily adjustable outer layers for enhancing warmth and comfort.

SECONDARY LAYERS

Shirts

Successful layering depends on the efficiency of each garment. If one layer fails to function properly, it dooms the entire system. This means that a "secondary" layer, such as a shirt, must provide warmth and ventilation without hindering mobility, and add as little weight as possible.

On very warm days, a short-sleeve knit shirt or a cotton T-shirt is appropriate. For a variety of activities including hiking and canoeing, they're lightweight, elastic, absorbent, generally cool and quite comfortable. However, many activities

require more protection. If there's danger of sunburn or attack by mosquitoes and black flies, add a long-sleeved shirt with a collar. It may be, too, that you'll need a little extra warmth, while paddling across a windswept lake or sitting around a campfire at night. Poplin shirts are a good choice, along with lightweight chambray and corduroy.

The variety among lightweight shirts is great but look for those with features adapted to outdoor wear. Some are known as "field" shirts, cut fully for ease of movement, with long tuck-in tails, two breast pockets with generous flaps, and even shoulder straps or epaulets. The latter might seem gimmicky, but they're not. They anchor camera and binocular straps. Double-needle stitched seams assure durability, and placket sleeves—those with overlapping button cuffs—are extra protection against insects.

As summer temperatures edge downward late in the season, medium-weight cotton-flannel and chamois-cloth shirts come into their own. These fabrics are soft to the touch and their napped surfaces provide warmth without bulk or undue weight. Flannel is usually napped on one side only, while chamois cloth is napped on both, the most common weights for each fabric running from seven to eight ounces per yard. Both drape nicely and grow more comfortable with wear.

An alternative to flannel or chamois cloth, especially for hard use (rock climbing, or woods work), is canvas, a preshrunk all-cotton fabric which, as its name implies, will withstand considerable abuse. The fabric is not napped and the weave is firmer. In keeping with its rugged design, most canvas shirts have double-stitched seams throughout. Some also have flapped button pockets and long tails.

Summer inevitably comes to an end. One day the sky is a little bluer than usual and the breeze out of the northwest has just a touch of nippiness to it. The time has come for wool garments.

The qualities, and the shortcomings, of wool have already been noted, but it bears repeating that wool is probably the most comfortable of all cool-weather shirt fabrics. A medium-weight shirt, for example, worn over fishnet underwear will probably keep you warm on any fall or spring day, providing it's topped by a windproof outer shell.

In colder weather, choose a heavier wool shirt. However, it's impossible to suggest a particular weight. There are too many variables—the warmth of your outer shell, the degree of activity, the temperature, even your metabolic rate. Allow for these variables—in other words, practice layering. For example, wear a medium-weight wool shirt over fishnet underwear, then a twenty-ounce stag shirt over that. Add a windproof parka, and you can probably withstand any type of arctic blast.

When buying a shirt, look for double stitching throughout. On wool shirts, nylon-lined collars and sometimes cuffs prevent chafing and save the wool itself from wear. Long tails, rather than the straight-cut type, stay tucked in—unless, of course, you prefer to let them flap freely in warm weather. Amply cut shoulders and deep arm holes insure freedom of movement. As with lighter shirts, placket cuffs protect against insects; placket fronts are sturdier and hold their shape well. There should be two pockets, each flapped with a secure button or other locking device to ward against loss of small items.

Trousers

In the outdoors, your legs do most of the work and take the greatest punishment. Since they are rarely covered by more than two layers, the abrasion resistance, protection, warmth and fit of the second layer is crucial.

Shorts provide minimum protection yet, when well cut, they are cool and impart a feeling of unhampered movement. While their use is limited to the "off-season" for biting insects, and along trails where the brush has been cut back, they are excellent for warm weather activities. Most are made of cotton, a cotton/polyester blend or denim. Those made of stretch fabrics are particularly comfortable. Several types of special "trail shorts," developed for hiking and active wear, have fully cut legs to reduce binding about the thighs. The seat is generous for easy crouching or bending. Some have cargo pockets, located at the front of the thighs, which are intended for light, generally flat items, such as a map and compass. Loading cargo pockets with heavy items—a jackknife or a metal match safe—will make for miserable hiking. No matter what you carry in them, such pockets require a secure closure such as a Velcro® patch.

Where more protection is required, whether it's from a searing sun, insects, brush, rain or cold, long pants are necessary. Among the relatively lightweight fabrics that stand up best are cotton/polyester twills, denims and poplin. Among the most practical are chinos—loose fitting, durable and comfortable—and jeans. The latter are so universally accepted that little needs to be said about them except that they are rugged. Other summer-weight pants are also available in stretch fabrics.

In the outdoors, trousers are likely to be subjected to hard use, so look for a double-fabric seat and, if possible, reinforced knees. While not an absolute necessity, the bellows-type cargo pockets are useful for carrying those small items such as fly dope, matches, a fly box or light snacks. Ideally, rear pockets should have button flaps to secure valuables. Check the interior pocket material, too. Pockets are inevitably the first part of trousers to wear out, so there is no justification for flimsy fabric here. Also look at the belt loops, especially if you prefer a wide belt from which to hang a canteen. Be sure the loops will accept your belt. Like good shirts, most utility pants of high quality are double-stitched and reinforced at stress points. Be sure, too, that the hips and legs are generously cut. Otherwise, the pants will bind at the thighs, hips and knees, perhaps a minor matter in camp, but misery on the trail. As for cuffs, avoid them. They serve only one purpose—to gather dirt, stones or snow.

You may have a few specialized requirements. Backpackers may find a belt uncomfortable under a pack's waistband. Look for an elasticized "beltless" trouser band. Suspenders remove pressure from the small of the back and enhance freedom of movement at the waist and hips. Where suspender buttons are provided, make sure they are well fastened.

Occasionally, there are situations involving cross-country travel—"bushwhacking"—where brush or brambles will raise havoc with wool or cotton trousers. Upland bird hunters frequently face such going, sometimes through wet brush. Wear "bush pants" made of army duck or poplin. The fronts of the legs are faced with a vinyl, heavy-coated nylon or a second layer of fabric for abrasion resistance and water repellency. Since the protective layers are attached only to the front, the trouser legs remain breathable.

When it comes to warmth and durability, it's difficult to improve on wool worsteds, which are more durable, lighter and more wind resistant than woolen trousers. When worn over wool underwear, they provide a splendid cold-weather combination. However, for extreme cold, true woolen trousers, worn over wool underwear, are the best protection short of insulated overpants.

There's a tremendous variety in weight among such pants, up to thirty-two

Bush Pants

ounces per yard. Buy wool pants with the same care as you buy summer-weight trousers, checking the pockets, belt loops and reinforced stress points. Suspender buttons of metal, riveted through the waistband, are decidedly superior to the plastic buttons that may be adequate for summer pants. A generous cut is even more important than in cotton trousers. You'll probably be wearing long, woolen underwear so that the slightest tendency toward binding is greatly increased by the friction developing between the two layers of wool. Some woolen pants have double fabric at the knees and in the seat. If you're a deer hunter who likes to sit by a deer run, that double seat adds warmth.

River drivers made a fetish of leg freedom; those who were not nimble died young. Driving logs on a springtime pitch meant being wet from the waist down all day long. Not surprisingly, the loggers' long stockings, underwear and pants were invariably made of wool. To avoid catching their boot calks in their pant legs, and to minimize the wool-against-wool binding problem, the men cut a foot or so from each pant leg. These were "stag pants." Thus, with full freedom they leaped about on the logs, the best of them bragging that they could "walk on the bubbles." Occasionally, however, a bubble walker made a misstep and was "sluiced." If his body were recovered, they buried it on the riverbank, hanging his calked boots on a limb over the grave. The log drive then resumed. The river wouldn't wait.

Wool pants are heavy, especially when wet. It's no surprise, then, that woods-men often wear both a belt and suspenders. The latter afford greater freedom of movement. The belt, loosely cinched, simply holds a sheath knife. The suspenders hold up the pants.

Knickers are the favorite of climbers and cross-country skiers, affording leg freedom and protection. For high-altitude summer climbing, corduroy knickers worn over polypropylene underwear are a good choice. Corduroy is also well adapted to cross-country skiing, though it is not as wind resistant as cotton/polyester poplin. For cold weather, wool knickers worn over polypropylene underwear are a good combination. All models can be easily ventilated by unfastening the leg cuff.

It's important that knickers fit well. If they are too short, they will bind severely at the knees. Proper fit calls for the leg closure to come between the calf and the knee, with the latter completely free to flex without hindrance. A Velcro ® closure is the most easily adjustable around the leg. Long stockings (see Chapter 3) are required, of course, and in deep snow you may want to add gaiters to prevent it from wetting your stockings or working its way into your boots. Rear pockets on any knickers should be equipped with button flaps.

For severe conditions, wear windpants or insulated overpants. Windpants are made of tightly woven nylon taffeta. Unlike rainpants, they are not excessively warm because the fabric is left uncoated. Insulated overpants are made of wind-resistant nylon or cotton/nylon, and lined with an eighth-inch layer of polyester or foam insulation. Both types of pants are designed to fit over regular trousers or knickers. Windpants are recommended for high-altitude camping where light-weight protection is needed, or for skiing, ice fishing and winter camping.

Sweaters, Pile Garments and Vests

Virtually everyone in the woods wears at least one shirt. As a second layer you may prefer a wool sweater. You'll find that a sweater restricts your arm move-ments very little. Sweaters ventilate well and have the insulating qualities of wool shirts. And, like most wool garments, they are quite water repellent. They won't double as raincoats, but they will shed a light drizzle.

The tighter the knit, the better the sweater will resist abrasion and turn the wind. A bulky but loosely knit sweater will tend to snag although it will be warmer under a windproof shell. You can determine the tightness of the knit simply by poking a finger into it. If you're looking for an abrasion-resistant sweater to be worn without a shell, a worsted wool sweater is best.

Avoid excessively heavy or bulky sweaters that defeat the layering concept.

Select those that slip on and off easily. Design is also important. Turtlenecks don't ventilate well. Among pullovers, buy one with a crew- or V-neck. Zip front cardigans and pullovers with button V-necks adapt well to cross-country skiing, hiking and other strenuous sports.

Pile Jacket

Pile garments lend themselves particularly well to layering. Pile is usually made of polyester, although varying amounts of nylon and acrylic may be blended into it. It provides the warmth of wool at about half its weight, dries quickly and, like wool, continues to insulate even when wet. It is not wind or water resistant, however. On cool days, a pile vest, jacket or pullover works nicely over a light shirt and under a windproof parka. It's a popular combination among climbers who wear it under a shell or mountain parka, as well as among fishermen in the North Atlantic who wear it under their raingear.

Vests are also excellent secondary layers. Basic models insulated with sewn-

Down Vest

through down or polyester quilting weigh little more than half a pound and compress into a bundle the size of a football. They provide body warmth without restricting arm movement. Wool-lined versions are slightly heavier but equally warm. Styling varies somewhat, with some having snap-closing fronts, others with zippers. Worthwhile, too, are covered pockets and an insulated kidney flap. High insulated collars are best if you expect to wear the vest under a shell-type outer garment. Flatter knit collars fit better under insulated outerwear.

THE OUTER LAYERS

Shells, Jackets, Anoraks and Mountain Parkas

A true shell is a lightweight uninsulated garment, usually of wind- and water-resistant fabric, in either a pullover style or with a zippered (or snap) front. While inner layers conserve and regulate body warmth and moisture, the outer layer—or shell—is the primary weather barrier turning wind and rain.

The shell should be geared both to weather and activity. Fortunately, there are many kinds, so that it's not difficult to locate an efficient one. Weight and compactness are vital. No one begrudges ounces on the trail as much as a backpacker, bicycler or cross-country skier. Some nylon shells weigh as little as eight to ten ounces, and several types can be folded or rolled to fit into one of their own pockets or stuffed into the side pocket of a pack. That's about as compact as you can get.

General durability and abrasion resistance are important, too. Otherwise, packstraps and trailside brush will ruin a shell. Several fabrics meet these requirements, including nylon, tightly woven cotton and cotton blends such as 65/35, 60/40 and 83/17. Most of the nylon shells are made of 2.3 ounce nylon taffeta. Zipper and snap models are certainly more convenient but some body warmth can escape through the closure. The pullover style should be large enough to fit over several inner layers without binding. Some sort of waist drawstring is desirable: snug it up when the wind is bitter, loosen it when you start to overheat. And, of course, a shell should be equipped with a hood, which can be pulled over a wind-porous wool watch cap or balaclava.

The anorak shell comes from the Far North, where no one has adapted as well to a hostile environment as the Eskimo. (He also gave us the kayak, probably the world's most seaworthy small boat.) Originally made of animal hide, the anorak was generously cut and loose-fitting for freedom of movement and ventilation. In a bitter wind, the anorak could be snugged up, its hood gathered about the face so that only the eyes and nose were exposed. The modern version bears a close resemblance to it in design, though the fabric is likely to be nylon or poplin. Some styles even have special front pockets cleverly rigged so that a packframe waist strap can be run through them without interfering with their use as hand warmers. This never occurred to the Eskimo, but then he never toted a pack. That was dog's work.

Anorak

Still more sophisticated than the anorak is the mountain parka—really a lined shell. Unlike other shells, it is a two-layer garment, the outer one made of tightly woven, cotton-blend fabric (or one of the new windproof, waterproof and breathable PTFE laminate fabrics such as Goretex® or Klimate®. See page 54). The body and the sleeves are lined with nylon or wool. Like the anorak, the mountain parka is amply cut to fit over bulky inner layers, yet it is longer in the body to provide better protection for the hips and lower torso. Most models have raglan sleeves to enhance shoulder and arm movement, adjustable gusseted cuffs and a number of handy pockets. Because it's a true parka, it has a hood, also lined with nylon or wool. The front zippered opening is covered by a snap-closing storm flap.

Felled Double-Needle
Seams

Raglan
Sleeves

Gussetted Cuffs with
Velcro® Closures

Cargo/Handwarmer
Pockets

Mountain Parka

If you're an upland hunter, stalking grouse, quail, pheasant or woodcock, you'll want to dress as lightly as possible yet you'll need protection against grasping bushes and brambles. Vests and jackets of cotton duck or heavyweight poplin are rugged and comfortable. Look for models with rubberized game pockets and "hunter orange" safety panels. Flapped pockets with ammunition shell loops are handy.

The warmth and quiet of wool are important when hunting in the woods. A big-game hunter in the high Rockies may wear a nylon shell because he'll be exposed to a variety of weather out in the open, but a deer hunter generally sticks to a heavy (thirty ounce) wool mackinaw or cruiser. No matter how often he brushes against tree limbs, the sound will be barely audible ten feet away. Wool mackinaws are rigged with numerous pockets for all sorts of gear—a compass and map, waterproof match case, a few spare cartridges—even a compact survival kit. Getting lost in the deep woods is a real possibility. If the jacket has a rear pocket, a lunch can be carried. A mackinaw may be relatively heavy, but a skilled deer hunter moves slowly and pauses frequently. He's not likely to work up a sweat.

Wool Mackinaw

The deer woods are generally well protected from strong winds; wind resistance is not as important as warmth. Wool mackinaws supply this and will shed a moderate rain.

Since November rain is cold, and there's always the chance of a wet snow, wear a wool jacket with a double yoke—that is, with two layers of fabric on the shoulders. The jacket may become quite heavy as it takes on moisture and will dry slowly, but it will keep you warm all the way back to camp.

Insulated Outerwear

Usually, insulated outerwear is unnecessary during spring, summer and fall. Even during the winter, many competent outdoorsmen keep comfortable with only a shell garment on top of as many as six or seven layers of clothing. However, when true arctic blasts are in the offing and activity is light or moderate, insulated garments are convenient. The loss of layering flexibility is more than made up by the lightweight warmth of these bulkier outer layers. As long as your inner and secondary layers are selected carefully, versatility is not lost.

Light- to medium-weight jackets and "sweaters" (containing six to nine ounces of down or nine to twelve of polyester fill) are adequate for all but extremely wintry weather. If six to nine ounces of down seem like spartan quantities, keep in mind down's superb lofting ability. It is not so much the weight of the fill that counts, but the loft that results. Such jackets or parkas, with shells of tightly woven nylon or a

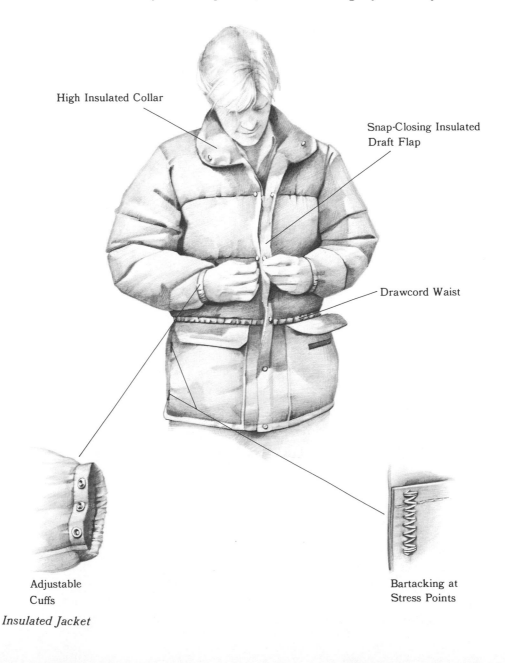

High Insulated Collar

Snap-Closing Insulated Draft Flap

Drawcord Waist

Adjustable Cuffs

Bartacking at Stress Points

Insulated Jacket

cotton blend, are light, compressible, abrasion resistant and fairly wind resistant. Sewn-through construction is fairly standard so consider carrying a full-cut shell garment such as a mountain parka in windy weather.

Three-layer constructed garments are warmer and more wind-resistant. Down parkas of this style generally contain eight to twelve ounces of down depending on their length; polyester insulated models are usually filled with two eight-ounce batts or a single ten-ounce batt. The fabric is usually poplin or a 60/40 cotton blend. Such jackets are considerably bulkier than their sewn-through counterparts so they're not normally carried on an extended trip. Nevertheless, for bitter cold, in camp or for casual wear, they're hard to beat.

There's a lot more to outerwear than fabrics and insulations, however. An overlapping draft flap, for example, that covers a zipper minimizes heat loss; if there's a button flap in addition to the zipper, so much the better. If one fails, you won't be stuck with a jacket that can't be closed. As for the zipper, choose nylon over metal. Nylon is smoother running, less likely to freeze or rust, and it's not as cold as metal on the fingers. There are three alternatives among nylon zippers— tooth and ladder, ladder coil, or continuous coil. The choice is not crucial, though the ladder is usually considered stronger and the coil type a little more flexible and smooth running. Two-way zippers are a worthwhile convenience on hip-length jackets and an absolute necessity on long models.

Cuffs vary, too, some rigged with button closures, some with snaps, others with Velcro® tape. Buttons may work loose and snaps can be balky in wintry weather. Velcro®, on the other hand, is reliable and easy to adjust. Some garments have cuffs with sewn-in wristlets. They're warm but hinder sleeve ventilation.

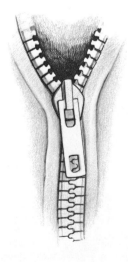 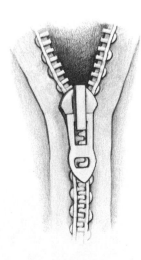 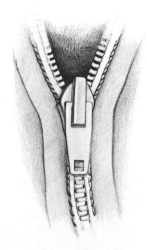

Tooth and Ladder Zipper   *Ladder Coil Zipper*   *Continuous Coil Zipper*

You may not always require a hood, but when you do, the need is likely to be urgent. A hood should be large enough to fit over a hat and should protrude a little over the face so that rain and snow are at least partially deflected. A drawstring is important to keep it in place on windy days.

Outerwear should be roomy enough to permit complete freedom of movement, yet be close-fitting to provide the best insulation. With the shoulders and upper back generously tailored, the arms remain free. Models with pleated or "bi-swing" shoulders eliminate any chance of the jacket binding. Elasticized "powder skirts" on the inside waist of the jacket snug it to your body and keep out snow and cold air. The bottom (or sweep) of the jacket must not bind the legs or hips.

The length of the jacket should match the activity for which it's intended. Backpackers, hunters and winter campers will likely prefer a jacket of slightly more than hip length. Shorter, trim-fitting jackets are excellent for skiers and cyclists who want to reduce bulk and air resistance and leave their legs free. Longer coats are best in extreme cold when activity is limited.

The outdoors has ceased to be the almost exclusive domain of the male, and it is no longer necessary for women to adapt men's outdoor apparel to their needs. In fact, women now find that the great variety of clothing tailored specifically for them is more comfortable, often more attractive and invariably more efficient, particularly in cold weather.

Specific needs may dictate color. Lighter shades reflect the sun's rays, dark colors absorb them. Dark blues and greens seem to attract black flies. Some fishermen even insist on "muted, earth-tone" colors, claiming these don't spook fish. Obviously, a duck hunter prefers camouflaged outerwear because it blends into the marshland background, whereas a mountaineer or backpacker may choose a brilliant orange or yellow—so that in a search-and-rescue situation, he'll be easy to spot from a distance. Big-game hunters also have preferences. Elk hunters maintain that grays, greens and dark reds blend better into wooded backgrounds than tans or light browns, which stand out vividly. And, of course, in many states, hunters are required to wear blaze orange for safety reasons.

Rainwear

When a Down East fisherman donned his oilskins, he called the procedure "oilin' up." He faced cold rain, sleet, snow and wind-driven salt spray, and though stiff and heavy, oilskins did a commendable job. But the seamen's oilskins were not practical in the woods and often the logger, trapper and timber cruiser relied on his heavy wool jack shirt or mackinaw to turn the rain. This worked well enough but eventually the wool was wet through. The drying process back in camp was a lengthy one. The poncho gained wide acceptance but, being rubberized or rub-ber-coated cotton, it was likely to be heavy. Some campers turned to the "slicker" of oiled cotton with a corduroy collar and numerous buckles down the front. It provided good protection as long as you undertook no serious chores; otherwise the wearer stewed in his own juices. It wasn't until the advent of modern coated fabrics that functional and practical woods-type raingear became available.

Today, there are various combinations of lightweight coated fabrics. Most are coated with neoprene, polyurethane or polyvinylchloride (PVC). Neoprene and polyurethane are generally applied to nylon, while PVC, also applied to nylon, is used on cotton and cotton blends.

PVC-coated cotton is a heavy-duty fabric, usually running two-and-a-half ounces per yard, and is slightly stiffer than neoprene- or polyurethane-coated nylon. PVC, however, is tough. It resists damage by oil, gasoline, grease and abrasion—which is why it's popular among sailors and commercial fishermen. Unlike the early oilskins, it doesn't become sticky nor is it likely to crack. "Oilin' up" today is easier, quicker, and the garments are more durable. Rainwear coated with PVC is generally of the slicker type—a jacket with a visored hood and rain pants. At first glance, such an outfit might seem ideal for all outdoor use. It's not. For any vigorous activity, lighter raingear is more easily ventilated.

Polyurethane-coated nylon is the lightest of rainwear fabrics, but it's susceptible to damage by oil, grease, gasoline and abrasion. Although some of the heavier grades can be heat-sealed at the seams, the lighter ones can't. Nonetheless, where weight is critical, and reasonable care can be given the garments, polyurethane-coated nylon provides adequate protection and reasonable durability. But before you buy polyurethane-coated nylon rainwear, check the seams. Two coatings of cement should be in evidence.

Probably the best all-round raingear is made of neoprene-coated nylon. In the lightest models, the jackets weigh as little as fourteen ounces, the pants, eleven. It's rugged stuff—light, flexible, abrasion resistant and even somewhat impervious to oil and grease. If you work around outboard motors in the rain, neoprene is a good choice. Because it's a rubber composition, the seams can be either cemented, machine-stitched and sealed, or simply vulcanized, making them more durable than those of polyurethane-coated nylons. Neoprene, however, cannot be dyed with the bright colors found in polyurethane raingear.

Basic rainsuits usually include a snap or zip front, hooded jacket or pullover and a pair of waist pants. The jacket should have covered pockets with the front closure backed by a storm flap. Elasticized cuffs inhibit ventilation; adjustable cuffs make ventilating easy. Although bib-type overalls are popular among fishermen and sailors who need more protection from spray and blowing rain, waist pants are more convenient and comfortable on land. Select a model with an elasticized drawstring waistband and generous leg widths so that the pants can be pulled on without having to remove your boots.

The "cagoule," a French design, is actually a pullover parka, often of two-and-a-half ounce nylon taffeta. *(Cagoule* is French slang for a hood once worn by bandits or monks.) However, it is much longer than a conventional parka, with a drawstring at its bottom hem. Since it is spaciously cut, you can actually sit in a

Cagoule

cagoule with your entire body protected from the rain; it's a sort of one-person portable tent. Otherwise, the bottom can be tied up so as not to interfere with walking.

Whatever type garment you choose, be sure that it's cut fully—generously, in fact. Not only does this allow full freedom of movement but it also enhances ventilation; loose-fitting rain garments have a "bellows" effect that helps wick away excess heat and body moisture.

Ponchos, long a favorite, seem to be falling into disuse, though some back-packers still favor them. Basically, a poncho is a flat sheet of waterproof fabric with a hole at its center through which the wearer's head protrudes. Most models come with a hood and open sides held together with a few snaps to form "sleeves." Backpacking models, longer and somewhat wider than the standard models, are designed to fit over a packframe. When used without a pack, the hem can be tied up like that of the cagoule.

The poncho has some advantages. It ventilates well. Most ponchos have corner grommets so that they can be rigged as emergency shelters or used as groundcloths. Most of them strive for lightness, so they're generally of polyurethane-coated nylon, some weighing as little as ten ounces. But there are some drawbacks. Ponchos protect the shoulders well but water running off them is likely to soak your exposed arms. On a windy day, they flap considerably. And their loose fit can be a hindrance when paddling a canoe, or hiking up a steep incline.

Whatever type of coated fabric you choose for raingear—PVC, neoprene or polyurethane—keep in mind that it's waterproof and does not breathe. If you exert yourself strenuously, perspiration and wet undergarments will result. If you must be active in the rain, try to pace yourself to minimize sweating and, as much as possible, ventilate. It may be, too, that you won't need as many layers under rainwear. On occasion, the old-time woodsman's philosophy will make sense—a damp wool shirt is better than a steamy raincoat.

But there is a new fabric used in raingear that is both breathable and waterproof. It's called PTFE and it is the basis of Goretex® and Klimate® garments. PTFE is a microporous film that allows the outward passage of perspiration vapor while turning away rain and other exterior moisture. The film is either laminated to a single outer shell such as lightweight nylon, or sandwiched between an outer layer of nylon or a nylon/cotton blend and a nylon tricot, depending on the weight and abrasion resistance you want. Although PTFE is designed as a breathable yet waterproof material, it has also evolved as a superior wind deterrent. PTFE fabrics are now frequently used in general outerwear for this reason.

Originally, PTFE laminate garments were made with either nylon taffeta or Taslan® (textured nylon) outer shells, the taffeta for its compressibility and light weight, the Taslan® for its pliability and abrasion resistance. Early PTFE garments had a reputation for being subject to contamination and abrasion; some required frequent cleaning with denatured alcohol to maintain their breathability/water repellency. However, subsequent PTFE laminates have been improved so that oil and dirt are no longer serious problems. Newer versions can be washed in warm water with mild detergents.

PTFE seams, like those in polyurethane raingear, must be sealed, and this is now done, to many of the better garments, at the factory. But an extra coating may still be advisable. PTFE laminate tape, recently developed, will probably eliminate the need for seam sealants in the future. Since it's a relatively new product, it may be some time before it becomes standard on all PTFE garments.

Hats and Caps

Hats are necessary protection against cold weather, rain, sun and biting insects. You'll rarely see a woodsman without a hat of some sort, and it's wise to follow his example.

For spring and summer wear, wool- and fur-felt hats are among the best types of headgear. Push the crown up into a dome, turn down the brim, and it doubles as

an excellent rain hat. Wool felt will shrink when wet so buy a size larger than you normally wear. Fur felt, on the other hand, while more costly, will not shrink and turns away rainfall like a tin roof. The brim should be generous, so that it doesn't channel water down the back of your neck. In a strong wind, add a chin strap. During the bug season, daub it copiously with fly dope. The felt will retain the repellent for some time.

There are numerous types of wool-felt hats, probably the most popular being the basic "crusher" hat. It's an age-old favorite of hikers and backpackers because it can be rolled up compactly and provides protection from sun, bugs and rain. Broad-brimmed, fur-felt western hats are excellent for canoeing, fishing and general outdoor wear but they're awkward in the woods and impossible to pack. Old fur-felt dress hats and European loden-cloth hats are practical substitutes.

Cotton and cotton-blend hats are lightweight, comfortable and water-repellent to varying degrees—fine for general warm-weather wear. However, during an all-day downpour, all of these will wet through, usually starting at a point where the brim joins the hat. You'll feel a tiny trickle down the back of your neck. If you're serious about being out in the rain, wear a good quality felt hat, a water-proof rain hat, or rely on a rain jacket with a hood.

Fishing in the rain, you will find a hood restricting. Consider the "sou'wester." It's still with us, only instead of oilskin, it's made of a coated nylon or cotton. It usually has a chin strap and with its wide, down-slanted brim extended at the back, it sheds rain in all directions. Under a hot sun, a fisherman's cap is ideal. This is made of water-repellent polyester/cotton poplin with an unusually large visor which helps to cut down on glare. One style has a rear visor to protect the back of your neck.

Another lightweight hat of poplin has a three-inch brim that can be tacked up on one side, Australian-style, a design borrowed from the military version developed for tropical climates. Within the crown is a fine mesh insect netting that can be dropped to protect the entire head. What's more, the hat has a chin strap. Since the wide brim shades the face and neck from a hot sun, it's ideal for canoe trippers.

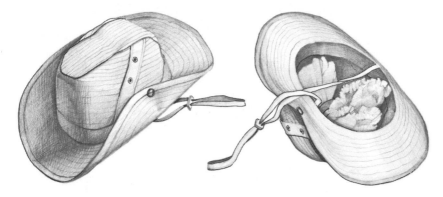

Australian-Style Hat with Headnet

Headgear takes on added importance as autumn and winter move in. For general wear at this time of year, there is the traditional wool hunter's cap with its visor, turned-up earmuffs and neck band, plus quilted lining. There are two types, usually available in a red/black plaid or a blaze orange fabric. One has earflaps that tuck up inside the cap. This often makes for a cap that's slightly too small and tight when the flaps are up, or too large and loose when they're down. The more practical version has ear flaps turned up on the outside. Tie tapes hold these up, or can be knotted under the chin. You're most likely to see such a cap in the November deer woods but when worn with ear flaps down and under a windproof hood, it'll keep your head and neck warm even in the fiercest wintry gale.

In severe weather, nothing will protect your head better than wool. For those who don't like the feel of it, acrylic knits are good substitutes. Knit wool headwear comes in several styles: watch caps, the knit "G.I." cap with its short visor, ski hats, or toques and the balaclava with its roll-down face mask. The denser and thicker the knit, the warmer the hat. The watch cap can be turned down to protect the ears and back of the neck. Wear it in your sleeping bag to stop heat loss through your head on a bitter-cold night. The balaclava helmet completely encloses the head except for the eye openings. Most models cover the nose and mouth but this does not hinder breathing, since air passes readily through the knit fabric. The balaclava can be rolled up, much like the watch cap. Any one of these caps worn under a windproof hood affords comfort in the worst possible weather.

Balaclava

For extremes—such as high-altitude winter climbing—an insulated hood may be worn over a wool cap or even over a balaclava helmet. Such a hood, whether insulated with down or one of the polyester fills, should be equipped with a drawstring for snugging it about the face. There is also a hunter's style cap insulated with polyester fill or down and equipped with ear flaps and neck bands lined with fleece or mouton. Such caps don't afford the protection and versatility of the balaclava helmet and insulated hood combination, but they are well suited to activities in which possible overheating is not of great concern.

Gloves and Mittens

Among the materials used in gloves and mittens are leather, wool and nylon, as well as down, polyester and pile insulations.

The leather category includes cowhide in various thicknesses and tannages, and deerskin. Both types are available in full-grain leather and in suede (degrained leather). Leather is generally quite durable, though it does not stand up well when exposed to prolonged rough work, such as the handling of large quantities of firewood. Leather also affords a firm grip. An axe handle will not easily slip from your grasp if you're wearing leather mittens—something that can't be said of wool or cotton gloves. And, if you want to protect your fingers and knuckles while doing heavy work, nothing beats heavy cowhide. Deerskin, on the other hand, is durable yet supple and is excellent for shooting gloves where fit and feel are important. Models that are inseam sewn are especially close-fitting.

Leather has its shortcomings, though. It doesn't retain body warmth very well so wool liners or some type of insulation are necessary. Furthermore, leather wets through fairly easily and dries slowly. In cold weather, wet leather mittens or gloves will freeze if left out overnight, so they're not recommended for winter camping. When dried, even slowly, all leather stiffens a bit, but softens when put back to work. Deerskin, however, can be restored to its original suppleness more quickly than cowhide.

Wool and wool-blend mittens or gloves are warm and durable but they generally need the wind and water protection of an outer shell. A favorite combination consists of buckskin mitts, known as "choppers," worn over ragg-knit wool mittens; this arrangement is about as warm as can be devised. If the choppers become wet you can simply slip in dry wool liners. Boiled wool and double-wool mitts are heavier and warmer than the ragg-wool liners used in most choppers. These are dense enough to be used without a shell for short periods of camp chores.

Among the insulations, down is used in mittens intended for wear in extreme cold, with an exterior fabric of deerskin, poplin or nylon. This is a warm combination but there is always the danger that if the down gets wet, it will lose virtually all of its insulation value. A polyester fill or a wool/synthetic pile blend is a better choice, since it absorbs little moisture and functions fairly well even when wet. For maximum protection in arctic conditions, a pair of nylon or Goretex® overmitts can be worn over your regular gloves.

The colder the weather, the more bulk you need. But with bulky gloves or mittens, it's virtually impossible to light a camp stove, operate a camera, set up a tent or fire a rifle. Specialty gloves and mittens have solved the problem. One of the cleverest designs is a wool or leather mitten with fleece lining and a Velcro® closing aperture in the palm. You need only cup your hand to pop open this aperture, and your fingers are free. For ice fishing and setting out decoys, there are waterproof insulated rubber gloves.

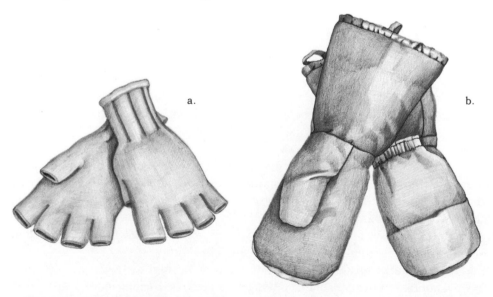

a.   b.

a. *Fingerless Ragg Gloves* b. *Overmitts*

For delicate work such as operating a camera, carry a pair of thin gloves of silk, nylon or olefin. Wear these as liners for heavier mittens or gloves, and remove the outer layer while you're photographing. The thinner gloves will keep your hands warm, at least for the few minutes it takes to get a picture. Fingerless ragg-wool gloves are also useful—particularly for fly fishermen who need their fingers free to tie on flies. Fingerless gloves are equally useful as glove liners for winter campers who may need the finger dexterity to tinker with a stove or adjust a ski binding.

It might seem that fit is not critically important with regard to bulky cold-weather gloves and mittens. However, reasonably good fit is vital. If handwear is too short, your fingertips will compress the insulation or crowd the outer fabric, inviting a rapid loss of warmth. Gloves or mittens that are too small will bind. Better that they be slightly too large than too small.

Which are preferable, mittens or gloves? Gloves provide greater finger dexterity. Mittens are a better choice for warmth because each finger shares the warmth of the others. Lastly, when winter camping or snowshoeing, borrow an idea used by arctic explorers and mothers with small children: tie your mitts to a cord that runs up one sleeve of your parka, across the shoulders and down to the other mitten. Or use short mitten straps to attach the mittens to your cuffs. A mitten lost in deep powdery snow or blown into a crevice can spell disaster on a winter trip.

ACCESSORIES

Bandannas are handy; they double nicely as a handkerchief, sweatband, tourniquet or pot holder. They're easy to wash out, dry quickly and tuck easily into a pocket. Many bandannas, however, are too small to be of much use. Choose an elephant size and take several if you're headed out on an extended trip.

Belts need not be much different from those worn every day except perhaps a bit heavier and more rugged. For summer use on lightweight trousers and shorts, woven jute, cotton web and stretch fabric belts are excellent. They're especially good for fishermen and canoeists because they dry more quickly than leather belts. For most other activities, leather is best. Backpackers, however, should select a belt with a small flat buckle; large buckles tend to interfere with the hip belt on packs. Suspenders are worthwhile on wool trousers.

During exposure to wind and extreme cold a face mask is useful. It provides better wind protection than does the knit-wool or acrylic balaclava. (Some can be worn over a balaclava.) Leather face masks are most common. Neoprene, like that used in wet suits, is also available.

GARMENT CARE

Clean garments are warmer, more breathable and last longer. In the field, however, cleaning may be difficult. Some light, uninsulated garments can be washed but others must wait to be cleaned at home. As a general rule, depend on the instructions in the garment. If these call for washing, use the hottest water that's safe for the fabric. Fabrics containing natural fibers should generally be washed more carefully than synthetics the first four or five times to avoid shrinkage. Wash wool by hand in cold water or have it dry cleaned.

Down-insulated garments can be hand washed and machine dried. (Put a sneaker in the dryer. As it tumbles with the garment, it will break up the clumps of wet down, thus helping the down to fluff out fully.) Down can also be dry cleaned. Avoid the use of harsh chemicals such as "perc," which remove the natural oils in the fill. Polyester insulations should be hand or machine washed and machine dried at a low heat setting. Avoid dry cleaning.

Be sure clothing is clean before storing. Some dirt and stains will set permanently if left untreated. Pack the clothes loosely in cardboard boxes or a trunk, out of direct sun, and away from heat sources such as radiators. Avoid plastic bags; they invite mildew. Wools should be mothproofed or treated by a professional cleaner for summer storage.

Buy clothes well suited to the weather and your activity. Make sure they fit properly. Give them reasonable care, and probably most important of all, buy the best quality you can afford. You'll save money in the long run.

Chapter 3

Boots and Shoes: Your Best Foot Forward

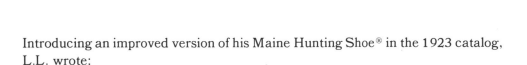

Introducing an improved version of his Maine Hunting Shoe® in the 1923 catalog, L.L. wrote:

> Outside of your gun, nothing is so important to your outfit as your footwear. You cannot expect success hunting big game if your feet are not properly dressed.

If L.L. were to make such a statement today, he would certainly include back-packing, fishing, canoeing and winter expeditions along with big-game hunting. No one knew better than L.L. that boots not suitable for the job, or ones that fit poorly, will detract from your enjoyment of the outdoors, and perhaps painfully so.

A pair of sneakers might be adequate for a weekend canoe trip. Except for launching your canoe and taking it out, most of your activity will consist of pad-dling while seated or kneeling. But for a month-long cruise in Canada, you had better look to sturdier footwear. You'll need a shoe that provides protection and support on lengthy portages, often over rocky terrain. Also, footwear should dry quickly—after you've "lined" or dragged your canoe, for example.

Whatever your activity, you'll need footwear chosen to match weather and terrain. But most important, it must fit comfortably.

THE FOOT AND THE FIT

The human foot consists of twenty-six bones, thirty-eight muscles and a vast array of intricately linked ligaments and tendons. Together they support and propel the body. It's a complex bit of anatomy. However, if you're seeking that "perfect fit" in a shoe or boot, you need only to recognize the foot's four basic parts: the weight-supporting heel, the longitudinal arch that transfers weight and thrust from your heel to the ball of your foot, the ball of your foot itself and the ankle that links the whole system to your leg.

You don't have to be a podiatrist to visualize the stress imposed on your feet as you walk, run, jump or climb. It's easy to see that the arch acts as a shock absorber when you hop on your toes from one rock to another to avoid a mudhole in the trail. The arch also lends resiliency or spring to your stride. It is remarkably strong. During a steep climb when you can only effect toe holds, the arch bears the full weight of your body and your pack. Obviously, then, you need the right boot, correctly fitted, to alleviate some of this stress. Otherwise you're heading for premature fatigue, and possibly even injury.

In separate but related incidents, two hikers proved this one day on the Tuckerman's Ravine Trail of New Hampshire's Mount Washington. The climb, except for the headwall, is not difficult. One hiker, a middle-aged man, reached the summit, wearing his favorite "woods boots"—a pair of ten-inch moccasin-types. His troubles started during his descent and by nightfall he was wincing at every step. He overtook a young woman, herself obviously in great pain, slowly walking backward. The two continued together, the last two hikers off the mountain that day. At the Appalachian Mountain Club's Pinkham Notch Camp, the reason for their agony became clear. The man, his feet sliding freely in his loose-fitting boots, had lost seven toenails. The woman moaned about her hiking boots: "They're too short. I should have listened!" She had lost six toenails.

There are two morals to this story. First, wear only boots that are appropriate to your activity. Climbing and descending require footwear designed for that purpose. And second, never settle for a pair that "fit pretty well." Pretty well is not good enough.

To get the best fit, it helps to know a little about footwear. A boot* consists of an "upper" that protects the foot and supports the ankle; a midsole or insole to cushion and support the heel, arch and toes; and an outsole to provide protection, give traction and absorb shock. The upper is molded over a "last," a wooden or plastic form resembling the human foot. Lasts vary, just as one size eleven-D human foot varies from another. For example, the length between the heel and the ball (or metatarsal arch) of the foot may differ, along with the girth at various points in the instep. Moreover, European lasts, used in a number of hiking and ski-touring boots, are generally wider in the heel and narrower at the ball than American lasts. Consequently, one manufacturer's size nine may fit you perfectly while another's will pinch your toes or blister your heel. As a result, you can't rely on your "normal" dress-shoe size when buying boots.

Overall length, heel-to-ball length, width and the arch fit are the critical points. A shoe clerk may measure your foot with a Brannock device to determine these but in the end, the process is one of trial and error. You'll probably do as well by trying on a boot about one-half size larger than your street shoes and switching sizes and styles until you find the one that feels just right. There is a mandatory

---

* While the term "boot" is used for the sake of brevity, this discussion applies equally to almost all footwear.

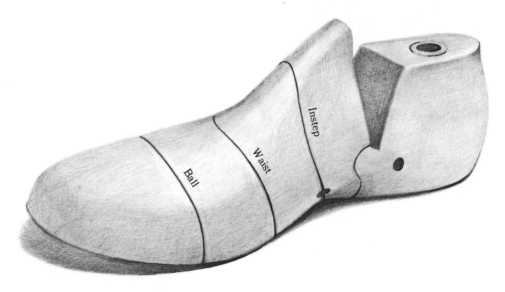

A Boot Last

precaution: always try on boots while wearing socks or the combination of socks you intend to wear afield.

When ordering from a mail-order outfitter, be sure to follow his directions. Most require a penciled outline of both your feet (some prefer that you wear socks when making this tracing, others do not.) Some indication of your dress-shoe size and your weight are also helpful. Given accurate information, outfitters can generally supply boots that fit properly.

Hiking boots require the most critical fitting, and there can be no margin of error. However, you might as well apply hiking-boot criteria to all types of outdoor footwear.

Start with the overall length. With the boot unlaced, drive your foot forward until your toes touch the front of the boot. Theoretically, you should be able to slip your index finger down behind the heel until it touches the sole—though this doesn't always work. Some index fingers resemble sausages; others are more like pencils. Generally, a space of three-eighths to one-half inch is acceptable. This allows your foot to spread somewhat in length, as it takes your weight. You can make this test while sitting, with the boot flat on the floor or while standing, in which case a friend or the salesclerk can insert his index finger. Be sure that your toes do not touch the front of the boot when it is laced.

Next, check for width. The heel should be snug but not tight. (The best way to test this is to lace the boot, and then do a half-dozen deep-knee bends. Your heel should lift no more than one-eighth inch or so within the shoe.) Proper width across the ball of your foot is vital, too. Here again, with the boot laced, bend your feet as much as possible at the toes. If the fit is too tight, the boot will bind and restrict circulation; if it is too loose and your foot moves freely within the boot at this point, the upper or "vamp" may buckle and later cause blisters at the base of your toes. Any undue side pressure against either the great or little toe indicates too narrow a boot. During these tests, your toes should remain flat within the shoe, without crowding.

Tongue

Outsole

Quarter

Counter

Vamp

The Parts of a Shoe

Fitting the arch requires great care as well. Ideally, the general arch area of your foot should be comfortably cradled in, and conform to, the boot's arch. At the same time, you should be able to flex your arch upward a little. It must not be locked in too firmly. If your instep feels uncomfortable, crowded or cramped at any point, try another boot. If the boot is right for you, the ball of your foot will fit perfectly into the ball-joint "pocket." If slightly ahead, or back, the fit is incorrect. Arch fit is critical. If it's not precisely right, you can count on such problems as cold feet, fatigue, blisters and corns.

Special foot problems require extra care in fitting. If you have a high arch, don't inflict a minimal built-in arch on it, thus depriving your foot of needed support. By the same token, a low, or fallen, arch jammed into a high-arch boot may doom you to painful hiking. Unusually bony or angular heels require compatible heel counters. For a pronounced ankle bone, you need a well-defined "ankle pocket" in the boot, perhaps even padding. Fit the boot to the foot—not the foot to the boot.

What do you do when one foot is larger than the other? Fit the larger foot. If the difference is minor, the smaller foot may still be comfortably supported. If the difference is great, you may be able to compensate by wearing a thicker sock on the smaller foot.

If the size of your feet differs so radically that you can't compensate with socks, try to buy a pair of mismatched boots. Some retailers, particularly those who make their own footwear, will sell you a different size boot for each foot at an extra charge. Do your best to fit both feet precisely.

It's interesting to note that the left foot of a right-handed person is likely to be the larger, and vice versa. The explanation, apparently, is that when a right-handed person's arm is under stress he tends to use his left foot for balance and stabilizing—while carrying a suitcase, for example. The opposite applies to a left-handed person.

Perhaps, after trying on several, you'll end up with a pair of boots that fit perfectly—except that they "pinch just a little." A shoe clerk may offer to stretch them for you. You'll have to buy the boots first, and once stretched, they're yours, even though they may still pinch. In time, leather shoes may stretch a little—usually very little—across the foot, but never in length. In no case accept a pair of boots that fits poorly, on the theory that they will eventually "mold to your feet." That's not likely to happen.

SELECTING THE RIGHT BOOT

In choosing outdoor footwear, first consider whether you'll be afoot under largely dry or wet conditions. Most boots are designed for one or the other. True, you will often encounter wet or muddy stretches along predominantly dry trails, and most quality leather boots will withstand an occasional soaking; you can even wade through a stream now and then. But for decidedly soggy underfooting, leather won't do. You need waterproof footwear.

When it comes to warmth and breathability, common sense takes over. Obviously, lightweight leather or fabric boots are fine for most summer wear. The breathable uppers will help to keep your feet cool. Even in moderately cold climates, an unlined upper may be preferable to help dispatch perspiration into the outer air. In truly cold weather, however, heavier boots are required, with extra innersoles and built-in insulation.

Next, consider the kind of terrain you expect to encounter. An elk hunter in Montana is likely to traverse extremely rocky, uneven ground, and will need boots that protect his feet, as well as provide ankle support. A deer hunter in New England will generally encounter a soft forest floor, or a wet—even muddy—woods road that calls for protection against moisture and good traction to minimize slipping.

Once you've decided on a type of boot, look for the lightest, most flexible one to do the job. You don't need stiff-soled, six-pound mountaineering boots for day hikes. Four-pounders, with reasonably flexible soles and supple yet firm uppers, are more than adequate and far less tiring on a long trek. Remember, one pound on your feet transmits the same stresses to your body as five pounds on your back.

If you want durability, be prepared to pay for it. Superior materials and craftsmanship cost more money initially but they effect a considerable saving in the long run, to say nothing of the added comfort and protection. A pair of boots that gives you five or six years of superior service is a far better value than one at half the price that must be replaced every year or two. Cheap boots are never a bargain.

TYPES OF FOOTWEAR

Visit any well-stocked outfitter's shoe department, or pore through any of the leading catalogs and you'll probably be overwhelmed by the variety of boots offered. The scope of materials, construction, designs and uses can be baffling. Classifying boots and shoes in any sort of logical manner is difficult.

The most useful categories we've found are: leather and fabric, leather top/ rubber bottom and all-rubber waterproof footwear. If you need guaranteed water protection, choose from the all-rubber category. Otherwise, review the other two, both of which include boots with some degree of water resistance. Let warmth and terrain be your primary guides.

Leather

On dry terrain, leather is unbeatable. It breathes, molds to the foot, is strong and durable, flexible and attractive. It even provides insulation of sorts, since close to 60 percent of its fibrous volume is trapped air space.

Most leather boots are made of cattlehide. Initially, hides are halved into "sides," then run through some twenty operations for cleaning, tanning, cutting and curing. Following a pickling process with various salts and acids, tanning agents are introduced to impart stability, strength, durability and flexibility. Although some leather is still oil-tanned, most tanning is now done with chromium sulfate, better known as "chrome"—hence, the expression "chrome-tanned" leather. It is then retanned, this time with a vegetable extract such as bark tannin. While the chrome process renders the leather supple through subsequent wettings, the vegetable tanning adds body and color. Waxes, oils and silicones may also be used during the retanning to impart water repellency.

Since side leather is too thick for use in footwear, it is split, usually between the tanning and retanning steps, to produce two different grades. The outer grain, or smooth side, is peeled from the inner flesh side. The outer leather is called "full-grain" leather; the inner flesh, a "split."

Full-grain leather is denser, stronger and more water repellent than split, and its smooth-grain surface is generally more attractive. In recent years, full-grain leather has been turned inside out to produce the "rough-out" or "reverse" leather used in many hiking boots. The reason for this is appearance. "Rough out" leather disguises scars. To make up for its lack of water resistance, it is usually impregnated with waxes, oils or fats. Split leather is inferior. It lacks strength, loses its shape and balks at water-repellent treatments. It is used primarily as a lining material in quality footwear.

Leather Boots

Construction methods for leather boots vary. Lightweight types are built with the moccasin or Littleway construction; heavier boots, with the Goodyear or Norwegian welt system. Workshoe-style boots and those designed for greater water repellency usually rely on two types of molded boot construction: injection molding or vulcanization.

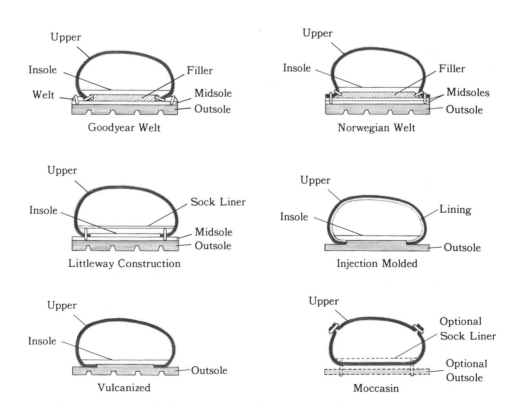

The Major Types of Shoe/Boot Construction

Moccasins were passed down to us by the North American Indian, along with the canoe and the snowshoe. Boots (and shoes) using the moccasin method of construction are made of a single piece of leather that cradles the foot and is drawn up to form the sides, or vamp, of the boot. A U-shaped plug is then hand-sewn into the throat area. Although machine stitching is possible, only firmly locked handsewing can make the seams tight and uniform.

Moccasin-style boots have been "modernized" to include heel counters, a steel shank in the arch and an innersole for added support. Better boots often have a handsewn overlapping seam around the vamp for extra strength, toe protection and water resistance. Soft, shallow lug-rubber compound or cushion crepe soles are added for flexibility, traction and walking comfort. Another feature of the better models is an outsole cemented to a midsole—which is then stitched to the bottom of the boot. When worn out, these outsoles can be easily replaced.

Six-inch-high moccasin boots with five or six eyelets are well suited to fairly active dry-weather activities. Still higher uppers, perhaps eight to ten inches, elevate the boots to field status—for upland bird hunting, for example. As light workboots, they are popular among woodsmen. The increased height of the uppers protects the ankle and shin, turns briars and low brush, and lends greater support.

Moccasin-type boots are light, weighing no more than two-and-a-half pounds per pair, and exceptionally comfortable. The flexible uppers mold nicely about the ankles and calf. Best of all, they require little breaking in. However, the numerous exposed stitch holes cause leaks, so it has been said, two days before it rains. Even walking through wet grass, you may get damp feet. Since these boots cannot be effectively insulated, they are basically for mild weather.

Another form of construction is the Littleway method, found in some light-weight hiking boots, usually with six-to-eight-inch uppers. On most models there is a firm heel counter, steel shank and box toes, along with a semihard rubber-compound lug outsole such as the Vibram Roccia® or Vibram Sunburst®. Little-way construction has two advantages over the moccasin method. The stitching that attaches the outsole is concealed within the boot and thus protected against abrasion and moisture. Littleway boots also provide firmer lateral support. Although they are not recommended for decidedly wet or cold conditions, they adapt well to moderately active wear such as light backpacking.

Boots for tough going are built using the Norwegian or Goodyear welt method. (The welt is the strip, usually of leather, set between the outsole of a shoe and the edges of its insole and upper.) In the Norwegian system the welt and the upper are slantstitched to the insole. A midsole (or two) is added, joined to the upper and welt with a lockstitch. Lug outsoles are then cemented (sometimes stitched) to the midsole. You can identify this construction by the two or three rows of stitching along the shelf of the boot where the sole meets the upper. An optional storm welt or capping may be added, running around this shelf.

Moccasin Field Boots

Goodyear welt construction employs both an inseam (interior) and an outseam (exterior) for attaching the sole to the upper. The inseam holds the welt, the upper and the insole together with chainstitching that passes obliquely through the underside of the insole. Thus, no seam is visible inside the boot. A lockstitched outseam then joins the welt to the outsole. On many Goodyear-welt hiking boots, the outseam joins the welt to one or two midsoles, to which a sturdy rubber compound or lug-type outsole is then cemented. Sometimes the cement is supplemented with stitching and/or screws.

Heavy, deeply lugged outsoles are applied to some (but not all) Norwegian and Goodyear welt boots. Such soles are necessary only on boots that you'll wear while toting hefty loads on steep or difficult terrain. They provide excellent traction, especially on loose talus and uneven rock surfaces. Color is an indication of hardness. The darker the outsole, the greater its carbon content, and the harder the sole. These soles can be slippery on wet surfaces, however. Worn where they are not needed, they may prove uncomfortably stiff and, because of the pronounced lugs, they contribute to trail deterioration, much as shod horses will chew up a path. They can destroy delicate vegetation above the tree line. The lugs also carry mud, stones and general dirt into tents or cabins. Softer rubber-compound soles with shallower tread patterns are more flexible and provide better traction on rock ledges and wet surfaces, and aren't so hard on ground cover.

The differences between Goodyear and Norwegian welt boots are for the most part insignificant. Both constructions are used in a number of heavy-duty field boots. These are good for everything from upland bird hunting or big-game hunting to snowshoeing. A good choice would be a boot six-to-ten inches high with box toes, two midsoles, a steel shank for arch support, sturdy heel counters and fully lined, padded uppers. A bellows tongue keeps out dirt and moisture while hard rubber soles protect your feet on rough terrain. If you intend to use the boots in cold weather, select a model that has been insulated with closed-cell foam. Uninsulated boots will not keep your feet warm during extended exposure to snow, ice and freezing temperatures. If you must select a pair of uninsulated leather boots, consider wearing a pair of insulated nylon or PTFE fabric overboots for extra protection.

For casual backpacking—weekend treks, day trips or other short jaunts—you'll find lightweight hiking boots weighing three-and-a-half to four pounds more than adequate. There is controversy as to whether uppers should be built from one piece of leather. Some quality hiking boots are built with pieced uppers. Generally, though, pieced uppers don't provide the support and durability of the one-piece design. Also look for a snug heel counter, a bellows tongue, a generous and well-stitched backstay, a box toe and a lined upper. A padded scree collar keeps out minor debris that becomes major when lodged under your foot. Padded ankles are also desirable. The steel shank renders the sole sufficiently rigid but not so much so that bending is inhibited. Some degree of rocker is also necessary. This is a slight upward curve in the outsole which provides "toe spring."

Medium- to heavyweight hiking boots weighing four to five-and-a-half pounds are well suited to long treks on steep and rocky trails, especially if you're carrying a pack of more than twenty-five pounds. Such boots provide greater protection, durability and lateral stability, and are more secure than lightweight models on shale and talus slopes—or on any rough terrain, for that matter. Look for the same desirable features found in lightweight boots, as well as such embellishments as heavier (eight- to twelve-ounce leather) uppers, extra padding at the ankles, a padded tongue, full-length steel, fiberglass or nylon arch support, two midsoles and a rockered outsole with deep lugs. Soles for use with crampons should be quite stiff.

When you examine heavier boots, those weighing six pounds or more, their obvious ruggedness may appeal to you. They are really mountaineering boots, and though you may envision far-off glaciers and Matterhorn-like peaks, beware. Such boots are designed for the severest of conditions where climbing a hundred feet on a steep slope is a major triumph. The soles are inflexible; the uppers are extremely rigid. In this type of footwear, a brisk hike is impossible. You plod.

Most leather boots are water resistant, not waterproof. They will keep your feet dry through an occasional puddle or muddy stretch; but sooner or later, because midsole or upper stitching cannot be sealed perfectly, the boots will soak through.

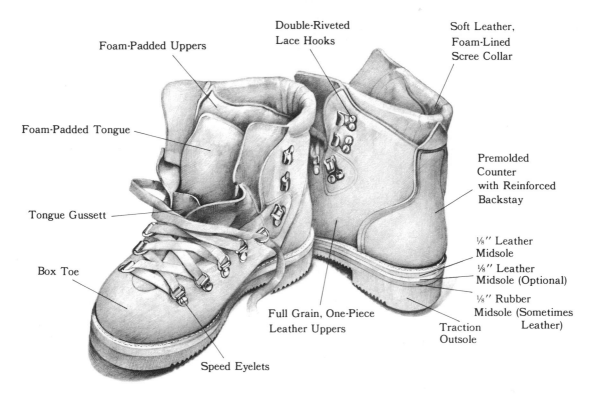

Foam-Padded Uppers

Double-Riveted
Lace Hooks

Soft Leather,
Foam-Lined
Scree Collar

Foam-Padded Tongue

Tongue Gussett

Box Toe

Premolded
Counter
with Reinforced
Backstay

⅛″ Leather
Midsole

⅛″ Leather
Midsole (Optional)

⅛″ Rubber
Midsole (Sometimes
Leather)

Full Grain, One-Piece
Leather Uppers

Traction
Outsole

Speed Eyelets

A Pair of Medium-Weight Hiking Boots

To capitalize on the breathability and general comfort of leather, while at the same time getting a boot that is waterproof, several types are built with an injection-molded PVC midsole. This is bonded directly to the leather upper without stitching. For traction, soft, shallow lug outsoles are cemented to the midsole.

Injection-molded leather boots should have silicone-tanned uppers for water protection, a box toe, a steel shank and a sturdy leather backstay to help retain the shape. Most models are built as field boots or workshoes. Two heights are usually available: the six-inch style works well for light hiking and general field wear, and the eight- to nine-inch boot for upland bird and big-game hunting. Those insulated with closed-cell foam can be used for snowshoeing and winter hiking.

Injection-molded leather boots offer a greater degree of water resistance than moccasin, Littleway and welted boots. They also provide fair ankle support, but are not without their limitations. The finest silicone-tanned leather cannot be immersed indefinitely without some leakage occurring. The degree of water resistance of the leather depends on frequent reapplications of silicone. For wear on exceptionally marshy ground and for winter camping trips, a rubber-bottom boot is preferable.

Fabric Boots

Most fabric boots have uppers of heavy, shrink-resistant cotton duck, double-stitched at stress points. During construction, latex cement is applied to the upper, which is then forced against a die-cut outsole and vulcanized to effect the bonding. Outsoles vary but they are generally of the rubber-compound lug type.

Ankle-high, six-eyelet fabric boots are excellent for camping, canoeing and light hiking. They're ideal for white-water canoeists. They grip well on slippery underwater rocks, a boon when you're trying to salvage a swamped canoe. Some innovative canoeists apply cement-on felt soles (originally designed for use on fishermen's waders and hip boots) to counter the slippery rock problem. Fabric boots dry rapidly and, ashore, they are comfortable, light and breathable: this makes them good summer footwear. However, they lack the durability, foot support and protection afforded by leather. As a result, they're not suited to cold-weather wear or to extended backpacking trips.

PTFE fabrics such as Goretex® and Klimate® are fairly new entries in the fabric boot market. Most PTFE boots are made of a three-layer Cordura® nylon-PTFE–nylon laminate. To lend shape and support and to protect the laminate, the uppers of better boots are reinforced with leather around the quarters and at the heel. The uppers are usually stitched directly to a midsole, to which lug outsoles are cemented.

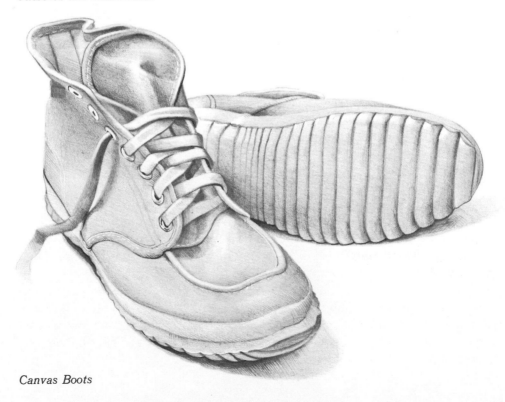

Canvas Boots

PTFE boots are light (their total weight varies from two-and-a-half to three pounds) and generally require less breaking in than most leather footwear. Their cost, however, is about 10 percent more than comparable leather boots. It should be understood that while PTFE fabric is waterproof, not all PTFE footwear is. The numerous stitchlines on most boots allow moisture to penetrate. Also, PTFE will not mold to your feet as well as leather. Its main advantage is its light weight.

Leather and Fabric Shoes

For ordinary dry, warm-weather wear, leather or fabric low-cuts can be a delight. Most leather shoes are built using either the moccasin or Goodyear construction. Moccasin-built shoes are lightweight, comfortable and adapt well to a wide variety of summer activities. After a day afield in heavy boots, change into clean, dry socks and slip into a pair of true moccasins. They are positively rejuvenating. Moccasins can be squeezed into the pocket of a pack or duffel. Models with the characteristic white nonskid soles are almost standard for boating. Depending on the amount of support you need, you can select moccasins in slip-on, two-eyelet and four-eyelet models.

Shoes built using the Goodyear welt method provide greater support and foot protection than their moccasin counterparts. They generally have four eyelets, a lining, full-grain uppers, an insole, arch support, sturdy midsole and a traction-tread-rubber outsole. (Slippery leather soles should not be used for outdoor activities.) Being stiffer and somewhat heavier than moccasins, Goodyear welt shoes are not as suitable for boating and canoeing, but they come into their own for light hiking on fairly level terrain and for skeet and field wear. They have limited use in cold and wet weather.

Four-Eyelet Leather Moccasins

The construction methods used on fabric shoes are similar to those on fabric boots. The uppers are usually heavy cotton duck. The soles are most frequently crepe or a lug-patterned, rubber composition. The uppers and soles are cemented and vulcanized.

Fabric shoes (or sneakers) are ideal for boating and light hiking. Fly fishermen and canoeists find that felt soles cemented to the bottoms of sneakers provide traction when wading rocky rivers. Heights vary. Regardless of the style you select, look for a shoe with a well-stitched, durable heel counter, and a cushion insole for comfort.

Leather-Top/Rubber-Bottom Boots

Leather-top/rubber-bottom boots combine waterproof underfooting with the breathability, support and protection of leather uppers. Although designated as the "Maine Hunting Shoe®," they are better known in the northern New England woods as the "Bean boot." One old-time guide boasted that he's worn the same pair for thirty-two years. "Had three new bottoms," he claimed, "an' two new tops." (There are several brands of leather-top/rubber-bottom boots distributed in the United States and Canada. Some are only intended for street wear, but most are quite durable.)

Since it was devised by L.L. in 1912, the Maine Hunting Shoe® has undergone considerable improvement. New technology in the field of rubber has produced more durable, ozone-resistant compounds for the sole, to which the well-known "chain pattern" crepe rubber outsole is attached. Advanced tanning processes now produce leather uppers that better resist moisture and cracking. The early weak point, the joining of the leather to the rubber, is no longer a problem for it is now bonded with rubber cement before stitching to create a permanent water-resistant bond.

Depending on the height of the uppers, which range from six to sixteen inches, the Maine Hunting Shoe® weighs from three to three-and-a-half pounds, remarkably light for such boots. The eight- to twelve-inch models are the most popular with the higher style preferred for wear in thick low-growing brush. Game wardens, guides, loggers, forest rangers and wildlife biologists are all "Bean boot" fans. You'll even run across "Bean boots" in a maple-sugar grove during the springtime "sugaring off," or at far-off military outposts. (Thousands of pairs were purchased in November 1973 for the Israeli army on the Golan Heights.) Deer hunters, who face every kind of weather, especially favor them.

The basic uninsulated "Bean boot" was not designed for extreme cold or rough mountain country, but subsequent models with closed-cell foam and wool-felt insulation, and another with lug outsoles, have been added for such purposes. The closed-cell foam-insulated boot provides warmth while snowshoeing, winter camping and hunting in the snow. For less active, extreme cold-weather wear such as winter camping and ice fishing, a boot with wool-felt liners (removable for

The Leather-Top/Rubber-Bottom Maine Hunting Shoe® Family: a. Basic Maine Hunting Shoe®; b. Vibram®-Soled Cold-Weather Boot; c. Vibram®-Soled Maine Hunting Shoe®; d. Gum Shoe; e. Lounger Boot

drying) was developed. Vibram® soles were added to certain models for big-game hunters who need boots for rocky, wet and steep terrain. And for canoeing, boating and general camp wear, there is a low-cut, ankle-high shoe. For camp wear in sloppy weather there is a pull-on model. All can be rebuilt when the bottoms wear out.

Leather/rubber boots are not suited for all types of outdoor activities. Foot protection and support are adequate for gentle terrain but they are not ideal for hiking on steep and rocky ground. Nor will leather/rubber footwear keep your feet dry during prolonged immersion.

All-Rubber Footwear

If you have to stand in water, only one type of boot will keep you dry—rubber.

In the manufacture of boots, rubber compounds, backed by nylon, are formed on aluminum frames, then bonded to outsoles either by vulcanization or injection molding. In the vulcanizing process, the upper is tacked to a midsole (sometimes to the insole) and the two are held together with adhesive. The lower edges of the upper are then roughed and cemented to the sole. Heat-setting completes the bonding. Injection molding differs slightly. The uppers are forced into a mold, into which an uncured sole compound is injected. A delicate balance of heat and pressure assures perfect bonding. In either case, sole hardness, welt design and tread pattern can be altered in the mold, or in the composition of the compound.

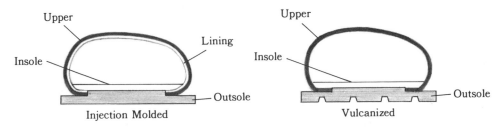

Injection Molded and Vulcanized

Rubber boots, whether calf-high, hip-length or chest waders, require a steel shank between the midsole and insole for arch support and protection. The outer sole should be rockered to ease walking. The heel counter, snug yet not too grasping, helps prevent chafing (heavy socks help, too). A heel backstay is vital, since rubber has little rigidity. Without one, the boot would collapse at the back of the ankle. In some boots, notably among calf-high styles with lacing, a gussetted tongue makes the boots easier to pull on and off and keeps out water.

For winter wear or cold-water wading, closed-cell foam in the vamp and uppers enhances warmth. Thick wool-felt innersoles, or those of foam (both removable) also add to warmth and provide cushioning. Wool felt is slightly warmer and more absorbent; the closed-cell foam better resists compression and dries more quickly.

Wherever the underfooting is sloppy from wet snow, slush, water or mud, rubber boots, which range in height from ten to sixteen inches, are the answer. Some are slip-ons (called "pacs") with only two or three eyelets; others are full-laced, giving both support and snugness around the ankle and calf. Another rubber boot is the "Arctic" which can be worn over regular boots or shoes; they are popular among farmers because they are easy to slip into or remove. Don't confuse these with the lightweight buckled or zippered overshoes, often called galoshes, which are designed for city or suburban wear; they are too flimsy for farm or trail. Pull-on rubber deck boots with non-skid soles serve well for boating and fishing.

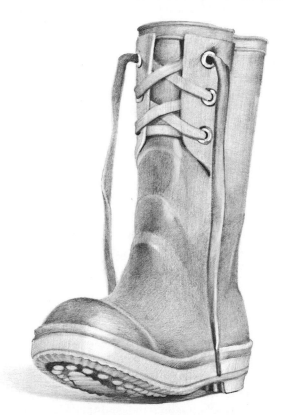

Rubber Shoepacs

Fishermen are fussy about hip boots. Wading in a rocky, turbulent stream, seeking to place a fly in an inviting but almost out-of-reach spot, calls for deft footwork. Bottom surfaces may be slick. Replaceable felt soles cling best on moss-covered ledges and algae-draped rocks, both notoriously slippery. For mud or gravel, cleated soles are better. Hip boots are not the sole prerogative of fishermen. For duck hunters, setting out decoys in the face of a November gale, there are insulated models with cleated soles for the cold, muddy waters of typical duck hang-outs.

Some hip boots have a loose, bulky instep, easy to slip into but less comfortable for walking and subject to "suction" in muddy or marshy ground. Those with a snug-fitting ankle and instep alleviate this problem but require a little more tugging to put on or remove.

Chest-high waders are more specialized than hip boots, and are worn mainly by stream and surf fishermen, as well as by some duck hunters. The advantage of waders over hip boots is obvious. You can wade into four-foot-deep water instead of limiting yourself to about twenty-four inches.

There are two types of waders: "boot foot" and "stocking foot." Boot-foot waders, which are more widely used, are simply boots extended upward to the chest and held up by suspenders. This type of wader is still made of a nylon-backed rubber compound, though it is gradually being replaced by one made of a sandwich material—rubber bonded between two facings of nylon. This newer material is generally more flexible, and better resists tearing, puncturing and snagging.

If you decide in favor of boot-foot waders, look for these features: a steel arch-support shank, a snug but comfortable heel counter and a cleated rockered sole. Padded ankles and reinforced toes provide good protection when you stumble against a midstream rock. If your fishing is done largely in waters noted for their slippery rocks and ledges, felt soles rather than cleated ones offer a firmer grip. For cold-water wading—winter steelhead fishing, for example—closed-cell foam insulation cuts the chilling effect of an icy river. Consider selecting waders that are a mite full through the trunk and legs, so that you can wear heavier clothing for added warmth. Two seemingly minor items are a convenience: an inside chest-pouch to hold tackle; and a drawstring top to snug the uppers about your chest, thus eliminating the chance that your waders may interfere with your casting. Some models are equipped with belt loops. Tightening your waders about your waist with a belt will cut down on "water intake" in case of a spill. Be sure to fit your inseam as well as your feet. A short inseam can bind uncomfortably. Inseams that are too long are bulky and make walking difficult; they can also cause leak-producing abrasion.

Stocking-foot waders have built-in feet over which you'll need to wear wading shoes. The major difference between these and the boot-foot waders lies in the fit and sure-footedness provided by the separate wader/shoe system. Most stocking-foot waders are made of either latex rubber or coated nylon. Both materials are flexible and lightweight and are cut close to the contours of your body to provide a closer fit that reduces drag in a swift current. The latex is elastic and stretches slightly as you move. Polyurethane-coated nylon waders are lighter (less than a pound vs. three-and-a-half to four pounds) and more abrasion resistant. Both types are easy to repair. Because the materials are thin, the waders fold up into a small bundle for pack-in fishermen. However, there is virtually no insulation against cold water.

a. *Boot-Foot Waders*   b. *Stocking-Foot Waders*

Most wading shoes have either leather, fabric or rubber/nylon uppers. However, the manner in which the shoe is made is more important than the material
that goes into it. Wading shoes undergo constant scuffing and abrasion, so the
uppers should be well-stitched and reinforced around the quarters with a layer of
leather or nylon. Box toes, reinforced heel counters and bellows tongues are
important—as are steel shanks between the insole and the midsole, which provide
support when you're wading, and shape retention when you're not. As for outsole
materials, wool felt is supposedly better for traction; synthetic felt is probably
more durable. It's a toss-up. A more critical feature is a sturdy rubber or leather
midsole. Without one, you'll find yourself replacing not just the outsole when it
wears out, but the whole shoe.

Purchase wading shoes large enough to accommodate two pairs of wool
socks—one to be worn between the shoe and your feet and one between the
waders and the shoe. This outer pair of socks reduces the abrasion caused by
"scree" that works its way into the space between shoes and waders. If you're

planning on cold-water fishing, you'll probably need extra warmth. A pair of wet-suit booties in place of the outer socks will help considerably.

One final note: all waders develop leaks in time. Put together a repair kit of patches and a small tube of cement. If you tear your waders hiking through a patch of brush, or discover a leaky seam, you'll be able to make streamside repairs.

SOCKS AND INNERSOLES

Think of socks as underwear for your feet. Like underwear for your body, they help retain body warmth and absorb or pull away moisture. The materials that go into socks, then, should have much the same characteristics as underwear fabrics.

On a mild summer day, when you're lounging around camp in your moccasins or loafers, almost any stocking will do. However, once you go out hiking, climbing, touring on skis or even cutting wood, socks begin to matter—and whether it's summer or winter, it's advisable to put on two pairs.

Consider first the inner ones. In hot weather, those of nylon or olefin are a good choice, since they pull away moisture into the outer socks. (By minimizing chafing, inner socks also prevent blisters.) For winter wear, inner socks may be of silk, olefin, nylon or wool. Silk is comfortable and warm because of its smooth, hollow fibers. Since they are highly absorbent, silk socks are at their best when worn with footwear that does not, like rubber, encourage perspiration. In rubber-bottom footwear, nylon and olefin work well, drawing moisture away from your feet and transferring it to your outer socks. Nylon and olefin are not particularly warm, however, and in the winter you'll probably prefer wool. Although wool socks tend to hold foot perspiration, they insulate better.

When it comes to outer socks, it's hard to improve on wool for any outdoor activity, summer or winter. Wool is more resilient, warmer and more absorbent than any other sock material. The bulk of wool protects the feet, provides greater comfort in cold weather—and warmth even when your feet are wet. Wool's only weakness—its lack of durability—is offset by blending it with nylon, sometimes throughout the sock, sometimes as a localized reinforcement in the heel and toe.

Cotton socks, soft and absorbent, soak up moisture. In warm weather, this leaves you with a clammy feeling and parboiled feet. During the winter, soggy cotton socks suck away your feet's warmth, sometimes at a dangerous rate. All in all, there is little to be said in favor of cotton socks for outdoor use at any time of year.

If you find wool uncomfortable on your skin, you can substitute acrylic knit socks, though they don't provide the warmth and absorbency of wool. A better remedy is to wear silk or nylon inner socks under your wool ones.

If you're active, there is no way you can keep perspiration and dirt from accumulating in your socks. These can cause skin irritation, blistering and a loss of insulation. The risk of such problems is greatest during the winter while you're wearing all-rubber, or leather/rubber boots. Frequent daily changes (with washings between wearings, if possible) are the solution, even when trekking in the snow. Changing your socks may be a frigid experience but you can do it quickly if you carry spares. A summertime backpacker can change and wash quite conveniently just about any time, hanging the wet socks on his pack frame to dry as he hikes along. But the possibility of a three-day rain always makes it advisable to take along a couple of extra pairs.

Wool socks are available in a number of heights and styles. For most outdoor activities socks under ten-inches high are worthless. In cold weather they're too short to keep you warm or to fit under a pair of boots. In warm weather they aren't high enough to provide adequate protection from insects. On early summer trips when the insects are particularly voracious, many outdoorsmen tuck their trousers into their socks. To do this, you'll need socks even higher than ten inches. However, ten-inch socks are adequate for most purposes. For higher boots and for cross-country skiing select fifteen-inch socks or knicker-height ones. Lastly, try to get the best fit possible. It may seem like a minor thing but socks that are too small or ones that bunch at the heel or across the instep are a primary cause of blisters and foot discomfort. When you're buying wool or silk socks, choose one size larger than normal to allow for shrinkage.

Removable innersoles pleasantly cushion your feet and better yet, in cold weather, they cut down heat loss through your boot soles. They also absorb moisture. Some wearers of rubber complain that it "draws my feet." Innersoles reduce the problem. Few woodsmen buy "Bean boots," for example, without purchasing two pairs of innersoles, wearing one while they dry the other.

The best innersoles are of wool pile, shearling, woven wool felt or closed-cell foam. For shape retention, the pile and shearling are usually attached to leather arch supports. Genuine wool shearling and woven-wool felt are warm, effectively trapping a layer of dead air space. And they perform equally well wet or dry. Synthetic shearling, usually a polyester pile, is as warm but less absorbent. Innersoles of closed-cell foam are also warm but do not compress significantly. However, they are totally nonabsorbent. Be sure your foam innersoles are of the closed-cell type. The open-cell variety absorbs moisture greedily (it's used for making sponges) and is worthless as an insulator.

ACCESSORIES

Boots are generally furnished with cotton, rawhide or nylon laces. The most durable and quick-drying are nylon—but since it doesn't hold knots well, tie double ones. And carry extra laces. You'll find a dozen emergency uses for them around camp or on the trail and, when you need a replacement, you won't have to improvise with a length of fish line.

Booties are to winter campers what moccasins are to summer backpackers. After a long day in a pair of cold-weather boots, booties are delightful foot relaxers. The best have above-the-ankle shells and Cordura®-covered soles that are insulated with closed-cell foam and down or polyester fill. They're warm, lightweight and can be stashed into a corner of your pack. They're also an excellent remedy for cold feet in a sleeping bag.

BOOT AND SHOE CARE

Moccasin-type and light-trail boots can usually be broken in during normal wear even in the field, providing the initial fit is correct. Even so, it's usually safer to break them in at home.

Heavier boots should be broken in gradually, increasing wearing time from a half hour or so to several hours, until the boots can be worn all day without discomfort. However, before tackling an extensive hike, try a day trek close to home, preferably under a moderately heavy pack. You can help the breaking-in process, and even accelerate it, by applying one of the many leather-conditioning agents. Use these sparingly, however. Too much dressing will soften the leather to the point where it loses its support.

Leather boots should be cleaned frequently with a damp cloth to remove dried mud, and other grit. Wet boots are best dried slowly, away from direct heat. Don't prop them on sticks close to a campfire. Too much heat will stiffen them and ruin the leather.

Once your boots are dry, condition and waterproof them with the proper solvent to restore and preserve the natural qualities of the leather. A compound such as saddle soap will loosen salt and dirt and restore the leather's natural nutrients. After cleaning, apply a waterproof dressing.

The boot dressing you use is determined by the tanning process. Oil-tanned leather requires an oil-base dressing such as mink oil or Scandinavian Boot Grease®. Chrome or silicone-tanned leathers should be treated with silicones or waxes, such as Snow-Seal®. Neatsfoot oil, long an old reliable, tends to over-soften leather, especially when you apply it too copiously. On the other hand, if comfort is more important than support or protection—along a woods trail, for example—Neatsfoot oil will keep the tops comfortably pliable. Regardless of the dressing you use, apply it sparingly and wipe away any excess. There is no need to saturate the leather. A toothbrush works well for cleaning seams and applying the dressing.

If your boots have rubber lug soles, be careful when you apply an oil-based dressing. The petroleum chemicals may rot the adhesive between the mid- and outsoles.

It's easier to care for canvas shoes. They can be hand or machine washed, and then dried at room temperature or in the sun.

Mud and dirt can be rinsed off rubber boots, of course. If yours have cemented rubber outsoles, keep them clear of petroleum-based products that can destroy adhesives. This includes gasoline, camp-stove fuel and kerosene. Although good rubber boots and waders are made of ozone-resistant rubber, prolonged exposure to air may eventually cause cracking. You can delay this by storing your boots in an airtight plastic bag.

FOOT CARE

Blisters are the most common foot injury, usually caused by a hole in your socks or by boots that are improperly fitted, poorly laced or not adequately broken in. Carry a first-aid kit that includes: "moleskin" (which is not really the skin of a mole but actually a heavy flannel with an adhesive backing), adhesive tape, gauze pads, an Ace bandage for minor sprains, a needle with which to pierce a blister (sterilize it first) and a disinfectant. And somewhere in your pack include a can of foot powder.

Other precautions include keeping your toenails trimmed, which not only saves your socks but prevents injury to your toes. The use of foot powder lends a feeling of comfort as well as reducing friction.

Chapter 4

Sleeping Bags: Slumber on the Trail

Back in 1917, Horace Kephart wrote:

> A man can stand almost any hardship by day and be none the worse for it, provided
> he gets a comfortable night's rest; but without sound sleep he will soon go to pieces,
> no matter how gritty he may be.

Sleeping gear in Kephart's time was, by today's standards, primitive. Two or
more wool blankets were often folded to form an envelope held together with
horse-blanket pins, sometimes encased in a canvas tarp or rubber poncho—the
total weighing twelve to twenty pounds. Then came sleeping bags insulated with
wool batts—warm but heavy and bulky—or filled with cotton quilting—equally
bulky, and inclined to become soggy. Later, bags were filled with kapok, a silklike
natural fiber. These were inexpensive, costing as little as $6 during the 1930's.
However, under the stress of the sleeper's weight, the kapok soon broke down
into powder and became useless as insulation. Down-filled "sleeping robes" were
also available; while they would be considered bargains now, their cost was
beyond the reach of the average outdoorsman forty-odd years ago.

In appraising the sleeping gear available to him, Kephart also wrote:

> Look for the most warmth with the least weight and bulk, for durability under hard
> usage, and for stuff [fill] that will not hold moisture, but will dry out easily.*

These are standards by which we still judge sleeping gear. What's more, modern technology now provides materials and designs that are thermally efficient,

* *Camping and Woodcraft* (New York: Macmillan, 1917), p. 125.

durable and moisture resistant, at about one third to one fourth the weight of Kephart's "portable bed." We have not only attained his specifications, we have exceeded them.

A sleeping bag is not unlike an insulated jacket, its function being to slow the loss of body warmth so that heat loss does not exceed heat production. The culprits that steal body warmth at night are the same as those that trouble us by day: radiation, convection, evaporation and conduction. The first three can be thwarted by encasing the body in a given thickness of insulation. Conductive loss can be prevented by inserting a pad or mattress between your sleeping bag and the ground.

MATERIALS: INSIDE AND OUT

Insulations and Thermal Efficiency

Thickness, or loft, determines the warmth of a sleeping bag. There are two ways of measuring loft. One measures the thickness of the bag from its inner to its outer shell; the other, the full profile of the bag, from the bottom to the top shell. Of prime concern, however, is the thickness of the top half. (The weight of your body will compress the lower half, rendering it less effective as an insulator.) Since outfitters use both methods in their specifications, be careful when comparing two or more bags. Generally, when loft in excess of four inches is indicated, it refers to the full profile of the bag. Also be aware that the lofts of the top and bottom shells are not necessarily equal. On many newer bags, 60 percent of the fill is put in the top. Once again, by comparing top-shell loft figures, you'll be able to make accurate comparisons.

The U.S. Army Quartermaster Corps has issued guidelines governing the amount of loft required at various temperatures if you sleep in a tent or camp. The suggested figures are for the thickness of the top shell only.

40°F	30°	20°	10°	0°	−10°	−20°	−30°
1½″	1¾″	2″	2¼″	2½″	2¾″	3″	3¼″

It should be noted that these widely cited figures are bare minimums; they are guidelines for survival, not luxurious comfort. However, our experience has shown that it's better to have two inches of loft in the top half of the bag at 40°F; two-and-a-half inches at 20°F; three inches at 0°F; three-and-a-quarter inches at −10°F; and three-and-three-quarters inches at −30°F.

Roughly speaking, each inch of loft will buy you about 27 degrees of protection below the body temperature of 98.6. For example—a bag with four inches of loft will usually be suitable to about 9 degrees below zero. (Multiply 4 inches by 27 degrees, which equals 108. Subtract this from 98.6, which rates the sleeping bag at 9 below). Consider a sleeping bag hood, too. This adds about 5 degrees of warmth and, if you're using a tent, add another 10 degrees, for a total rating of −24. Don't consider this formula as a hard and fast rule, however. It's simply a guideline.

In theory at least, all insulations of equal thickness provide equal warmth, whether it's two inches of down, polyester or even sawdust. However, since you may have to tote your sleeping bag some distance, you'll want the lightest possible two inches. This ratio of warmth-to-weight is known as "thermal efficiency."

Of the two major sleeping bag insulations—down and polyester—down is more thermally efficient. (See Chapter 2; pgs. 31–35, for the discussion of down vs. polyester.) Polyester, including PolarGuard® and Hollofil II®, is somewhat less so. Although the percentages may be subject to challenge, it is safe to say that a quality down bag provides the warmth of a polyester bag that is 25 to 30 percent heavier.

Then there's the matter of bulk and compressibility. In selecting a sleeping bag for backpacking or bicycle touring, choose one that is lightweight and compresses into the smallest bundle possible. Down's compressibility exceeds that of polyester, and it is remarkably resilient. A down bag can be stuffed into a sack not much larger than a loaf of bread yet, when spread out, it lofts (or "fluffs" out) to its full original thickness. Polyester bags may require a stuff sack twice the size. Thinsulate® insulation, which is found in a number of outerwear garments, has not been used successfully to date in sleeping bags. Bulk/compressibility ratio is the major problem.

Moisture

During recent years, the question of moisture as it affects sleeping bags has been much exaggerated by those who favor polyester-filled bags. Nonetheless, some of the arguments are valid, particularly if your sleeping bag will be exposed to water or high humidity.

Sleeping bags are usually carried in stuff sacks or simply jammed into a pack. But stuff sacks and most packs are not waterproof. A spill in the rapids, a sudden heavy downpour or even hiking in a thick fog can result in a soggy, or very damp, sleeping bag. When wet, down mats severely, losing more than 80 percent of its insulating value. What's more, drying may take several days. Even when down is merely damp, its efficiency rating drops 20 percent. Should this occur in the mountains or during a springtime river trip when temperatures can dip into the forties or lower, a night of discomfort is guaranteed, and hypothermia is a distinct possibility.

On the other hand, polyester-filled bags lose only about 5 percent of their loft when saturated and maintain close to 75 percent of their insulating value. Granted, a night out in a sopping polyester bag is not an enticing prospect but you will, nonetheless, survive nicely. Come morning, and sunlight—or even a moderate breeze—and it won't take long for your polyester bag to dry thoroughly, lofting to its original shape.

However, since there are waterproof packs (see Chapter 6) which will protect your sleeping bag against wetting, the moisture issue is more of a warning than a criterion of selection. Nevertheless, when you're headed for a white-water canoe trip, overnight sailing, winter camping or backpacking in a wet region such as the Pacific Northwest, it may be well worth your while to consider polyester.

Cost/Durability

The price of a down sleeping bag is roughly double that of a polyester model of comparable loft and quality, the difference lying in the cost of fills. As of 1981, the goose down used in better sleeping bags ran $28 to $38 per pound with duck down slightly cheaper; polyester fills, such as PolarGuard® or Hollofil II®, cost only about $2.50 per pound. Obviously then, if a bag requires two to three pounds of fill, the cost differential is substantial.

Surprisingly, construction costs of high-grade down and polyester bags are comparable. Down bags must be compartmentalized to control shifting and to assure even lofting. Otherwise the down will tend to bunch at one end or the other, leaving parts of the bag insulated poorly, or not at all. But polyester, in the form of batts, must be stabilized by sewing its edges or by means of a sandwich construction. The cost of stabilizing matches that of sewing compartments.

Initial cost is only part of the story. Evidence suggests that polyester's insulation value deteriorates in time. This loss can be accelerated by exposure to heat—a laundry dryer, for instance, or being left in a car trunk under a hot sun. Temperatures in excess of 140 degrees Fahrenheit will speed polyester's inherent tendency to lose the crimp imparted to the fibers. This results in a flattening of the batts and a loss of loft. For a polyester bag, a reasonable life expectancy is only about three years at 100 percent efficiency, even with the best of care. After that, look for a gradual decrease in loft. A down bag, properly cared for, will maintain its loft indefinitely.

Shells and Linings

Most sleeping bag shells are of 2.3-ounce nylon taffeta or 1.9-ounce nylon rip-stop. The latter is usually "calendared"—that is, passed through heated rollers—or chemically treated to make it "downproof." Taffeta is naturally downproof because of its extremely tight weave. Nylsilk®, an all-nylon taffeta of extra-tight weave with a silklike feel, is also commonly used for shells. Lighter weight, more compressible nylons such as 1.5-ounce rip-stop are used on down bags designed for bicycle touring and backpacking. Bags for fixed camp or car camping often have durable but relatively heavy poplin shells.

PTFE fabrics have recently been used on a number of sleeping bags, but with limited success. While PTFE breathes and turns away exterior moisture, it has not been found particularly effective in cold weather. As the difference in temperature within and without the bag increases, body moisture, seeking to escape through the fabric, strikes the inside of the colder exterior shell and tends to condense. In droplet form, water can't penetrate the PTFE. So the moisture accumulates, wetting the insulation and even freezing.

The inner linings of most bags match the shell fabric. Nylon, whether rip-stop or taffeta, is ideal for this. Once warmed by the body—and this takes only moments—it provides a soft, pleasant feel to the skin. And best of all, it's slippery, so that you can twist and turn in your sleep without entangling yourself with the bag.

Trinyl®—a blend of cotton, nylon and polyester—is also used for lining. The cotton presents a comfortable sheetlike feel and boosts absorbency. Because this material is not naturally downproof, it should be calendared before being used in down bags. A few other bags have linings of cotton blends, especially the full-cut polyester bags suitable for fixed camps and family-type camping. Such linings are delightfully comfortable, being both absorbent and breathable. Pleasant to the touch and warm, flannel is also used as lining in inexpensive family camping-type sleeping bags.

DESIGN

Shape

There are three basic shapes among sleeping bags—mummy, rectangular and barrel. As its name implies, the mummy type conforms most closely to the body's contours and because free-flowing air around the body is kept to a minimum, it's the most efficient. This is vital in cold weather, since the head and shoulders provide a massive escape route for body warmth unless protected. Most mummy bags are rigged with hoods, which can be drawn snugly about the head and neck, further increasing the bag's efficiency. Reduced volume also means reduced weight and bulk.

Rectangular bags, squared off full width at the head and foot, are the roomiest. In some respects, these bags are more comfortable than the mummy type since you can roll over inside them. Roll over in a mummy bag and the bag rolls with you. However, this generous space can be a drawback. Air moves freely around your body, resulting in loss of warmth. Most rectangular bags have no hoods—but they do have full-length zippers that allow them to be used as quilts in camp or at home.

The barrel-shaped bag is a compromise between the roomy comfort of the rectangular and the thermal efficiency of the mummy. The barrel style is cut more

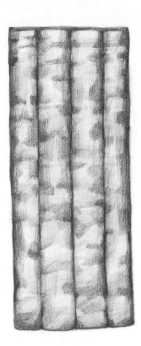

Sleeping-Bag Shapes

fully than the mummy around the feet and torso, yet is not squared off as widely at the head and foot. Some come with hoods, others without.

There are a number of variations of the basic shapes including modified mummy, semirectangular and tapered bags. The modified mummy combines the best features of the mummy and the barrel. Although it's somewhat fuller at the hips, it's distinctly a mummy, with both a hood and bottle-shaped foot. The semirectangular bag is simply a more generously cut barrel model, while the tapered bag is nothing more than the rectangular bag tapered so that the foot is slightly narrower than the shoulder.

Cut and Construction

For a sleeping bag to be at its best, the insulation must be free to loft and must be distributed evenly throughout. If the insulation is compressed in any manner between the outer shell and the lining, or if it shifts too easily, cold spots will develop. The compression problem is eliminated in some better bags by "differential cut," in which the circumference of the bag's inner shell is cut substantially smaller than that of the outer. This prevents compression of the insulation against the outer shell everywhere except under your body. Many of the better bags supplement the differential cut with a box or oval foot section, which allows the feet to rest upright without driving the inner shell against the outer.

Differential Cut

To keep it from shifting, down is quilted or compartmentalized. The simplest method, sewn-through construction, is acceptable only on summer bags and sleeping-bag liners. Down is distributed evenly throughout, and the inner and outer shells are then stitched together. This makes for a lightweight bag but the sewn-through seams do not stop the escape of body warmth. The double-offset method used in some insulated outerwear (see Chapter 2, p. 33) eliminates heat loss through the seams but the result is a relatively heavy and bulky bag. And, like sewn-through quilting, it inhibits natural lofting.

Better sleeping bags rely on one of three types of baffle construction to hold the down in place. These baffles are fabric dividers located between the outer and inner shells, and are usually made of nylon tricot or mesh netting. Stretch fabrics are now used in many bags to reduce stress on the quilt stitching.

The simplest of the three is the box baffle in which the baffles are sewn to the inner and outer shells at right angles. This encourages full lofting but cold spots may develop if the compartments are not adequately filled with down. Slant-wall construction is identical except that the baffles meet the inner and outer shells at 45° angles, forming parallelogram-shaped tubes that allow the down to loft while distributing it more evenly.

The most effective baffle method involves V-tube construction. If the tubes could be seen from one end, the baffles would appear to zig-zag between the inner and outer shells, forming triangular compartments so that no seam is without full down backing. It is a costly process. The numerous baffles require more fabric and considerably more stitching, which add slightly to weight and bulk. However, they produce a superior sleeping bag, particularly for winter use. Incidentally, the tubes—whether box, slant or V—do not run lengthwise on the bag, but circumscribe it.

Most down bags are of slant-wall construction, the best compromise among warmth, weight and cost. Manufacturers' specifications generally indicate the type of tube employed, but it's relatively easy to determine this for yourself. Grasp the stitch line on the outer shell in one hand and the stitch line on the inner shell with the other, and pull them apart gently. If the seams appear directly opposed, it's a box-baffle bag. If they are diagonally opposed, it's a slant-wall construction. Seams that appear to be interconnected indicate a V-tube design. Note also the

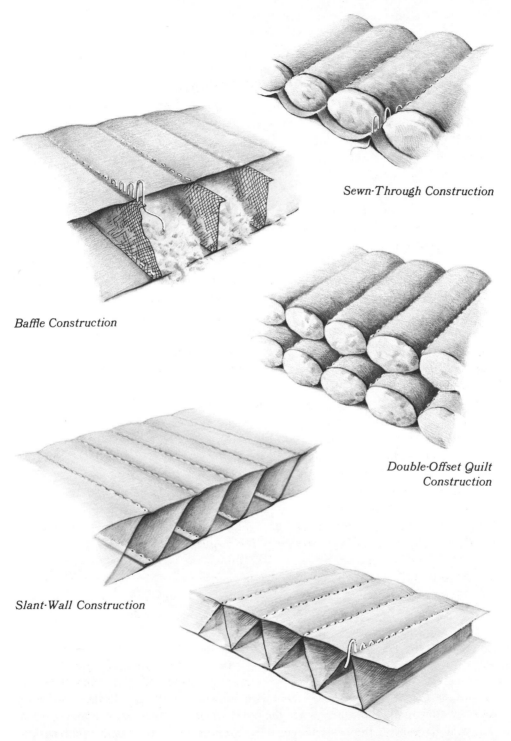

Sewn-Through Construction

Baffle Construction

Double-Offset Quilt
Construction

Slant-Wall Construction

V-Tube Construction

width of the baffles, or compartments. On better down bags, the width of the tubes should not exceed seven inches—but if they do, the tubes must be filled with extra down to provide proper lofting and to eliminate the chance of cold spots.

Because polyester insulation comes in batts—flat sheets of matted fibers—rather than in batches of loose fibers and clusters, compartments are unnecessary. The batts merely need to be anchored in place. Inexpensive polyester-fill sleeping bags are of sewn-through, quilted construction. They have the same disadvantages as sewn-through down bags. Polyester bags of better quality are likely to employ double-offset quilting, edge stabilization or sandwich construction. In the edge-stabilized construction, the batts are layered and stitched to the edge of the bag's shell: along the zipper tape and across the foot and the head of the bag. Thus, there are no quilting seams to compress the batts. This type of construction has one disadvantage. Since there is considerable shifting between the batts and the shell, the bag loses its shape when washed or stuffed. The shape can be restored, of course, by working the batts back into place with the hands, but this is a considerable chore. Multilayer or sandwich construction combines the no-shift advantage of quilting with the full lofting of edge stabilizing. The insulation is layered (two to four layers in both the bottom and top halves of the bag), the outer layer quilted to the outer shell. The innermost layer is then quilted to the lining and the middle layer edge-stabilized, which holds the batts firmly in place and allows for full lofting. This construction is used in better polyester-filled bags.

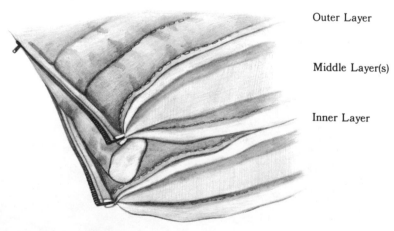

Outer Layer

Middle Layer(s)

Inner Layer

Sandwich Construction

Another design is shingle construction, in which batts of PolarGuard® are overlapped, shinglelike, and sewn to the inner and outer shells at regularly spaced intervals. By varying the amount of overlap, weight and loft are controlled, resulting in a durable and efficient sleeping bag.

Shingle Construction

WHICH BAG IS BEST FOR YOU?

Before deciding on a bag, ask yourself three questions: Will you carry the bag on your back or in a boat or car? What temperature ranges do you anticipate? How much can you afford to pay?

If neither weight nor bulk is a problem and you don't need a bag that provides maximum warmth, choose the comfort and roominess of a full-size rectangular bag. However, for backpacking, cycling or canoe trips involving lengthy or diffi-cult portages, the bulk and weight of such a bag are out of the question. You can reduce this bulk and weight without sacrificing warmth by selecting a mummy-type down bag. If such a down bag is beyond your means, the best alternative is a mummy-shaped polyester-filled bag.

Weight and temperature range are closely interrelated so that sleeping bags fall into three broad temperature-range categories: summer, three-season and four-season. A summer bag will loft about one-and-a-half to two inches (top shell) and will be comfortable down to 30 to 40 degrees Fahrenheit. The weight of the bag can vary considerably, from as little as two pounds in a down mummy model suitable for backpacking to as much as three-and-a-half pounds in a more full cut PolarGuard® or Hollofil II® model. A three-season bag with two-and-a-half to three inches of loft and a temperature rating of about 10 degrees will weigh in the neighborhood of four pounds with a down filling in the mummy style; or up to six pounds in a polyester-filled, rectangular model. Four-season bags, suitable for the coldest weather, loft to approximately three to three-and-a-half inches and are comfortable to about −10 degrees. Weight is generally in excess of five pounds in the polyester bags, and over four pounds in the down models. Still warmer bags with greater loft and somewhat increased weight are used under extreme condi-tions, such as mountain climbing or arctic expeditions.

If you're strictly a warm-weather camper, there's no reason to buy anything other than a summer bag. For winter camping, a four-season bag is a must. But if you want to get started as early as possible in the spring and are reluctant to abandon the big woods after Labor Day, the best all-around choice is a hooded, barrel-shaped, three-season bag. It will keep you warm during a chilly April night and, if left unzipped, it's comfortable at 60 degrees in the summer. Come fall, you can sleep in it for a few extra weeks. And, your three-season model will work well into the winter if you slip a liner or down summer bag into it. Most liners will increase the temperature range of a bag by up to 20 degrees.

A quality sleeping bag is a costly but worthwhile investment. Buy the best you can possibly afford, perhaps even temporarily foregoing some other item.

Finally, never overestimate your needs. Buying too much bag can be as great a mistake as buying too little. If temperatures plummet abnormally, you can always add a layer of clothing. That's better than roasting in an oversize expedition bag at 40 degrees.

Checking Out a Sleeping Bag

When you've narrowed your choice to three or four sleeping bags, all may appear to be similar in design, loft, weight and perhaps even color. Look more closely. You'll find important differences. Start with the stitching on the zipper tape, the hood (if any) and the inside of the foot. Stitches should run evenly, eight to ten to the inch, with no bunching or skipping. If the stitching winds on and off the edge of the fabric, eliminate the bag immediately. This is a sign of sloppy workmanship. Stress points, such as each end of the zipper, should be bartacked or reinforced.

The next step is to get into the bag. Pull the hood tightly about your head and shoulders to be sure it fits. The drawstring should stay securely snugged up, with no slippage. A cord lock, operable from the inside, is a necessity. Proper size is easy to determine. If, with the bag snugged securely about your shoulders, your feet feel crowded against the bottom of the bag, or if there is too much pressure about your shoulders, the bag is probably too small. This snugness may not seem objectionable during a brief test in a store, but it will prove downright uncomfortable during a long, cold night. What's more, it will detract from the bag's warmth. On the other hand, if the bag seems overly large, try one that is less generously cut. There is no sense in having extra free-flowing air within the bag that your body will have to heat.

Since your feet are quick to feel a chill, check the foot section carefully. The easiest way to build a sleeping bag is to sew the bottom and top halves together with a single, simple seam. This provides no room for the feet and causes compression of the insulation. Better bags, especially those intended for cold weather use, have a box or oval foot section. This creates a compartment that allows your feet to rest upright without undue tension against the inner shell—and ultimately, the outer one. In a down bag, this foot compartment should incorporate a horizontal baffle to keep the down filler from settling.

Turn the bag inside out, still concentrating your attention on the foot. Seams should not be exposed, or loose. Stuffing and restuffing the bag into its carrying

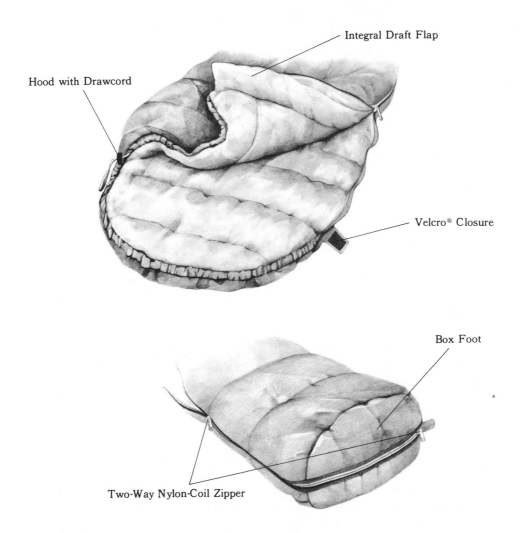

Integral Draft Flap

Hood with Drawcord

Velcro® Closure

Box Foot

Two-Way Nylon-Coil Zipper

Sleeping-Bag Features

sack will loosen, and eventually break, insecure seams. Now examine the longitudinal seam opposite the zipper. This seam joins the top and bottom halves of the
bag. The least efficient way to sew these together is with a simple sewn-through
stitch, which will allow precious body heat to escape. Better bags have a sidewall
baffle here. You can check it in the same manner you determined the type of baffle
design. If there is a baffle joining the inner and outer shells, the bag will husband
body warmth more efficiently.

Zippers are generally either of metal or nylon. Metal is cold, temperamental,
and may freeze or corrode. Nylon, not subject to freezing or corrosion, is more
reliable. As with apparel there are two basic nylon zipper designs—the tooth-and-
ladder, in which teeth interlock when the slider is pulled, and the coil, which is

less likely to get stuck. The coil zipper is "self-repairing," and will continue to run smoothly even though it may have suffered some minor damage. It's less prone to snagging and is somewhat more airtight, important on a cold night. A zipper that can be opened from either end, the foot or the head, more readily permits ventilation. Naturally, any sleeping-bag zipper should have pull-tabs on both the inside and outside, along with a Velcro® closure to keep it from opening while you sleep.

By way of size designation, zippers are numbered, but it's a baffling system. The No. 5, No. 7 and No. 10 nylon coil zippers used on sleeping bags vary in size from one manufacturer to another. The best way for a layman to judge is to appraise the heft and apparent durability of the teeth or coils. A light zipper, adequate for a pair of trousers, has no place on a sleeping bag.

Sleeping-bag zippers vary in length, too. Those on mummy, modified-mummy and barrel-shaped bags are usually three-quarter length, leaving the foot of the bag completely enclosed. Most other styles have full-length zippers, extending down one side and across the foot; this permits you to use the bag as a comforter. Many sleeping bags can be mated to form double bags, provided the zippers are exactly alike. Mating two mummy, modified-mummy or barrel bags, however, requires that you buy one bag with a left-hand zipper, and the other with a right-hand one; both of course, should have similar zippers.

Considerable heat can be lost through zippers. To arrest this loss, an insulated draft flap is sewn on the inside of the bag behind the zipper. If this flap is sewn through to the upper shell along the same seam that attaches the zipper, the seam will leak heat to the outside. A more effective draft flap is one sewn to the upper inside shell; thus, the flap will cover not only the zipper but also the seam that attaches the zipper to the bag. More sophisticated systems are used in bags designed for extreme conditions, such as a double-zipper system with a draft flap locked securely between them—or even in some instances, double flaps. A draft flap should always have a sewn-in fabric stiffener to keep the zipper from snagging it. Also, a gussett at the foot of the bag, where the flap and zipper meet, eliminates any flow of cold air at this point.

When ordering from a mail-order firm, check the catalog's specifications carefully; the chances are that they will answer most of your questions. Then choose the model that seems best to fill your needs. Upon delivery, conduct your own "in-person" tests. If the bag does not meet your expectations, return it with a letter pointing out what you consider to be deficiencies. Reputable mail-order firms will then provide a bag to suit you.

SLEEPING-BAG CARE

Your new sleeping bag will probably come with a "stuff bag." Use it. Generally made of coated nylon, with a flap that tucks under a drawstring closure, it protects the bag against snagging or other damage. It also keeps the sleeping bag dry and clean. It's called a stuff bag for good reason. Don't try to roll or fold your bag. Stuff it—literally. Do this gently, starting at the foot to avoid trapping air. Thrust the sleeping bag into the stuff bag, one fistful at a time, compressing it firmly. In removing the sleeping bag, draw it out carefully. This is not to imply that sleeping bags are fragile. They are not. However, overly rough handling can damage them. On the trail, unstuff your bag as soon as you arrive in camp to allow the filler to attain full loft before you turn in.

At home, remove the sleeping bag from its stuff bag for storage. Otherwise, lengthy compression will reduce both down's and polyester's lofting capacity. Store the bag loosely folded on a shelf in a dry area. Keep it away from direct sunlight or extreme heat: both will dry out the natural oils that give down its resilience and destroy the crimp and bonding agents in polyester fills.

A sleeping bag need not be washed after every trip but it should be aired out before storage. If outdoor airing isn't possible, run it through a machine dryer at a low-heat setting. Eventually, though, your down sleeping bag will need washing. Do this by hand, not in a machine. Lay the bag in a few inches of lukewarm water in the bathtub, using a mild soap—Ivory®, Woolite® or one of the special down soaps available from most outfitters. Push the bag up and down, gently working in the suds. Localized dirt can be sponged. As the suds and water begin to appear dirty, drain the tub and refill it with clean water, repeating the process until dirt no longer discolors the water. Rinse thoroughly, again by pressing the bag with the flat of your hands as the tub drains.

To remove the bag, cradle it in your hands and arms. Never lift it by one end, or the soggy (and heavy) clumps of down may damage the baffles. It can be dried outdoors, laying it flat on the ground, but this may require several days. It's better to use a large dryer with a low-heat setting, under 140 degrees. As the down begins to dry, toss in a sneaker (minus laces) in order to break up the clumps of down and to fluff up the plumules.

If you choose to have your down bag dry-cleaned be sure that a special down-cleaning fluid, such as Stoddard's Fluid, is used. Most other commercial cleaning solvents will remove the natural oils in down. Air your bag thoroughly before using it. Otherwise, residue fumes from the dry-cleaning fluid could make you ill.

A polyester bag can be hand washed, or if you prefer, machine washed on a gentle setting. Use warm water, not hot, which will ruin polyester's crimp. To dry, hang the bag outdoors or tumble dry at a low-heat setting. Do not dry-clean polyester bags.

PADS AND MATTRESSES

In *Hunting—Fishing and Camping,* L.L. told how to build a bough bed. He attached no romance or mystique to it. Like other woodsmen of his era, he took the bough bed for granted. It required spruce boughs, curved and springy, piled to a depth of about twelve inches, with about six inches of smaller and more flexible fir boughs placed over them for cushioning. This matter-of-fact heap provided an experience one long remembered. Wrapped in wool blankets, with the aroma of balsam blending with that of wood smoke, a camper's life was serene indeed. Alas, the bough bed is no longer with us. If we all built bough beds, we'd soon denude the forests along our travel routes. Not only is the bough bed now frowned upon, but it's also illegal in some areas.

So, we turn to other types of sleeping bag cushioning—foam pads and air mattresses. These not only soften the bumps and gouges of the earth's surface but also reduce conductive heat loss. And they protect a sleeping bag against ground dirt, moisture and abrasion.

For use at a trailside camp, the most popular type is a foam pad. Of the two broad categories—closed-cell and open-cell foam—the closed-cell models are lighter, more compact and provide the best insulation. They are ideal for canoeing and fishing trips since their closed-cell structure will not soak up water.

There are two types of closed-cell foam—polyvinyl chloride (Ensolite®, Airex®) and polyethylene (Volarafoam®, Blue Foam®). Polyvinyl chloride pads are heavier yet more durable. They are also easier to roll up. Some, like Ensolite®, however, become brittle in cold weather and are subject to deterioration if exposed to the sun for long periods. Polyethylene pads are lighter and less expensive. But they gouge and tear more easily than those of polyvinyl chloride.

Don't look for the comfort of a luxury mattress and box spring when you sleep on closed-cell foam pads. They are usually three-eighths inch thick, little more than basic, spartanlike beds, which can be rolled compactly for backpacking.

More comfortable are one-and-a-half to two-and-a-half inch thick open-cell pads of polyurethane foam. While this is soft and flexible, open-cell foam does not insulate as well and readily absorbs moisture, much like a sponge. For this reason, it should be used only with some sort of waterproof sheet or cover. The best

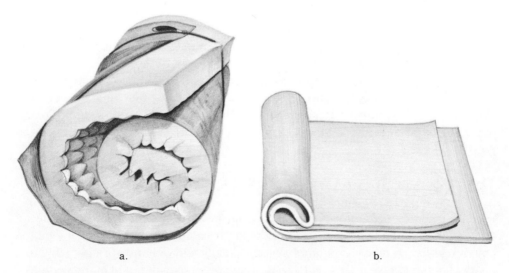

a.   b.

Two Types of Foam Pads a. *Open Cell* b. *Closed Cell*

covers envelop the pad, have waterproof-coated nylon bottoms and breathable tops. Models with cotton-blend tops are less slippery than those with nylon taffeta shells.

There are pads that combine both types of foam. One of these includes a quarter inch of closed-cell foam, for protection against moisture, and one-and-a-quarter inches of open-cell foam for added cushioning. This style of pad, while slightly bulky, is well suited to cold weather camping.

Foam Pad Specifications

Type	*Approximate Dimensions**	*Approximate Weight**
P.V.C.—¾ length	56″ x 21″ x ⅜″	20 ounces
P.V.C.—full length	84″ x 21″ x ⅜″	30 ounces
Polyethylene—¾ length	54″ x 24″ x ⅜″	9 ounces
Polyethylene—full length	70″ x 24″ x ⅜″	11 ounces
Polyurethane—¾ length	48″ x 27″ x 2½″	40 ounces
Polyurethane—full length	75″ x 27″ x 2½″	64 ounces
Combination P.V.C./Poly-urethane—¾ length	48″ x 20″ x 1½″	24 ounces
Combination P.V.C./Poly-urethane—full length	72″ x 20″ x 1½″	40 ounces
Air Mattress—¾ length	44″ x 28″	7 ounces
Air Mattress—full length	72″ x 28″	11 ounces
Therm-A-Rest®—¾ length	48″ x 20″ x 1½″	23 ounces
Therm-A-Rest®—full length	72″ x 20″ x 1½″	36 ounces

* Sizes and weight may vary depending on the manufacturer.

Air mattresses are comfortable, they roll or fold into a much more compact bundle than is possible with foam, their weight runs as little as seven to twelve ounces and so far as bulk is concerned, they are probably the best choice among trail beds. However, the free-flowing air within provides little, if any, insulation and they are slow to inflate and deflate. And, of course, they're subject to leaks. Among the more reliable air mattresses are those with tubes that are inflated separately and can be easily removed for repair or replacement. Carry a repair kit.

Incidentally, beginners are inclined to overinflate air mattresses, producing a sleeping surface little more comfortable than bare ground. Sleep in an air mattress, not on it. When testing it, lie on it full length. Probing it with a fist or knee only leads to pumping in more air than is needed.

A novel and effective design is the recently developed Therm-A-Rest® foam pad, which is encased in a coated-nylon shell. The pad consists of an open-cell interior which, when a valve is opened, causes foam to suck in air—in other words, to self-inflate—thus combining the insulation value of foam with the adaptability of the air mattress. Therm-A-Rest® pads are light and convenient but narrow—and, with their nylon shell, slippery. It's a bit of a challenge to stay centered on one for a full night.

Hammocks are a practical alternative to trail beds in tropical climates. Strung between two trees they keep well off the damp ground, and out of reach of pests. Some hammocks weigh no more than a polyurethane pad and can be tucked into an already full pack. If insects are abroad, you'll need some sort of headnet for protection. Obviously, hammocks are unsuitable in the rain.

NIGHT COMFORT

Spend enough time on the trail and sooner or later you'll hit an unexpected cold snap during which your sleeping bag may prove inadequate. All is not lost.

Choose campsites carefully. Cold air settles into low-lying valleys while, at high elevations, exposure to wind has a chilling effect. Select campsites located somewhere between these, on a hillside, for example.

Always use a tent. It will add about ten degrees of warmth. Lacking a tent, rig a lean-to shelter with a tarp, ground cloth or poncho to deflect the wind. Use a ground pad under your sleeping bag to slow conductive heat loss. When the weather is unusually bitter, slip an extra insulated jacket or vest under your body.

Moisture is the prime thief of insulation. Keep your sleeping bag dry at all cost. During the summer, air it whenever possible, during breakfast, for instance. While sleeping out in the winter, avoid snugging the bag around your nose and mouth, so that vapor from your breathing is not trapped. Some moisture build-up stemming from body vapor is inevitable, of course. Ventilation will minimize this. And, before stuffing the bag for the day's trek, brush all frost from it.

You can also add to your warmth by practicing layering. Don two layers of underwear, pull on an extra pair of socks or booties, wear a wool cap, snug the bag's hood about your head. If you're still cold, add more layers.

Speed up your metabolism rate before retiring by exercising mildly, or by eating foods that are high in fat and carbohydrate value. Hot chocolate helps greatly.

Chapter 5

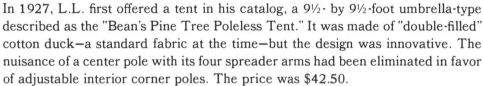

Shelter: Tents for All Seasons

In 1927, L.L. first offered a tent in his catalog, a 9½- by 9½-foot umbrella-type described as the "Bean's Pine Tree Poleless Tent." It was made of "double-filled" cotton duck—a standard fabric at the time—but the design was innovative. The nuisance of a center pole with its four spreader arms had been eliminated in favor of adjustable interior corner poles. The price was $42.50.

Times change. And so have tents. But not the need for them. Sleeping under the stars can be a delightful experience, but in most parts of North America a shelter is necessary. We need a tent for the same reasons that we wear clothes—as protection against wind, rain or snow, and to some degree for warmth. Then, of course, there are the insects, the biting kind which are often more active at night than by day. Except in certain arid regions, camping out or traveling in the backcountry without some kind of shelter verges on the foolhardy. Since modern fabrics and designs have resulted in lightweight, highly portable tents, there's little justification for doing without.

Tents can be separated into three basic categories: lightweight, three-season tents; expedition models for winter or high-altitude use; and fixed-camp tents. The three-season models are the most popular, being suitable for the majority of camping activities. Expedition tents are largely three-season models that have been beefed up to withstand hard use and embellished with special features. Fixed-camp tents are large and preferred by hunters, fishermen, family and auto campers to whom extra space is more important than light weight and ease of carrying. Tents in all three categories are generally made of the same materials and share similar construction features.

MATERIALS

Fabrics

Until the early 1960s there were few radical changes in materials, tentmakers having been limited to using cotton, commonly—but often incorrectly—referred to as "canvas." Today, the few cotton tents that are still made are generally for fixed-camp use. Most of these are of poplin which weighs seven to eight ounces per yard, is tightly woven, quite wind resistant and moderately lightweight—at least as compared to old-time double-filled duck, a true but heavy canvas. Cotton is also remarkably breathable. There is no condensation problem even on wet and humid nights, a drawback of many nylon tents.

Cotton poses problems, however. In a heavy rain, it may "mist," a fine, foglike moisture penetrating the fabric. Touching the inside of the roof can create a leak caused by capillary action. A cotton tent, therefore, really needs a waterproof fly. Another drawback to cotton is its susceptibility to mildew and rot. It requires special care such as thorough drying before storage. Still, if weight and bulk are not objectionable, a number of cotton poplin tents are well suited to stationary camping.

For most other uses, there are numerous tents of lighter, more durable fabrics—principally nylon. Nylon is stronger, as breathable when uncoated, less bulky and adaptable to designs that are more wind resistant. Mildew doesn't bother nylon. It does have shortcomings, though. Under constant exposure to the sun's ultra-violet rays, nylon tends to deteriorate, something which mountaineers have noticed at high altitudes where sunrays are stronger. In some lightweight tents, polyester has been introduced to combat this problem.

As a tent fabric, nylon did not get off to a promising start. In Italy during World War II, ski troopers of the 10th Mountain Division were issued tightly enclosed, single-wall nylon tents. These sweated badly on the interior and, in cold weather, the men often found themselves encased in ice come morning. The fabric simply did not breathe. As recently as 1960, umbrella tents of nylon developed interior puddles of moisture for the same reasons. Today, the problem has been solved by double-wall construction. Uncoated—and therefore breathable—nylons such as rip-stop and taffeta are used in the side walls and roofs over which a polyurethane-coated nylon fly is draped. With this combination, the inner tent releases interior moisture while the outer wall or fly repels rain and snow. This double-wall design also creates a thin insulating barrier between the fly and walls that helps reduce interior condensation and heat loss. Ground moisture is kept at bay by sewed-in coated nylon floors.

PTFE fabrics, widely used in apparel and in some sleeping bags, are also found in a limited number of tents. The PTFE film is usually sandwiched between a nylon shell and a nylon or polyester lining, resulting in a fabric combination

Double-Wall Tent

weighing about four ounces more per yard than plain nylon. As noted in Chapter 2, PTFE fabrics are breathable yet repel rain, eliminating the need for a fly, and would seem ideal for tents. However, problems seem to occur in cold weather when the difference between interior and exterior temperatures becomes pronounced. Condensation accumulates on the inside tent walls and, sooner or later, it freezes, thus inhibiting the fabric's breathability. Moreover, PTFE tent seams are not sealed at the factory. You must do this yourself. And PTFE tents are expensive, about double the price of similar nylon shelters.

Legislation enacted in many states during the early 1970s requires that most tent materials be flame retardant. While the treatment does not make tents fireproof, treated fabrics will self-extinguish once the flame source is removed. Early flame-retardant treatments used on cotton tents added up to 20 percent in weight and increased costs by 10 to 15 percent. But newer treatments for nylon have little adverse effect on either weight or cost.

Poles and Stakes

Virtually all modern tents are suspended from interior or exterior frames, or held in position by sectional "wands" inserted into fabric sleeves. The term "pole," however, continues in use.

Most frames are of aluminum alloy in sections of varying lengths, some connected by shockcord so that no segment of the pole assembly can be lost easily. (Also, with this shockcord connection, you don't have to figure out which section goes where.) Fiberglass is used, too, one type being tubular to allow for shockcord-section connections. Solid rod fiberglass, one-half inch thick, while less expensive, is somewhat heavier.

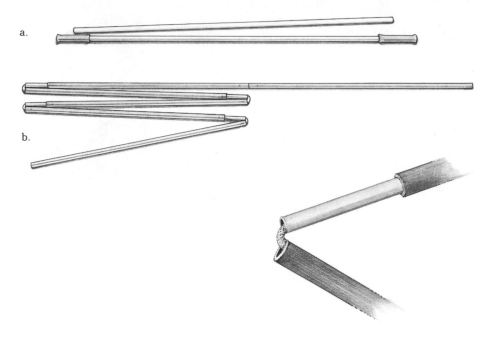

Tent Poles a. *Fiberglass Wands* b. *Shockcord-Connected Aluminum Poles*

Flexible pole sections, whether of aluminum or fiberglass, have made possible the design of tents with curved walls and arched ridgelines. Such frames actually flex to conform to the general shape of the shelter, easing tension and taking up slack. Generally, fiberglass is more flexible and can be bent into the tighter arc so necessary for modern geodesic-design tents. Both aluminum or fiberglass frames are remarkably durable, compact and easy to carry. Frames require some care, of course. Aluminum sections can be bent beyond their limit, and fiberglass tips can be damaged through cracking or chipping.

Not too many years ago, most tents came with wooden poles, usually two pieces joined by means of a ferrule. These were heavy and bulky. Many campers discarded them, preferring to cut poles at the campsite, or to string their tents between two trees. With today's tents, such "jerry rigs" are possible in an emergency, of course, but it makes more sense to use the frame assembly provided with them. Because both frames and tents are designed to "give" in strong winds, any sort of rigid improvisation could result in damage to the fabric.

Most of today's tent-pole sections run anywhere from fourteen to twenty inches when dismantled. This should present no problem in packing. Pole sections can be rolled within the tent, but it's better to use a pole bag, usually provided with the shelter, to prevent the relatively sharp pole ends from damaging the fabric. Before leaving on a trip, check your tent frame to be sure all sections are present. Many frames cannot be assembled if they lack even a single section.

Examine the stakes that are supplied with your new tent. These are often metal skewers, commonly provided with backpacking tents. Although they will hold fairly well in packed earth, they are worthless in sand or snow. Replace them with nine- to twelve-inch plastic stakes, which are virtually unbreakable and tough enough to withstand being driven with a hatchet or stake mallet into gravel or even lightly frozen earth. When you buy replacement stakes, be sure that they fit through the beckets (stake loops) of your tent.

In deep snow, stakes will not hold, but snow anchors or wide-shafted aluminum "flukes" will usually do the job if driven deeply enough. Makeshift snow anchors or "deadmen" are often more effective. Branches, stone-filled stuff sacks, rocks, skis, ski poles, even snowshoes, to which guy lines are attached, can be buried in the snow and then packed down by treading.

Whatever kinds of stakes or anchors you use, carry them in a separate bag to protect the fabric against soiling, puncturing or abrasion. If no such bag is provided with your tent, you can make one from a strip of poplin or cotton duck.

Many of today's tents are "free-standing," and supposedly require no guy lines. This may be fine at a sheltered campsite, but if your tent is exposed to strong winds—on a lakeshore or above the timberline—it's wise to rig guy lines. Many tents come equipped with such lines, but carry extra cord so that, if need be, you can extend them to reach trees, stumps or rocks. This extra cord can also be used to anchor ridgelines, wall pullouts and awning poles. Adjustable guys, with a section of shockcord tied in, eliminate the need for fussing with knots in windy or cold weather. Be sure that guy-line tighteners are attached to the lines so that they can't be lost.

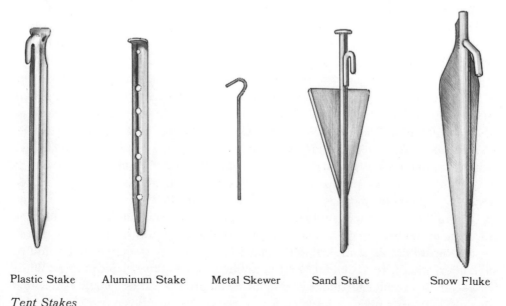

Plastic Stake   Aluminum Stake   Metal Skewer   Sand Stake   Snow Fluke

Tent Stakes

Netting

Since most tents now come equipped with nylon insect netting on the windows and doors, we tend to take this protection for granted. However, not all tents are equipped with "no-see-um" netting, a finer variety than the open-mesh mosquito netting found in less expensive tents. While slightly denser no-see-um netting cuts down ventilation a little, it will keep out black flies, midges and other tiny pests and is practically mandatory if you plan to camp during the early summer in regions where insects may prove a serious nuisance. In certain areas some varieties of black flies persist through the entire summer season.

Zippers

The nylon coil zippers described in Chapter 2 (page 50) are fairly standard on most high-quality tents. They are smooth-running, dependable and flexible enough to be used in curved doors and windows even in cold weather. The exact size isn't important so long as the zipper appears sturdy and has a slider tab large enough to grasp when you're wearing gloves. Metal zippers are not recommended. They're less reliable than nylon and are inclined to jam.

CONSTRUCTION

Even a well-cared-for tent is subject to considerable abuse from heavy snows and especially from gusty winds. The walls may "balloon" or "parachute," straining seams at the corners, peaks and pullouts. During the normal process of pitching or breaking camp, weakened seams may part, or poorly reinforced stake pockets may tear out. Obviously, workmanship—stitching, seam construction and the reinforcements of stress points—is critical.

The most secure seams are sewn with a cotton-covered polyester core thread. Eight to ten stitches per inch are required, although this may range from as few as six to as many as twelve. Fewer than six to seven stitches per inch will not hold in a high wind; more than twelve tends to weaken the fabric along the stitch line.

Double-needle stitching is important, too. This appears as two rows of parallel stitches running evenly along the seams, with no loose threads or puckering in evidence. Stitches running off the seam are a sign of shoddy workmanship. Lockstitching is generally more secure than chainstitching. With the latter, if one stitch is broken the sewing may unravel. On the other hand, chainstitching may be used on some of the less exposed seams because of the "give" it provides under strain.

The most durable seam is the lap-fell. Here, the edges of the fabric are folded and interlocked with each other so that stitching passes through four layers. While this seam is recommended for nylon tents, it can prove needlessly bulky on cotton models. Instead, a plain or flat-fell seam is used on cotton. This is a simple overlap of fabric backed on the inside with cotton tape and double-needle stitched. The interior tape backing enhances the seam's strength tremendously.

While some nylon tents have factory-sealed seams, others are sold with a tube of seam sealant to be applied by the buyer. Regardless, the seams of every new tent should be sealed before your first night out. If you use the tent regularly, reseal the seams every six to twelve months.

All stress points require reinforcement. The peaks and corners should incorporate a double layer of fabric to distribute tension. Pole sleeves and corner pole pockets of exterior-frame tents should be securely backstitched. If the poles are anchored in grommets, these should be set in an extra layer of fabric, or in a heavier material such as nylon oxford. Zipper tapes and stake loops should be bartacked or boxtacked.

DESIGN

Nylon, fiberglass and flexible aluminum have broadened horizons for tent designers. Early tentmakers were restricted to working with planes and peaks; domes and spheres could not be properly suspended by rigid wooden poles. While some of the basic plane surfaces are still in use, designs today are limited only by the tentmaker's imagination. Wind-shedding arches and domes are now commonplace. New materials have resulted in better ventilation, greater weather resistance, improved durability and more efficient use of interior space. Weight and bulk have also been reduced remarkably.

Compare, for example, a modern geodesic, two-man tent weighing slightly more than seven pounds to the two-man model designed by the noted British mountaineer, Edward Whymper, for climbing in the Alps. In 1862, Whymper announced proudly that, at long last, he had devised the ideal tent. It weighed 23 pounds and he had to hire a porter to tote it for him.

Design determines how well—or how poorly—a tent will perform. Performance involves weather resistance, ventilation, weight and to a lesser degree, aesthetics, or the general "feel" of a tent.

Among the lightweight three-season, expedition and fixed-camp tents, there are a great number of styles. Considerable overlap exists between the three-season and expedition tent categories: A-frame, dome and tunnel designs are found in both. Fixed-camp tents, including umbrella, cabin, baker and wall models, are in a class by themselves.

One of the oldest of all designs is the A-frame or wedge tent. It was originally rigged with an interior pole at each end which was guyed to a stake. Subsequent models had exterior inverted V-poles, thus eliminating the nuisance of a pole bisecting the entrance. The newest A-frame tents are totally self-supporting, require no guy lines and utilize an adjustable ridgepole to hold inverted V-poles in place at each end.

Dome and tunnel tents are relative newcomers, their design using the concept of the arch. The dome model relies on basic geodesic lines for support. Three or four flexible wands, inserted into sleeves on the tent's exterior, form a series of crossing arches from which the tent is suspended. (The design may be "new" but the Eskimo adapted it to blocks of snow to build his igloo long before the Vikings probed the North Atlantic coast.) The tunnel tent resembles the Quonset hut of World War II and is suspended on two or three "hoops." Unlike the dome tent, it is not free-standing. A guy line is required at each end. Most fixed-camp tents are hung from exterior frames by means of shockcords; the modern umbrella tent is a good example, as is the cabin tent. Neither generally requires guy lines, although these are advisable in high wind.

Weather Resistance

While double-wall construction pretty much assures a weatherproof tent, proper window and door design also contribute to this. Zippered closures, for example, should be operable from the inside. If the tent is equipped with a fly that extends out over the windows, so much the better. Since U-shaped or triangular-style

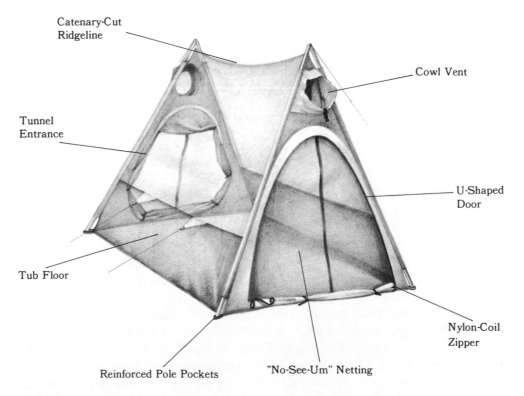

Catenary-Cut
Ridgeline

Cowl Vent

Tunnel
Entrance

U-Shaped
Door

Tub Floor

Nylon-Coil
Zipper

Reinforced Pole Pockets   "No-See-Um" Netting

Tent Features

doorways have zippers that open from the top, such doorways afford good protection against rain or snow. When snow has drifted up against the door you can exit without the nuisance of snow tumbling into the tent. During warm weather, the top of the door can be left open for ventilation on a rainy night without fear of water dripping into the shelter. Perhaps the least desirable type of entry is the inverted "T" in which one zipper bisects the door vertically and two shorter ones close across the bottom. Not only must you contend with three zippers but the bottom closure invites snow and rain to enter. Also, horizontal zippers are prone to leaking.

Not all moisture comes from the sky or from interior condensation. There is considerable moisture in the ground, to say nothing of rain run-off; both can seep into the tent. This problem is solved in cotton and nylon tents by a sewn-in, coated nylon floor, the waterproof fabric running up the sides from six to twelve inches to form a "tub bottom," or a "wraparound floor." The seams in such a floor are sealed, although some tub bottoms are of one-piece design without seams. You can clean such a floor simply by wiping it occasionally with a damp cloth, a blessing during a rainy spell when boots track in mud and debris.

For winter camping, a tunnel entrance virtually eliminates rain or snow from the tent's interior—although crawling through such an entry can be a somewhat awkward procedure. Most such tents are also provided with an additional U-shaped or triangular entrance for mild-weather use.

In order for stress to be distributed properly and for a tent to withstand buffeting by the wind, its surfaces should be taut or wrinkle-free. This depends on the cut of the tent and the design of the support system. On A-style and exterior-frame tents, the ridgeline should incorporate a "catenary cut" in which the natural sag of the ridgeline is built in, so that the walls of the tent can be pitched tautly. This minimizes noisy flapping in the wind and reduces strain on the fabric and the frame. Best of all, you'll get a better night's sleep. A camper unfamiliar with the catenary cut may attempt to straighten the ridgeline. Don't. You may tear the fabric.

The sturdiest tents are those rigged on rigid exterior frames, which can withstand strong wind gusts. Tents supported by flexible poles such as the dome and tunnel models are easily distorted in high winds unless they are rigged with guy lines. Larger tents will not spill wind as readily but their rigid frames hold firmly.

Ventilation

Even with interior vapor escaping through the fabric, a fully enclosed tent can become uncomfortably stuffy. You'll want a well-designed system of vents or windows to bring in fresh air, especially on a warm night. Vents placed so that they create a cross-draft are ideal. Opening a pair of doors, or a door and a window on opposite sides of the shelter, also provides a cross-draft. Some of the better tents incorporate ridge (cowl) vents in addition to one or more doors and windows; these vents are sheltered by the fly and backed with no-see-um netting.

Ventilating dome tents can be more difficult. Some of them have a ceiling vent, which is of limited value because of the close-fitting fly. Windows spaced around the tent's perimeter may also be covered by the fly or outer wall. And, because these are low, opening them in bad weather can cause drafts, and snow can drift in through them. The best solution is a dome tent with slightly raised zip-down windows and doors on opposite sides to provide controlled cross-ventilation.

Size, Shape and Volume

By nature, a tent is a portable shelter, convenient to carry whether on a pack-frame, in a canoe or boat, on a bicycle or in a car. The degree of portability limits the weight. Weight in turn limits volume, or the usable space within the tent.

Unfortunately, the cubic-foot volume of the interior doesn't always accurately convey the amount of usable space. The key word here is *usable*. Some styles make better use of interior volume than others; some are convenient, others are not. Check the interior. Is there room for each occupant's sleeping bag, with sufficient space left over for packs? Can you dress or undress conveniently? If you're choosing a tent for mountaineering or winter camping, does it give you a claustrophobic feeling? Remember that bad weather may keep you inside for one, two or even more days.

Usable space includes "living space"—where you can sit around chatting, playing cards, reading and, if necessary, cooking—as well as sleeping space. There are no set guidelines for space, but if you're so crowded that you have to go outside to roll over, tempers will fray.

Tents with external frames and vertical sides—cabin and cottage types, for example—and those with nearly vertical sides—such as the umbrella tents—provide the greatest usable space. Dome tents provide a good apportionment of living space, but sleeping bags aligned along the perimeter may make them a bit crowded. A-tents, within their designated size limitations, of course, provide ample sleeping- and gear-storage area, but little else.

What about color? Tan, red, orange, green, gray, blue and yellow—all of these are "standard" shades. Color should be more than just a matter of personal taste. For example, darker shades blend into the landscape, especially in forest settings, which is fine if you prefer a "hidden camp." Dark colors make a tent seem cooler—but they also make it seem smaller and gloomier. On the other hand, a light color—the popular tan shade of many poplins, for example—makes a tent seem quite spacious and well-lighted. The more startling colors such as red and yellow are good choices for tents that you might have to seek out in snowy or foggy weather. And, in the event of a search and rescue situation, brightly-colored tents are more easily spotted by aircraft. All in all, though, color is really a secondary consideration. Choose the tent that will best serve your purposes, rather than one that's pleasing to the eye.

TENT TYPES

Lightweight, Three-Season Tents

Lightweight, three-season tents comprise the largest category of tents and include A-frame, dome, and tunnel-style tents with sizes ranging from one-man shelters to minimum-weight multiperson models.

The lightest and most compact among them are the "tube tents" of absolutely minimum weight, usually two or three pounds. They also provide a minimum of protection—as a camper once said, "They're great in a light dew." Costing as little as $5, most tube tents are simply open-end plastic tubes that can be hung between two trees with the sides anchored to the ground by whatever means are available. Rocks will do. Improved versions may have one end closed, the other draped with insect netting. Tube tents, however, are spartanlike shelters, not recommended for serious camping.

The one-man bivouac sack, basically an oversize sleeping bag cover with the head section enclosed and protected by netting, is as portable as the tube tent but considerably more functional. The floor is usually of coated nylon, while the cover itself is of waterproof and breathable PTFE. If you're traveling alone during the spring, summer or fall, the bivouac sack allows you to hike with a two-pound shelter rather than a six-pounder. However, because of its limited storage space, the bivouac sack is not adequate for winter use.

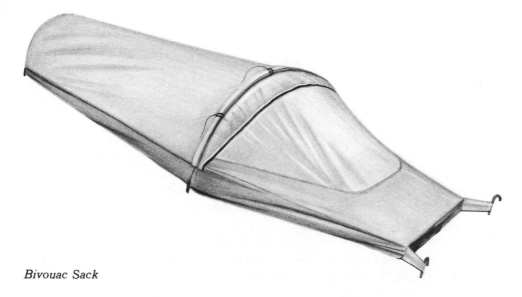

Bivouac Sack

A-frame tents are well adapted to backpacking and canoe trips—and in fact are well suited to almost all types of camping. Capacity ranges from two to six persons. Nylon is the predominant fabric used, and the best models are those of double-wall construction with an easy-to-assemble exterior frame of inverted V poles, no-see-um netting, triangular doors and a tub bottom. Self-supporting frames, even if they must occasionally be guyed in strong winds, liberalize your choice of campsites. An A-style tent can be set up almost anywhere. Soft ground, for example, is no problem. When you're carrying extra gear or supplies, consider adding a vestibule, a sort of "extra room" that can be attached to one end of many A-style tents for storage use. This will free the tent of clutter and provide more sleeping space. Also, the vestibule can be used for cooking if you become socked in by bad weather. As for the vestibule's added weight, it's trifling—one to two pounds.

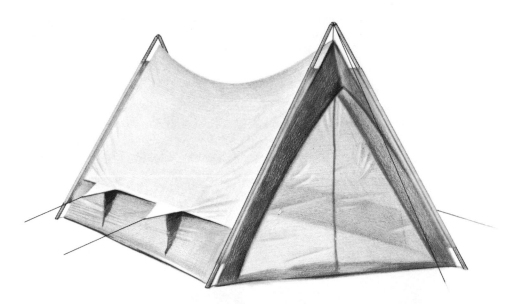

Basic Exterior-Frame A-Style Tent Without Fly

Another A-style shelter is the net tent with a tub bottom, a good choice for nights out in a humid, tropical climate. Even in the North, it's a delightful shelter that literally allows you to sleep under the stars protected from the insects. A coated nylon fly can be rigged should wind and rain occur. Net tents are now becoming available in dome designs.

Dome tents provide the most favorable interior space-to-weight ratio, not only physically but psychologically. Somehow, a dome's interior gives a feeling of spaciousness; and, because most of them are free-standing, they can be pitched

Dome Tent Without Fly

almost anywhere. Surprisingly, those equipped with four or more fiberglass or aluminum poles are often more easily and quickly set up than the seemingly simple A-style shelters.

Tunnel tents, because of their curved-side surfaces, shed wind, and also provide a good ratio of space-to-weight. The Quonset-like slope of the walls carries this spaciousness well up the sides so that there is ample head and shoulder room. When two doors are provided, one at each end, they are easier to ventilate than dome tents.

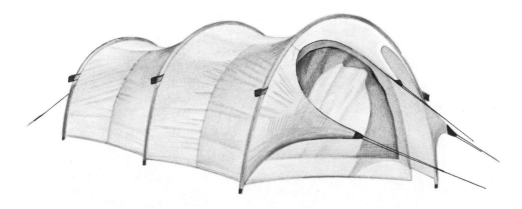

Tunnel Tent with Integral Fly

Expedition, Winter and High-Altitude Tents

Expedition, winter and high-altitude tents are basically lightweight three-season models that have been adapted to withstand the rigors of wind and snow. Even at relatively low altitudes winter winds can be vicious and, during a snowstorm, your tent may be all but buried, the weight of wet snow straining the fabric and frame to the verge of destruction. A winter tent must be rugged.

A winter or high-altitude tent must be somewhat larger than its summer version to accommodate gear that cannot be left outside. You'll need a variety of ventilation options, too. Some of the vents will have to be closed to keep out flying snow while others, on the lee side, must be kept open for fresh air.

Finally, you'll want a tent that goes up easily and quickly. The frame should be as simple as possible. With frost nipping at your fingers you won't want to waste time figuring out how section A fits into section B. Shockcord-connected poles help tremendously. Also, the frame should be sturdy or flexible enough so that your tent can better spill the wind. If the shelter is hung from the frame with shockcord, carry a couple of extra loops. It's easier to replace one than to repair it. Carry at least twenty-five to fifty feet of nylon line for use as emergency guy line.

If possible, choose a tent that has two entrances, one of them of the tunnel type. In driving snow you may prefer to enter or exit through the entrance in the lee of the wind.

Frostliners are of questionable value. These are detachable cotton mesh sheets that are draped along the inside walls to provide an extra layer of insulation and absorb condensation that would otherwise freeze on the tent fabric. Frostliners mean extra weight and bulk in your pack, though, and they cut down somewhat on interior space. Worse, they are difficult to dry in cold weather. Many campers choose to leave frostliners at home.

Winter Tent with Snow-Tunnel Entrance (Fly Removed)

Fixed-Camp Tents

Fixed-camp tents are at their best as semipermanent set-ups. Their bulk is considerable and so is their weight; generally you can use them only when you travel by car, boat, pack train or plane. Most are made of nylon or poplin, sometimes a combination of the two. Characteristically, they are spacious, large enough to permit the use of folding cots and tables.

The four basic types are the umbrella, the cabin, the baker and the wall tent.

The umbrella model, with its four steeply sloping side walls and pyramidal roof, is a favorite. Its exterior frame makes for easy setting up, it's remarkably stable and, depending on its size, it will house two to eight persons. Weight runs from eighteen to sixty pounds depending on size and fabric. The better makes have a waterproof tub bottom, a generous awning extending out over the door, fine-mesh insect netting and storm flaps that can be zippered shut from the inside. Large windows provide ventilation and cooling on a warm night. Among the nylon models, the walls are of fully waterproof coated fabric; the top is made of breathable nylon so that interior moisture can escape. A waterproof fly is fitted over the top. Poplin models, too, should have a separate fly. Guy lines are not usually needed but may be attached.

Umbrella Tent

Cabin and cottage tents are the roomiest of all. Their vertical walls permit the use of double-deck folding bunks to increase capacity. The difference between a cabin and a cottage tent is probably a matter of semantics—although some regard the cottage tent as the larger version; interior fabric partitions provide two or more "rooms." Both types are supported by exterior frames plus an aluminum ridgepole. The system is self-standing with guy lines added only when needed.

Some have walls of waterproof nylon with the roof panels of breathable nylon;

thus a waterproof fly is required. Nylon keeps the weight of such large tents within reasonable limits—slightly over twenty-eight pounds for a nine- by twelve-foot model.

Most cabin or cottage tents can be rigged with an awning extending over the front to provide space for cooking in bad weather or for lounging in the shade on a hot day. All of the desirable features found in an umbrella tent are generally present in a quality cabin or cottage shelter, including a tub bottom.

Cabin Tent

The baker tent is an old-timer associated with wilderness camping. A seven- by seven-foot version of coated nylon weighs slightly under twelve pounds. The baker catches the spirit of "camping out," since one wall can be left completely open—not advisable during the bug season, of course, unless a netting enclosure is added. The baker is often portrayed with a campfire blazing directly in front of it—again, not a recommended practice, because sparks can readily melt tiny holes in the nylon. The front wall can be raised horizontally to form an awning or it may be dropped to enclose the tent completely. The baker has been modernized to include a sewed-in waterproof nylon floor, and a netting enclosure that can be fitted under the awning to form an additional "room." The baker, naturally, is not as weatherproof as the more fully enclosed tents, nor is it really a safe haven from insects. Setting it up is a time-consuming chore, especially in windy weather.

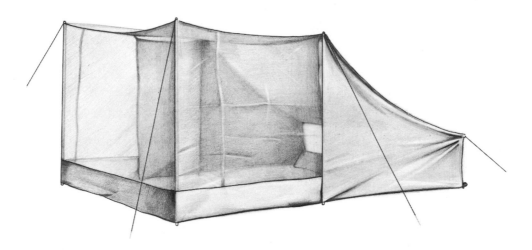

Baker Tent

Perhaps the most "woodsy" tent is the Whelen lean-to, devised by the late Colonel Townsend Whelen in 1925. Whelen adapted his design from a lean-to he had heard about in British Columbia. It differs from other lean-tos (the baker, for example) in that the side walls splay outwardly, thus providing three surfaces that reflect a campfire's warmth into the shelter. While the back wall is only about six feet long, the front opening between the two splayed-out side walls is almost twice that.

Whelen's original model is reproduced today in nylon (his was "balloon silk," a fine, tightly woven Egyptian cotton) and weighs three-and-a-half pounds. Its special roof ridge makes it possible to suspend the tent on lines or with poles.

Obviously, the Whelen is not suitable for camping at the height of the insect season nor is it particularly adapted to inclement weather. However, it serves well as a shelter in warm weather and doubles as a dining fly or extra shelter for gear storage. The Whelen should be pitched with its back to the wind so that it slides up and over the rear sloping wall. Pitched to face into the wind, the Whelen will "parachute."

The old-fashioned wall tent is now used primarily among western outfitters who guide big-game hunters into the backcountry on pack horses. They often pitch two or more such tents, one for sleeping, the other as a cook house and dining room. Wall tents are made exclusively of cotton and are large enough to house up to eight cots and a woodstove. They're not easily set up, requiring "two men and a boy" to accomplish the chore. Their use is limited almost exclusively to base camps.

Wall Tent

CHOOSING THE RIGHT TENT

While tents can be classified according to size, shape, portability, ease of erection, wind resistance and weight, choosing the right model is easier if you think of tents in terms of the use to which they best adapt.

For example, lightweight models are mandatory for backpacking but also serve well for bicycle touring and canoe trips. Tents designed for winter camping are ideal, of course, for ski touring, provided they are light enough. If canoe travel is your prime sport, you can carry a somewhat roomier shelter, but you'll want one that can be erected quickly and comes down just as easily. For base-camp hunting or fishing, there's no reason why you can't enjoy the luxury of a cabin or cottage tent, especially if your campsite is accessible by some sort of vehicle or power boat. Car campers—a family on a visit to a series of national parks, for example— want roominess, yet minimal weight and bulk for toting in today's compact automobiles. For fixed-camp use, the optimum shelter is a nylon umbrella or cabin model. Incidentally, if you'd prefer one of these yet are hesitant because you drive a small car, consider a car-top carrier, or even a small utility trailer.

In seeking to fit the right tent to your specific activities, consider the following:

- Means of travel: afoot, skis, canoe, car, four-wheel drive vehicle, packtrain, bicycle, airplane.
- Time of year: climate, anticipated weather (warm with insects or cold with snow), exposure to high winds.
- Destination: mountains, Far North, canoe routes, backpacking trails, wilderness, state parks.

Short of having a tent custom-made, you may not find one that incorporates every possible feature you want. So the trick is to choose the shelter that comes closest to filling all of your requirements.

Most tents appear reasonably spacious on a showroom floor but this spaciousness tends to dwindle once the shelter is pitched at a campsite. Unless your travel plans impose serious weight limitations, be cautious about buying a tent that may be too small for your needs. Going light is important but there's no use sacrificing more weight than is necessary. Quite often, the addition of a mere pound can make the difference between a comfortable camp-out and an unpleasant, overcrowded bivouac.

The following chart, based on three size variations of a popular A-style tent, illustrates the need for caution when judging the size of a tent.

Rated Capacity	Floor Dimensions	Floor Area	Per-Person Area	Weight
Two-man	5'3" x 7'2"	37.6 sq.ft.	18.8 sq.ft.	7 lbs. 14 ozs.
Four-man	7'2" x 8'9"	62.7 sq.ft.	15.7 sq.ft.	9 lbs. 14 ozs.
Six-man	10'3" x 8'6"	87.1 sq.ft.	14.5 sq.ft.	17 lbs. 10 ozs.

The larger the tent, the less per-person floor space you'll have when it's fully occupied. A four-man tent, for example, will not be twice as large as a two-man model.

Consider that you'll need a bare minimum of twelve square feet per person for sleeping, not a generous allotment when you consider that most of us toss and turn in the night. The two-man model would then have two persons using twenty-four square feet for sleep, thus leaving about thirteen square feet for storage of two packs, probably more than ample for backpackers.

In the four-man tent, forty-eight square feet would be occupied by sleeping bags, leaving roughly fourteen square feet for storage. This, at a glance, seems a more generous allocation. But, remember, with four persons in the group, there will probably be four packs in that fourteen-square-foot space. The six-man tent is even less generous. Some seventy-two square feet will be used for sleeping, leaving only fifteen square feet for the storage of six packs.

On the basis of the foregoing comparisons and chart, you may decide, for example, that two two-man tents are better suited to your trek than a single four-man model. Or you may decide to gain extra room by adding a vestibule or taking a three-man tent for each party of two. These alternatives are worth considering.

Once you've considered size, weight and style, look to the special features. Inside pockets are handy places to store your knife, glasses or flashlight during the night. Door and screen tiebacks not only make it easier to ventilate but they're a convenience when it comes to brushing the tent out. D-rings sewn to the inside ceiling make it possible to stretch a clothesline on which to hang wet socks and gloves.

TARPAULINS

Probably no single item of outdoor gear is as versatile as a tarp. It can be rigged as an improvised tent, dining fly, windbreak, groundcloth, wrapper for a canoe's cargo or as a cover for the woodpile. Since a tarp is an auxiliary item rather than a basic necessity, we tend to seek out the lightest possible waterproof fabric. There are clear polyethylene nine- by twelve-foot sheets weighing a mere six ounces but these are of questionable value. They're easily damaged and it's virtually impossible to tie one down adequately against even a light breeze. Slightly better are the two- and four-mil sheets, weighing about three pounds, and not unlike painter's dropcloths. These, too, are prone to tearing and are difficult to anchor but are adequate when used as wrappers or groundcloths.

If you're looking for something inexpensive, consider plastic tarps that are reinforced with a gridlike pattern of nylon yarns on the same order as rip-stop nylon. Such models are not particularly light, a twelve- by twelve-foot sheet weighing about four pounds. These are not equipped with edge grommets through which lines might be strung. But, by using twisties or a piece of line enclosing a small rock within the plastic, a relatively secure covering can be rigged. However, the weight of this material and its bulk make packing difficult.

Somewhat more costly (but worth every penny) is the coated rip-stop nylon tarp available in a number of sizes, ranging from six by twelve foot to ten by twelve foot (weighing thirteen to thirty ounces), and equipped with edge grommets. These you can anchor firmly and they will withstand considerable abuse. Another style of rip-stop nylon lacks grommets, but is equipped with numerous tie-tapes along its edges and at several other locations on its surface so that it can be rigged as a shelter of almost any shape. This type weighs about thirty-six ounces.

Larger tarps of cotton duck are used for commercial and industrial purposes, their weight making them impractical for recreational use. However, those of lighter cotton drill or poplin (six to seven-and-a-half ounces per yard) are highly practical, available in sizes ranging up to twelve by eighteen feet. One note of caution. When buying a cotton tarp, make sure that all the grommets are firmly set in leather reinforcement patches. Otherwise, the grommets will pull out under stress. Incidentally, don't use a cotton tarp as a wrapper for gear in a canoe. It is not waterproof (only water repellent) and spray accumulating in the bilge will seep through, wetting your gear.

TENT CARE AND REPAIR

If a cotton tent is stored while wet or damp, mildew will quite likely ravage its entire surface; or if it's left erected for long periods, the lower hem of the walls will quickly mildew—unless, of course, the tent is equipped with a coated-nylon tub bottom. Before storing it, be sure your tent is thoroughly dried, particularly along the hems and seams that tend to hold moisture. If you remain in camp for some time, raise the bottom hems of the walls a few inches every two or three days. Prop them up to dry thoroughly.

If mildew does develop, wash the affected areas with naphtha soap, dry them thoroughly, then apply waterproofing that contains mildew inhibitors. If you're also having trouble with leaks, spray the exterior of the tent with a water repellent such as Scotchguard® or Zepel®, then roll or fold it loosely in a plastic trash bag. Let it stand at room temperature for a few days. This will allow the waterproofing to permeate the fabric and the seams. Your tent is then ready for use again.

If you find that some leakage persists—it's usually localized—apply beeswax or waxstick. This is particularly effective if leaks occur along the needle holes in a seam.

When in camp, use insect or hair sprays carefully within the tent. The propellent in some of these sprays will damage the water-resistant treatment. If you must spray the interior to get rid of insects, direct the repellent into the center of the tent, away from the walls. Be sparing of it, too. Most of us overdo bug spraying.

Fewer precautions are needed for all-nylon tents. They are not damaged by mildew. True, mildew may form as a whitish-green powder that gives off an unpleasant odor, but it doesn't eat into the fabric. Brushing and airing usually eliminate the odor.

Nylon tents, even new ones, may develop minor leaks through the seams. A seam sealant such as Sealtite®, K-Kote® or Seamstuff® is easily applied and is an effective remedy. Every year or two, depending on use, reseal all seams, especially those in the floor. Soiled spots on the fabric can be sponged clean with a cloth soaked in warm water and lathered with a mild soap. If this fails, it's generally best to allow the spot to remain. The use of cleaning fluids or strong detergents may damage the finish of the nylon.

During a bad blow, you may elect to cook inside your tent. Don't fuel, or refuel, your stove inside. Spilled gasoline or naphtha may injure the coated floor. Citric acid is also harmful, so sip orange juice carefully.

In striking camp, whether your tent is nylon or cotton, brush it free of all grit, twigs, tiny pebbles or other ground debris. These can damage the fabric during transport. Damage can also be avoided when setting up by clearing all sharp stones, sticks or tiny brush stumps that could cut into the floor fabric.

Using a groundcloth will extend the life of your tent floor. It should be slightly smaller than the shelter's floor area, otherwise rain running off the tent will gather and—if there is no tub bottom—seep inside. If necessary, fold the groundcloth to the right size, then set up the tent over it. Any of the plastic materials or tarps described earlier make excellent groundcloths.

Despite all precautions, expect some damage if you camp out often. Unless it is massive, there's no need to interrupt your vacation. Repairs in the field are feasible. Carry a small repair kit including such items as the already-mentioned seam sealant, fabric cement such as Spee-Dee®, rip-stop nylon tape with adhesive backing or duct tape, a small piece of fabric matching that of your tent, a needle and thread and beeswax or waxstick. The Speedy Stitcher® is a handy awl-like device with which you can sew a lock stitch, the thread feeding from a bobbin within the wooden handle.

All in all, a good tent is one of the best investments you can make in outdoor gear. Choose carefully, buy the finest you can afford, take care of it and it will last many years.

Chapter 6

Packing Gear: Afoot and Afloat

Dillon Wallace summed it up pretty well when he wrote almost seventy years ago in *Packing and Portaging:* "The one chief problem that confronts the wilderness traveler is that of how to reduce the weight of his outfit to the minimum with the least sacrifice of comfort." Packs have changed but not the problem. In fact, most of us now carry more individual items of gear than did the early woods trekkers.

True, modern technology has miniaturized, lightened and compacted our camping gear. Yet some of us continue to struggle with overweight packs, and we paddle canoes literally loaded to the gunwales. We start with the absolute essentials—an extra wool shirt, a sweater, a nylon shell, a map and compass, a rain jacket, extra socks and underwear, fishing tackle and insect repellent. These combined with a tent and sleeping bag, plus grub, all add up. At this point, determining what goes and what stays becomes an exercise in discipline. The temptation is to include small luxuries, nonessentials that loom as essentials, and soon the pack creaks when you lift it. The disease is insidious, and learning to control it comes only with experience.

No pack or duffel bag will lighten weight or cut down on bulk—that's up to you—but a well-selected pack will generally handle even overenthusiastic loads with a minimum of strain to your muscles and sinews. Basically, a pack should be large enough to accommodate your gear, convenient to load and unload, durable and comfortable to carry. There are special considerations, of course. For a canoe trip you'll want a pack that will keep your gear dry. Cross-country skiers and rock climbers require a pack that rides low and close to their backs so that it will not affect balance.

Packs are available in two broad categories: those for foot travel and those intended primarily for water travel. Packs designed for foot travel vary in design and capacity. The smallest—day and overnight packs—are frameless, with a capacity of five to twenty pounds. Volume usually runs less than 2000 cubic inches.

Internal-frame packs, as the name suggests, have flexible interior frames that lend greater support. Sizes vary considerably from compact weekend types with volumes of 1,900 to 2,200 cubic inches to expedition models of up to 4,200 cubic inches; the most popular are in the 3,000 cubic-inch range. Average weight capacities run between twenty-five and forty-five pounds. However, well-designed and properly fitted exterior-frame packs handle heavy loads best. Bag capacities average between 2,500 and 3,500 cubic inches, but gear—a sleeping bag, for example—can be lashed to the exterior frame, thus freeing space for other equipment. In this respect, an external-frame pack can be said to boast greater capacity than an internal-frame model of the same size.

MATERIALS AND CONSTRUCTION

While cotton army duck is used on a small number of rucksack-type day packs and frameless overnight models, most packs are made of nylon. This is lighter, stronger, more durable and requires less care. Despite the great number of manufacturers and the wide range of designs, only two types of nylon are used on most packs—eight ounce nylon duck (commonly referred to as "parapack") and ten to eleven ounce Cordura® nylon. Both fabrics are rugged and serviceable; they are usually coated with polyurethane to make them waterproof. (Note: a waterproof fabric obviously won't guarantee a waterproof pack. Zippers and seams are likely to leak. In heavy rain, you'll need a cover, tarp or a backpacker's poncho for complete protection.)

Internal and external frames can be plastic, wood or aluminum; the latter is most common. Internal frames usually consist of two to four "stays" that are fitted into the back panel of the pack. These are flexible and can be bent to provide a custom fit.

External frames are ordinarily made with frames of five-eighths to one inch aluminum alloy tubing with heli-arc welded joints. Nonwelded flexible plastic joints are also used. Advocates of this type of frame claim it flexes with body movements, is equally durable and slightly more comfortable to carry. Less expensive frames are often brazed or lightly soldered—but most are also less durable.

Details such as zippers and buckles often set one pack or bag apart from another. Nylon coil zippers are used on most newer packs because they run smoothly, especially on curved flaps and openings. Durable plastic quick-lock buckles, cordlocks and Velcro® strips make opening and closing a pack easy. Quick-release belt buckles are an important safety feature as well as a convenience. With these you can divest yourself of your pack quickly should you lose your balance while crossing a stream or while climbing a steep trail.

Quality construction is largely a matter of good stitching and proper reinforcing. Better packs are stitched with eight to ten stitches per inch and are bartacked, "box-tacked" or backstitched at all areas of stress—the ends of the zipper tapes, at the point where the packstraps or handles join the bag, and at the ends of major seams. Pay particular attention to the manner in which the packbag is joined to the frame or harness assembly. If clevis pins are used (as on most external-frame packs) be sure that the grommet holes in the bag are set in two layers of fabric. If the harness system is stitched directly to the bag (internal-frame packs) look for a rugged, well-reinforced seam. On many better packs, leather or nylon patches distribute stress. Check also the stitching on the hip belt. If the buckle does not appear to be well-stitched to the belt, move on to another pack.

Check the seams carefully on packs designed for water travel. These are usually heat-molded to make them waterproof. Bubbles or weak points could cause the seam to split open.

PACKS AFOOT

Day Packs and Overnight Packs

Among the many day packs, the rucksack of canvas or nylon is of European origin. Rucksack-type day packs are inexpensive, top-loading bags with draw-string closures and buckle-down flaps; the better grades are reinforced with leather at stress points. They are designed to ride close to the body. One popular model, the tear-drop, named for its shape, has a shallow profile that keeps its contents low and closer to your back. The shoulder straps and back panel are cushioned with foam. Some of the larger tear-drop packs may also have a front-buckling belt (otherwise known as a belly band) to hold them close and to keep them from swinging. This makes them well-suited to hiking, skiing and bicycling. The capacities of such packs range from about 700 to 1,000 cubic inches. Most will carry up to ten pounds comfortably.

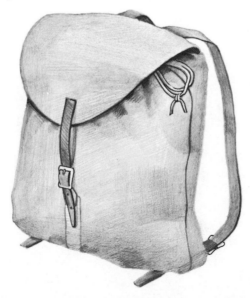

Canvas Rucksack

Teardrop Daypack

Slightly larger than day packs are the frameless weekend-type models. Capacity ranges from 1,000 to 2,000 cubic inches and they will carry up to twenty pounds, including a change of clothes, a small shelter and a meal or two. Most are top-loading bags with drawcord necks and zippered top flaps. A down sleeping bag can usually be lashed to the outside.

Frameless Weekend Pack

Since most day and overnight packs lack a frame, load them with care. The thin foam membrane on the back panel offers little protection from the bouncing of a camera or stove against your spinal cord. Pad all hard items and load your clothing next to your back. Incidentally, these packs are at their best when full, not necessarily at their weight capacity, but when the pouch is filled out with bulk. To prevent a half-dozen loosely stashed items from bouncing around, add a light sweater or a similar bit of clothing as padding.

Internal-Frame Packs

Internal-frame packs are usually two to three times the size of most overnight models. They are designed to hold weight close to the body so that it has minimal adverse effect on balance. They are "fluid," conforming to the movements of your arms, shoulders and torso. Because of this, internal-frame packs are especially preferred by climbers and cross-country skiers. Another asset of internal-frame packs is that they are easily stored in car trunks and under airplane seats. They double nicely as travel bags.

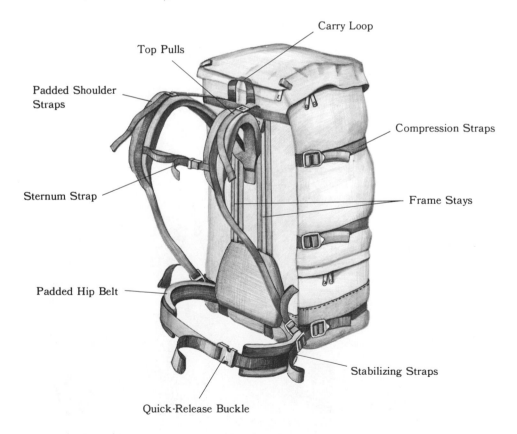

Internal-Frame Pack

By way of contrast, external-frame packs call for placing most of the weight high, at shoulder level and higher, which makes for less tiring packing on relatively good trails, but for some instability when footing is precarious.

Internal-frame packs usually employ a number of aluminum "stays" set into sleeves in the back panels to help control and shape the load. These stays are most commonly arranged parallel to each other or in an "X" fashion. Of the two designs, packs with parallel stays are generally more fluid—they twist and bend with your body movements. They also fold easily for storage. X-frame packs, on the other hand, provide greater load control because the crossed stays extend to the corners of the pack.

Bag design is a matter of convenience and personal preference. Internal-frame packs (and external-frame ones as well) load either from the top or the front. Top-loading models generally hold more gear. Extra clothing, a tent or a sleeping bag can always be stuffed under the top flap. The front-loading system allows you to lay the pack flat like a suitcase so that you can remove a sweater or down vest without having to empty the entire contents. Regardless of the system you choose, pick a pack with compressor straps to help cinch the contents against your back. These not only give you better control over the load, but prevent loose items such as stoves and binoculars from "traveling" inside the pack.

The interior of packbags may be divided. Such packs allow you to sort gear into different compartments. For example, you can stuff your food and stove into the top compartment, reserving the bottom one for clothing. Undivided packs are

Front-Loading Pack

Top-Loading Pack

usually preferred by those who like to sort their clothing and supplies in individual stuff bags. Some models are now being made with large zipper-divided compartments to combine the flexibility of both systems.

Exterior pockets should be big enough for extra wool socks, a fuel or water bottle, a flashlight or a rain suit. Removable pockets are especially handy. They can be detached and strapped to your belt for use as belt packs on short day trips. Some pockets are designed to hold skis or a fishing pole inserted in a slot between the pocket and pack. Other styles have ice-axe loops, lash patches for attaching a tent or sleeping bags, and carrying handles for travel use.

An internal-frame pack should have a well-padded back panel and padded shoulder straps anchored securely. Of greater importance, however, is a well-designed, padded hip belt. This should be placed so that it carries roughly 70 percent of the pack's weight on the hips with the shoulder straps carrying the remaining 30 percent. With a properly fitted pack, you should be able to make adjustments between the shoulder and hip suspension to suit your activity. You may find that you'll want to make this adjustment as you travel, to ease weariness in your shoulders or your hips and legs.

In trying out a pack at the time of purchase, be as fussy about fit as you are when choosing hiking boots. First load the pack to the approximate weight you'll be toting in the field. If you feel undue pressure on your shoulders but little on your hips, the distance between the shoulder straps and hip belt is too short. This can be remedied by adjusting either the shoulder straps and the hip belt, or both. If the adjustments don't remedy the discomfort, or if you continue to feel a definite imbalance between the weight on your shoulders and hips, discard the pack and try another.

The best internal-frame packs can be "fine tuned" to provide an almost perfect fit—especially for women. Sternum straps make it easy to regulate shoulder and chest tension. Top-pull straps and stabilizing straps help to stabilize the load and redistribute the ratio of weight between shoulders and hips.

External-Frame Packs

In the days when African safaris were still foot treks, dozens of porters toted your gear, each carrying one pack on his head. These may have been primitive people but long experience taught them that the weight of a pack on the head rested directly over the spinal cord as they walked erect, and was directed to the hips and legs. There was no wasted energy. The noted backpacking equipment designer, Gerry Cunningham, pointed this out, citing as an example the overhead portaging of a canoe. The weight is on a canoeist's shoulders, not his head, but nonetheless he walks erect, just like the old African porters. Conversely, any pack that causes you to lean forward wastes energy. You have to counter not only the downward thrust of the weight, but also the forward thrust of your leaning body. All of which brings us to the external-frame pack.

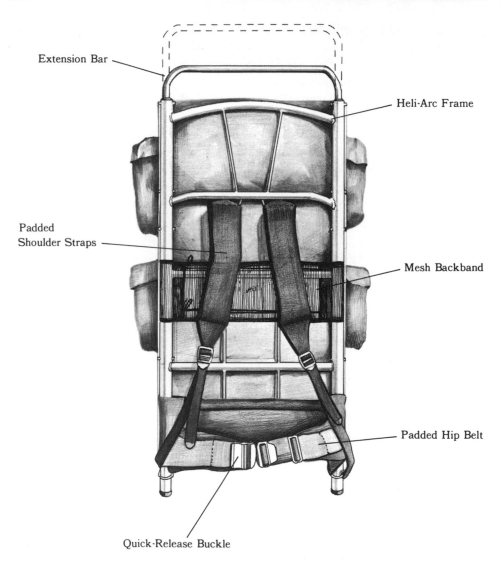

Extension Bar

Heli-Arc Frame

Padded
Shoulder Straps

Mesh Backband

Padded Hip Belt

Quick-Release Buckle

External-Frame Pack

The frame, ideally, is contoured to fit the natural curvature of your back. When rigged with a suitable bag, the weight is located high and close to your shoulders; at the same time, the padded hip-belt transmits its share of the weight directly to your legs. With this rig, there is relatively little forward lean. You walk nearly erect, wasting little energy.

One of the original external-frame packs was the Alaskan, or Trapper Nelson, a wooden frame with canvas shoulder straps. It could be used with a large canvas bag, or separately as a packboard to carry bulky items. Then came the World War II Army packframe, which was made of molded plywood; some are still in use today. Such rigs are suitable for short jaunts, portaging and for packing out game. On the whole, though, modern aluminum-frame/nylon-bag combinations are lighter, more comfortable and certainly more convenient. It's worth pointing out again that, compared to internal-frame packs, they generally have greater carrying capacities. And because the frame keeps the bag away from your back, thus allowing air to circulate, it is more comfortable in warm weather.

There are three basic frame shapes: straight, S-shaped and hip-wrap. The straight style is the least efficient. Because it permits more space between the pack and your back, the packbag tends to pull away from your shoulders. The S-shaped frame is contoured to fit the natural curves of a person's back, keeping the load close while still holding the bag slightly away for ventilation. The hip-wrap frame is a basically straight frame that bends in at the waist and partially encompasses the hips. Unlike the other two types of frames, the hip-wrap features a free-floating hip belt that is designed to carry a greater proportion of the load comfortably. For absolute comfort, however, you'll need just about a perfect fit. Some backpackers feel that the hip-wrap model is not suited to loads of more than thirty-five to forty-five pounds. But the truth is that with any frame such weight will likely prove uncomfortable on a long trek unless you've built up your muscles during frequent trips under heavy loads. Whenever you load beyond forty-five pounds, you can justly consider the pack "hefty." Colin Fletcher, during his walk through the Grand Canyon, started out with sixty-six-and-a-half pounds which, he later wrote, "just about takes the joy out of walking."

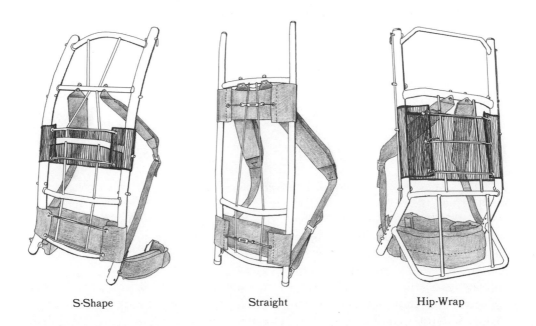

S-Shape   Straight   Hip-Wrap

Types of External Frames

External-frame packs are designed to carry a larger proportion of your load on your hips. Most backpackers try for about an 85–15 split. In order to attain the correct shoulder/hip weight distribution the distance between the upper terminal of the shoulder straps and the hip belt must correspond to the length of the trunk of your body. Once the hip belt is secured, the cross member to which the shoulder straps are attached should be just about level with your shoulders. If the weight seems properly distributed between your shoulders and hips and there are no points of discomfort, the frame is the correct length. You might also check the backbands. These are stretched horizontally between the frame's two upright members; lacing or possibly even small turnbuckles develop considerable tension. It is these backbands that hold the frame away from your spinal cord. They may have to be adjusted up or down, but this is easily done. Make sure that the shoulder straps are properly spaced. If you are heavy-necked, for example, the straps may be too close together. On the other hand, if they are too far apart so that they cut across the outside of your shoulders, the pack will strain your neck and shoulder muscles. The better frames avoid this by providing a number of points on the upper crossbar where shoulder straps can be attached.

Earlier comments about the features of internal-frame packbags apply equally to external-frame ones. An ice-axe loop is not only handy for an ice axe but works well for carrying rope. Lashing patches are convenient for ice crampons, snow-shoes, camp saws, grids, wet sneakers, sleeping bags and foam pads. A map pocket set into the top flap of the bag, within easy reach, is also worthwhile.

Suppose, however, you want a pack frame for use without a bag. For packing bulky equipment to a remote cabin or for packing out game after a backcountry hunt, a bag is more hindrance than help. You can, of course, remove it, but most pack frames are not designed to double as pack boards. There is, however, an aluminum contoured frame for such use. It has a platform at its base on which the load can be set and there are D-rings for lashing. Better yet, the platform can be raised or lowered for the best possible positioning of the load. If you decide later on to add a bag to the frame, you can easily attach one.

PACKING IT RIGHT

When backpacking, balance and convenience are critical. If you expect good footing, load the pack so that the heavier items are high and close to your back. The tent and food are usually the heaviest things you'll carry; try to load these near the top. Clothing is usually lighter and can be packed lower down. Your sleeping bag can be lashed to the bottom of the frame. Try to get as much of your load forward as possible. And don't overlook side-to-side balance. If you put your stove and fuel on the left side of the pack, try to balance it out with the flashlight and camera on the right. Rock climbers and cross-country skiers will usually want a slightly lower center of gravity. Forty pounds at shoulder height doesn't do much for balance. Internal-frame packs ride better when the weight is low and more evenly distributed. In such cases pack the tent under the food and stove. In anticipation of weather changes, stow your raingear, extra wool shirt and nylon shell in outside pockets or wherever you can get at them easily without disrupting the entire pack.

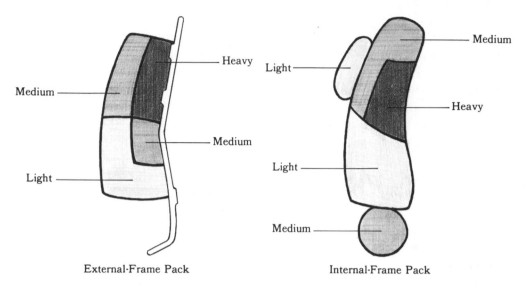

External·Frame Pack   Internal·Frame Pack

Proper Weight Distribution

PACKS AFLOAT

There's a certain perversity about water, be it rain, spray or splashes from a standing wave. Once in the canoe, water will invariably seek out your sleeping bag, your grub supply and your spare wool shirt. Thus, a pack for water travel must be as nearly waterproof as possible. And, since few canoe trips are without portages, the pack must also be reasonably portable.

External·frame packs are used by some canoeists because the frames serve as a convenient place to lash on bailers, fishing equipment and other loose articles during portaging. However, larger models with extension bars interfere with carrying a canoe. Also, they fit poorly under canoe thwarts. If you prefer frame packs, select smaller versions that will fit crosswise. Two can be fitted amidship so that the frames bridge the bilge keeping the packs four to six inches above any water that may accumulate. Internal·frame packs are easier to position in a canoe, and do not interfere with portaging. Outside pockets on either type are a great convenience aboard a canoe. You can stash a drinking cup, suntan lotion, sunglasses, a rain suit, map and compass, and even gorp for snacks within easy reach.

But even the best backpacks are not waterproof. They'll repel a light rain but that's about all. The fabric may be waterproof; the zippers are not. How, then, can such packs be waterproofed? Simply store clothing, sleeping bags, food and other items in appropriate-size plastic bags and tie the openings as tightly as possible. Merely wrapping in plastic sheets is not enough. If you swamp or tip over, water will find its way into such wrappings.

You may also pack canoe gear in duffel bags. While several styles are of waterproof coated nylon, with a bottom of nylon Cordura® (for abrasion and water resistance), they are not truly waterproof. Equipped with a full-length zipper and a Velcro® overlap, they are easy to load but, again, the zippers will leak. You'll have to resort to the plastic bags already suggested.

There are bags intended to be truly waterproof, including the urethane-coated nylon duffels that can be obtained from military equipment surplus stores. These duffels should be tested for leaks, however. Plastic liner bags may still be needed.

For portaging, take along an Army packboard or aluminum packframe in each canoe. Bags, duffels and assorted loose gear such as an axe, saw and fishing tackle can be lashed to these. Thus there is no clutter on the carries and no need for a second trip.

More convenient and durable are the large waterproof river bags that resemble World War II military "wetpacks," popular among western river outfitters for rafting expeditions. They are made of a PVC-coated polyester and have watertight buckle closures. Some models have padded shoulder straps for portaging. Since items must be thrust loosely into the bag, it's difficult to pack your gear in an orderly manner. However, using boxes and packing tins can somewhat overcome this problem.

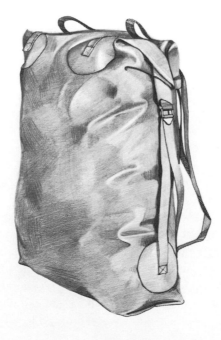

Waterproof River Bag

Until recent years, the Duluth pack was an old standby for canoeists. Available in several sizes, the largest being about twenty-eight by thirty inches, it is little more than a flat canvas envelope with a generous flap that is closed with three straps and buckles. It has shoulder straps and a tumpline that fits across the upper forehead so that much of the weight is borne by the carrier's neck. Trail-toughened canoeists often tossed one Duluth pack atop another to minimize trips across a carry. The tumpline, unless you're toughened to it, is an instrument of torture and it has virtually disappeared. So has the original Duluth pack.

Today, there are modernized versions with bellows sides and, among some models, a bottom half of waterproof fabric. If this sort of pack appeals to you (you can almost always jam "one more" bit of gear into it), line it with two heavy-duty 3-mil plastic trash bags, one inside the other, and seal the top with one of those little "twisters."

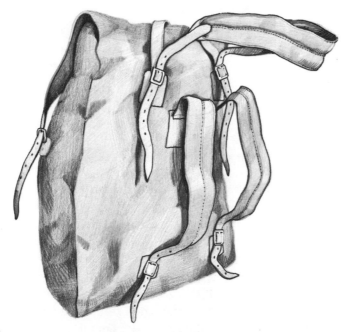

Duluth Pack

In the Northeast and parts of eastern Canada the packbasket remains popular among woodsmen and trappers. Woven of rattan and split ash, it is sturdy yet flexible, in time molding itself to your back. It affords good protection for fragile items. Old-timers often had their wives make them an oil-cloth cover to ward off rain but the packbasket has never been truly waterproofed—short of lining it with plastic bags. The packbasket serves well under moderate loads, but because of its tendency to pull away from the shoulders, it can be quite uncomfortable under a heavy burden.

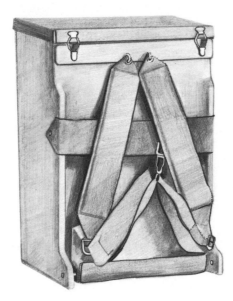

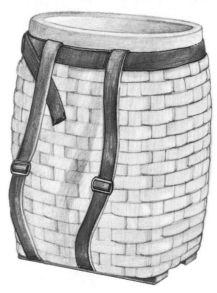

Polyethylene Plastic Pack   Packbasket

There is a modern polyethylene plastic replacement for the packbasket. Its top is gasket-sealed and it's equipped with shoulder straps, a padded hip belt and a backband. It's tough enough so that you can sit on it and, if not too heavily laden, it will float. It carries fairly well, protects fragile contents and is relatively water-proof if accidentally dumped overboard. It's not designed for white-water trips, though, since it will take on water if submerged for long—under an overturned canoe, for example.

Another traditional "pack" among canoeists is the "wanigan" or "chuck box." This is usually homemade of wood, sometimes with a rounded bottom to fit cross-wise in a canoe. Generally, wanigans are used to pack the grub supply and kitchen utensils, so the interior may have divided compartments to accommodate cooking utensils and assorted foodstuffs. Some are equipped with a rope handle at each end, others with a shoulder harness for portaging. However, it is never a joy to tote a wanigan over a long portage. For lengthy lake or flat-water river trips, with few portages, the wanigan is a superb "pack," but for rough water or for tedious portages, conventional canoe packs assure better protection against wet-ting and make portaging a bit more bearable.

No matter what you choose for a canoe pack, give some thought to color. Blue, black or brown packs that get dumped into a swift-flowing river may be hard to locate. Quite often, they'll look like just another rock in the water and you may paddle right by them. Bright colors—orange, yellow or brilliant red—are easier to spot.

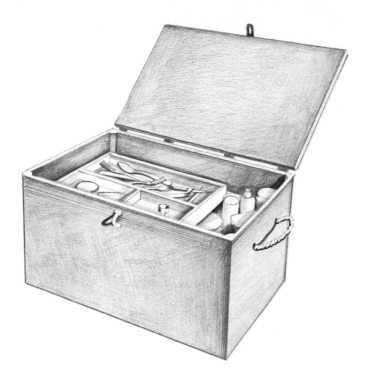

Wanigan

MISCELLANEOUS PACKS AND BAGS

For day outings, the nylon or leather belt pouch can be handy. It slips onto your belt and is meant to carry small items such as ski wax, map and compass, fishing tackle or perhaps trail snacks. It eliminates the need for stuffing jacket and trouser pockets.

Belt Pouch

The belt or "fanny" pack is a step upward in capacity, capable of carrying about three times as much as the belt pouch. It's the pack that the National Ski Patrol uses to carry first-aid equipment. Most models run about fifteen inches long, four to five inches high and six inches deep. It is rigged on a padded belt that buckles at the front. To reach the contents easily, you can loosen the belt and slide the pouch forward. Better models usually incorporate one main compartment and a number of smaller side pockets. Exterior D-rings allow you to lash on bulkier gear or clothing outside. Cross-country skiers and cyclists find the belt pack particularly convenient because it leaves the arms and shoulders free.

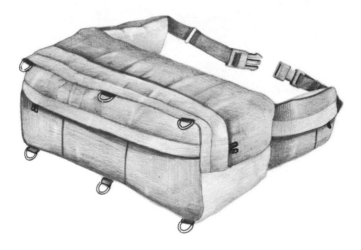

Belt Pack

For fixed camps, canoe trips and general outdoor activities, canvas tote bags are excellent. Canoeists can carry loose kitchen gear; auto campers, food; and boaters, extra clothing. For ammunition, first-aid supplies and valuables, there are World War II Army surplus waterproof steel ammunition boxes. Cameras, film and binoculars can be protected in watertight heavy vinyl bags. Special models are designed with two "bladders"—one bag inside the other. By filling the space between the two with air you can protect the valuables from breakage as well as from water.

Chapter 7

Pots, Pans and Stoves: Dining Under the Sky

The old-time mainstays of camp fare—beans, bacon and biscuits—are still with us, but nowadays the three B's can be interspersed with menu possibilities that fall just short of gourmet cooking. You can enjoy beef stroganoff, chicken almondine, shrimp creole and a raspberry smash for dessert a half-hour after pitching camp. Thanks to modern food processing, ingredients may weigh mere ounces, and a person can be well-fed on as little as two pounds per day during a summertime trek, and on only slightly more during cold weather. While many of these wonder foods are freeze-dried and prepared especially for backpackers, you'll find delicious and equally lightweight fare on supermarket shelves.

THE BASICS

Planning camp meals involves more than buying foods that everyone in the party will like. The more strenuous (or lengthy) the trip, and the colder the weather, the more carefully grub should be chosen—not only for its nutritional value but also for its portability and ease of preparation.

On a backpacking trip you'll probably consume 3,200 to 3,800 calories per day. Lounging on your cabin porch, you'll use up less than half this number. Obviously then, your food supply should be tailored to your activity, and your calorie sources should be suitably proportioned. A good rule of thumb calls for 60 percent carbohydrates, with proteins and fats at about 20 percent each.

Carbohydrates are found in candy, vegetables, fruit and cereals. They are quick-energy producers, good trail snacks for an instant pick-me-up. Backpackers have developed "gorp"—"good old raisins and peanuts"—which has a high carbohydrate content (though it does include some fats and proteins), takes up little space and goes a long way. Gorp is generally homemade, a mixture of nuts, sunflower seeds, pumpkin seeds, banana chips, dates, raisins, dried pears and figs. Not all of these ingredients appeal to everyone, of course, so most of us have developed combinations to our liking. Bits of candy and chocolate can be in-cluded. Although most of the ingredients are available at supermarkets, you may have to get some at a health-food store.

Gorp is meant for munching on the trail when you begin to feel "gaunt in the middle." However, you need not wait for hunger pangs. Snack lightly to avoid them. But don't overdo it. It's generally better to travel feeling just a bit hungry (so long as your energy level is adequate) than it is to arrive in camp with your belt let out an extra notch. Naturally, some judgment is called for. If the going is strenu-ous, or if the weather is cold, munch whenever you feel the need and drink lots of water.

Proteins, present in milk, fish, eggs, lean meats, cheese, legumes, grains and nuts, rebuild body tissues and muscle strength. They develop body energy at a slower rate than do carbohydrates, but they stick with you longer: hence the importance of proteins at breakfast—and for lunch, too, if a rugged afternoon's trek lies ahead.

Fats are indispensable for winter activity, because they provide the greatest concentration of calories. They are found in bacon, butter, margarine, cheese, salami, pork, beef, ham, nuts and chocolate.

Some foods may be rich in proteins as well as fats, or carbohydrates, while others, such as peanut butter, are amply endowed with all three. Thus the lowly peanut-butter sandwich is a good snack for an active person.

Vitamins and minerals are less critical; the common fare of most outdoorsmen provides enough. Vitamin C, for example, is present in citrus drinks, although ascorbic acid tablets can sometimes be substituted.

Salt is also vital to your well-being. When the loss of salt through perspiration is excessive, headaches, stomach cramps, diarrhea and general exhaustion result. With a properly balanced field diet, however, such an extreme loss is not likely to occur. (In unusually hot weather, salt tablets can be taken if necessary.)

Don't overlook the need for liquids. At high altitudes, in arid regions, in the tropics and even in very cold weather your body can pass off moisture at an alarming rate, resulting in dehydration. Once your body becomes dehydrated, it can no longer cool or warm itself effectively. Dehydration can be subtle. You may not feel particularly thirsty. Whether it's cold and dry or very hot, you'll probably need up to four quarts of liquid per day. Many hikers carry a Sierra cup at their belts so they can readily dip into mountain streams or bubbling woodland brooks and springs. If the watering holes are few and far between, carry a canteen. There are no calories in water, so if you want to increase your intake of these and at the same time enjoy a flavorsome drink, carry soluble beverage crystals, which dilute almost instantly to produce flavors that include orange, grape, grapefruit, straw-berry and lemon. You can even produce a tomato-juice cocktail at trailside, or, with powdered milk, a chocolate or strawberry milkshake. And for cold weather there are the old standbys—tea, instant coffee, and cocoa. Hot flavored gelatin is also excellent.

THE GRUB SUPPLY

At a backwoods cabin accessible by car or boat or at a family-type campground, weight and bulk pose no problem. Short of a leg of lamb, you can probably enjoy home cooking much of the time. You can also select most of your menu at the supermarket before you leave home. Even fresh meats and vegetables keep well in campers' ice chests.

Weight and bulk are critical to a backpacker, however, and if there are arduous portages a canoeist may cuss copiously at being overloaded with the wrong assortment of grub. Dehydrated and freeze-dried foods are the answer, not only because they are light and compact, but also because they need no refrigeration.

At a fixed camp, or during leisurely travel, you can indulge yourself in complex, five-course productions. However, when the miles beckon and everyone is "fierce to go," you'll want meals that are quickly and easily prepared. In fixing quick meals, there's often a tendency toward sloppiness, and even if the fare is nourishing, it may seem boring or unappetizing. Remember that during a long trek or a lengthy stay in camp, meals are one of the high spots of the day, to be savored and relished. Don't experiment with new techniques or recipes on the trail. Stick to foods that you know how to cook. If you want to try a new recipe, first master it at home. Trailside failures make dismal fare. Vary the menu. Corned-beef hash two days in a row may be grudgingly accepted but it will surely provoke rebellion if it appears on the third.

Be sure that supplies are ample. In remote areas, what you eat is what you bring along. Although there may be no danger of starvation, running out of basic ingredients can shorten tempers. Don't plan to live off the land, even partially. Fish and game have a knack of disappearing when you need them most. Also, they may be out of season. No matter how hungry you claim to be, you'll find game wardens unreceptive to this alibi.

Most outdoor cookbooks include a master list of foods from which you can plan a menu. However, there's a better way. Many outfitters who sell freeze-dried foods supply a menu planner—a worksheet with which you can plan for each meal, with additional space for snacks. Of course, you need not stick to the menu sequence; a catch of trout can be substituted for beef stew, and certainly there's no reason why you can't have freeze-dried chili on Tuesday instead of Thursday. The menu planner simply insures that you take along sufficient grub. When you eat it is up to you.

In planning the menu, consider the fact that lunch in camp is often a light meal, quickly prepared and quickly eaten. There may be miles to travel down the river, or fish to be caught. Few want to spend a great deal of time whipping up full-fledged meals at noontime. On the other hand, if the afternoon's travel promises to be arduous, don't skimp on the "noonin' " meal. You'll need all the energy you can garner.

Finally, the need for snacks is often underestimated and they are likely to run out. So include a good supply, including cheese, crackers, jerky, raisins, nuts, dried fruit and candy.

Sample Menu Plan for a Four-Day
Backpacking Trip

	Day 1	*Day 2*	*Day 3*	*Day 4*
B		Orange Drink, Pancakes, Hash Browns, Coffee, Tea, Hot Chocolate	Applesauce, Scrambled Eggs, Toast, Coffee, Tea, Hot Chocolate	Granola or Hot Cereal, Fried Spam, Hot Jello, Orange Drink
L	Deviled Ham Sandwiches, Fresh Fruit, Grape Drink	Split Pea Soup, Tuna Sandwiches, Lemonade	Vegetable Beef Soup, Gorp, Fruit Drink	Saltines, Peanut Butter and Jelly Sandwiches, Fruit Drink
D	Cream of Asparagus Soup, Shrimp Creole, Rice, Raspberry Smash, Coffee, Tea, Fruit Drink	French Onion Soup, Beef Stroganoff, Green Beans, Hot Apple Cobbler, Coffee, Tea, Fruit Drink	Leek Soup, Turkey Tetrazzini, Corn, Chocolate Pudding, Coffee, Tea, Fruit Drink	

Sample Menu Plan for a Four-Day
Canoe Trip

	Day 1	*Day 2*	*Day 3*	*Day 4*
B		Orange Drink, Fresh Bacon, French Toast, Tea, Coffee, Hot Chocolate	Grapefruit Drink, Eggs, Fried Salami, Toast and Honey, Tea, Coffee, Hot Chocolate	Orange Drink, Pancakes, Cream of Wheat, Canned Bacon, Tea, Coffee, Hot Chocolate
L	Cold-Cut Sandwiches, Cookies, Grape Drink	Peanut Butter and Jelly Sandwiches, Cookies, Fruit Drink	Beef Boullion, Tuna Sandwiches, Chocolate, Fruit Drink	Chicken Noodle Soup, Peanut Butter and Jelly Sandwiches, Fruit Drink
D	Steak, Home Fries, Canned Peaches, Juice, Hot Chocolate	Clam Chowder, Canned Ham, Baked Beans, Gingerbread, Fruit Juice, Coffee, Hot Chocolate	Chicken Noodle Soup, Spaghetti and Sausage, Spice Cake, Fruit Juice, Coffee, Hot Chocolate	

Freeze-dried and Dehydrated Foods

"Freeze-dried" and "dehydrated" are sometimes used interchangeably. This is incorrect. Freeze-dried foods are quick-frozen, then placed in a vacuum chamber where moisture is removed, thus cutting weight by more than 70 percent. In some instances, a further step includes compressing freeze-dried foods into space-saving patties. For example, a green-bean patty, weighing a mere 1.6 ounces, one-half to three-quarter inches thick and barely three-and-a-half inches in diameter, reconstitutes to twenty ounces of beans, enough for six one-cup servings.

Freeze-dried foods generally retain their shape, flavor and color. There are two types. One requires water for reconstitution after which it is cooked as fresh food—broiled, fried, grilled, stewed or whatever. The second is "instant." This is precooked as well as freeze-dried, requiring only the addition of hot water before eating.

Dehydrated foods are not frozen but merely dried by one of several methods. The process is highly successful with fruits and vegetables but not with meats. As a result, some trail-food processors include a soybean-based textured vegetable protein (TVP) substitute which duplicates the texture and taste of meat, has a high protein content and is easily and quickly readied. This "artificiality" need not deter you. It's surprisingly tasty.

Generally, freeze-dried foods are sold by outfitters. The cost is considerably higher than that of fresh foods and of most dehydrated items, yet they provide several big advantages. Not only has weight been cut and flavor retained but there's no waste, and much, if not all, of the preparation has been done for you. What's more, there's no need for refrigeration.

The variety of freeze-dried foods is great. Some are packaged as complete, one-pot meals—chicken stew, beans and franks, ham and potatoes, ham and eggs, cheese omelets, beef hash and chili with beans, to name only a few. Even greater is the variety of ingredients that can be combined. These include ground beef, sausage patties, diced turkey, shrimp, vegetables and fruits.

Dehydrated foods are also sold by outfitters but there's usually a wider assortment on supermarket shelves. Among the "instant" or "quick" foods used extensively in home kitchens, you'll find soups, spaghetti dinners, potatoes (scalloped, hash brown, au gratin and mashed), puddings, powdered fruit drinks and milk.

Which Foods to Take?

For ski touring, cycling or a backpacking trip of more than a couple of days, freeze-dried and dehydrated foods are virtually a must. However there's no reason why some fresh foods cannot be included for use during the first few meals. It's a matter of weight. If you'd like a steak broiled over hot coals the first night out, why not? The dehydrated or freeze-dried steak that can match the flavor of a fresh one has not yet been developed.

For canoe treks and family camping, there's even greater flexibility of choice. Some trippers carry a camper's ice chest in which they pack such items as a frozen gallon of milk, frozen spaghetti sauce or meats, first "precooling" the chest. When fully packed a block of dry ice is added, then the chest is sealed with duct tape. Fresh foods, packed in this manner, will last six to seven days or longer. And, of course, if the anticipated portages are not too gruelling, you can stow a couple of tins of canned peaches in your duffel for a backcountry dessert.

What you carry for food is determined by your mode of travel and how long you'll be away from a source of supply. Even then, you can give in to your whims if you keep them reasonable.

ORGANIZING AND IMPLEMENTING THE MENU

Organizing the commissary for two or three persons headed out on a brief excursion is a simple matter. A short checklist will expedite the process. However, for a larger group or for an extended trip, a nearly foolproof method is to appoint a camp "steward." He outlines a proposed menu which, when approved by the team members, is then transformed into a shopping list. The steward makes the purchases and packs the grub. He is also responsible for utensils, tableware, dishwashing detergents, dish mops, towels and whatever else is deemed necessary.

In some instances, the steward is also the chef. This may seem like an undue burden to place on one person's shoulders, but most skilled outdoor cooks prefer to do their own buying and packing. Since he has done the packing, the chef knows where to find the ingredients for each meal.

Among some groups, the cook handles the cooking and only the cooking. Other members of the party gather firewood, haul water and assist in any way the chef might request. When the meal is eaten, he gets his reward. He washes no dishes, wipes none. Other party members clean up. The cook relaxes, and deserves to.

This arrangement can be varied, of course. The steward need not also be the chef. Members of the group can rotate assignments. However you arrange things an orderly set-up is vital, including planning the menu, making food purchases, packing the grub, cooking it, then cleaning up afterward. An organized meal is likely to be an enjoyable one.

Packing It Right

For a short overnight hike or a weekend canoe trip, packing your gear more or less helter-skelter probably won't create a great deal of inconvenience. It's another matter when a long trip lies ahead or when eight to ten persons and four to five canoes make up your party. Setting up nightly camps and preparing the evening meal is easier if you know which pack(s) contains the butter and sugar, the spaghetti sauce, the beef stew and the pancake mix. A campsite, after a long day's trek or miles of paddling, is no place for confusion, organized or otherwise.

Save yourself time and weight by repacking food at home before you leave. Juice mix can be transferred from cans (you then won't have to pack these out) to plastic bags, peanut butter and jelly (who needs glass jars?) into plastic food boxes or Gerry® tubes, pancake mix (the cardboard box will probably get soggy and fall apart anyway) into nylon food bags. If you use instant coffee, measure out what you'll need, add a little extra to be safe, pack it in a plastic bag and leave the jar at home. Eggs can be prebroken, put into plastic bags, sealed and then placed in a container. Spices can be stored in an empty 35mm film container. Strip off excess wrappings from such items as powdered soups, taking along only the inner pouches. The various plastic bags and food canisters can be labeled with an indelible felt-tip marker. Be sure to save the directions. Cooking powdered spaghetti sauce while following a recipe for hot apple cobbler makes for a rather thick sauce.

Next try to organize your meals according to ingredients. Pack the spaghetti sauce with the spaghetti; measure out powdered milk and stash it with the pancake mix. No one likes to wait interminably at the end of a long day while ingredients are assembled for supper.

How you divide up the commissary among the packs seems to be a matter of opinion. Backpackers and climbers generally prefer to split up the grub and kitchen gear among members of the party so that no one person carries everything. This not only distributes the load fairly, but in the event that one person is separated from the main party, nobody goes hungry. On canoe trips where tough portages or feisty white water are not anticipated, food and kitchen gear are often concentrated in a single duffel (or two) or a wanigan. If your canoe trip is headed for "big water," it's a good idea to distribute the grub supply among several boats so that if one canoe does flip, the others can still provision the trip. Even more important, be sure that the most critical items are in the canoes handled by the party's best canoeists. Obviously, circumstances—and personal opinion—dictate the distribution. However you do it, the secret lies in knowing where everything is.

Experienced canoeists have learned to delegate duties in advance. As soon as the flotilla lands at a campsite, one man lifts out the food and kitchen supplies, starts a fire (or lights the stove) and gets supper underway. The rest of the party divides the chores, one member assisting the cook while others set up the tent(s) and unfurl the sleeping bags (one person, of course, should see that the canoes are secure for the night). By the time these assignments are completed, supper is just about ready. This may seem like oversimplification but it's the basis for a successful trip.

POTS AND PANS

Early cook kits were of dubious value. They nested cleverly and the kettles were useful but that was it. Aluminum cups burned your lips, aluminum plates wafted away the food's warmth before you could finish your meal and aluminum fry pans that doubled as kettle covers scorched foods. Today's cook kits are a vast improvement. Their makeup may vary slightly as to the utensils included, but dinner plates are now made of plastic, which retains food warmth quite well. Plastic cups do not burn the lips. Better kits include one or two Teflon®-lined fry pans. A typical six-person kit consists of three kettles, the largest having about a ten-quart capacity; two Teflon®-lined skillets with removable handles; a coffee pot with a bail, pouring handle and spout; six plates and six cups. The entire outfit nests into the largest kettle, which then fits into a cloth carrying bag.

A cook kit may be looked on as a "starter set." It provides only basic utensils. You'll want to add to it. In fact, many outdoor cooks prefer to assemble their own kits. It's impossible for a nesting cook kit to include all the implements a skilled camp chef requires.

For a kettle, woodsmen often use a No. 10 can, with a capacity of about one gallon, to which is added a bail of stove-pipe wire. Known as a "tea pail," its price is hard to beat, since it adapts to steeping tea, boiling coffee, heating soup or concocting a trout chowder.

Backpackers and other outdoorsmen worried about the weight they'll have to carry often look to the "billy," which came from the Australian Outback. It resembles the tea pail but is made of aluminum with a fold-down bail handle and a snug-fitting lid. Several, ranging from a one- to six-quart capacity, nest one into the other. The innermost billy can hold a backpacker's stove or tableware. Thanks to the lid, it heats more quickly than the primitive tea pail, and, since the bottom edges are rounded, it's easily washed.

For lifting pots and kettles too hot to handle, use a pot lifter. This resembles a pair of pump pliers that grip the edge of the utensil. Some Maine Guides swear by vice-grip pliers, pointing out that these will lift almost any pot without fear of

Nesting Billy Pots

dropping it. And the pliers double as a useful camp tool. Traditionally, Maine Guides have also cut themselves a pair of pot lifters, simply two forked sticks (alder is excellent) one used to lift, the other to pour.

In this day of instant coffee, any pot is suitable for heating water. However, if you prefer "perked" coffee, buy a wide-based pot. It's less likely to tip over and heats water more quickly than the vertical-sided pots provided in many kits. There's an excellent wide-base, porcelain pot available, with a basket strainer, glass percolator dome, bail and a side handle for pouring.

When it comes to fry pans, skillets or "spiders"—call them what you will—there are many choices. It's been demonstrated that aluminum is a poor one. Teflon®-lined fry pans, while a vast improvement, are limited to about ten inches, inadequate for large parties but ample for two or three persons. The old-fashioned pressed-steel fry pan, still available in country stores, distributes heat well and is relatively inexpensive, but its permanent handle can be a nuisance when packing.

Those who cook for large parties, guides and pack-train grub wranglers, favor steel skillets no thinner than fourteen gauge. These distribute heat beautifully but they are heavy, a ten-inch size weighing five pounds. Where weight is no problem, it's difficult to improve on them. Some range up to twenty inches in diameter, and, since they are big enough to double as a griddle for mass-producing pancakes, they are a boon to the breakfast cook.

Hardly suitable for backpacking or other light travel, cast-iron skillets are ideal for fixed camp or cabin use. No metal more evenly distributes heat and, best of all, a cast-iron cooking surface improves with use, soon acquiring a smooth, polished finish. Such cookwear comes preseasoned but further seasoning is needed before using. Simply apply a light coating of unsalted grease (not bacon fat) and allow the utensil to stand at room temperature, or in a low oven for an hour or more. Repeat the process daily for a week or so, taking care to wipe out the remaining grease between each application. Avoid washing cast iron in strong detergents, which will damage the seasoned finish. If possible, merely wipe out with a dry cloth or a paper towel. If food sticks, scrub it with a wet cloth and a mild soap.

Because of weight, backpackers, cyclists and cross-country skiers have a limited choice of fry pans. Virtually all are of aluminum, though there are Teflon®-lined saucepans that double as small skillets. Few hikers want to carry full-sized skillets, which add weight and bulk to their packs and, what's more, fit poorly over the burners of tiny stoves. The little six-inch fry pans provided in some cook kits are well adapted but their capacity is somewhat limited. Backpackers have generally learned to live with such limitations.

At breakfast time, especially if weight is no object, you may prefer to use a griddle rather than two or three fry pans. For preparing eggs, bacon, ham and pancakes you can turn out larger quantities simultaneously. It works well for other meals, too—for fried potatoes or fish, for instance.

Here again, cast iron is best but a ten-by-twenty-inch model weighs about fifteen pounds. A griddle of cast aluminum, not to be confused with the thin aluminum used in fry pans, weighs about five pounds in the same size. Another type is Teflon®-coated. Whether you use cast iron or aluminum, be sure the griddle has a shallow groove around its outer perimeter to help drain excess grease.

Even at a remote campsite you can enjoy freshly baked biscuits and muffins—or cake. The most intriguing utensil for achieving these is the reflector oven or "shed baker," an outgrowth of the "tin kitchen" used by colonial wives on the hearths of their great fireplaces. The modern reflector (most of which fold) with its sloping back surfaces reflects a campfire's heat upward and downward, directing it to the center shelf. Baking time is about that required in a kitchen range. Incredibly, a reflector oven is capable of six hundred degrees. Heat is governed by moving the oven closer to, or farther from the fire; since the "makings" are visible, there's little guesswork involved. The secret to success is maintaining flames about the height of the oven. Keeping the interior reflecting surfaces polished will boost efficiency about 30 percent over that of a rusted or discolored oven. If you're not inclined toward such neatness, line the interior with aluminum foil.

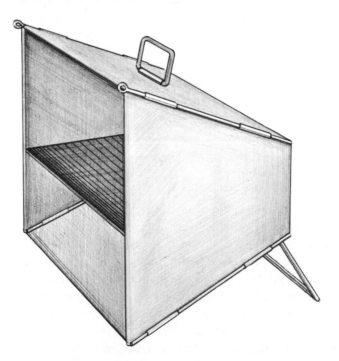

Folding Reflector Oven

The Dutch oven has been standard among western pack-train cooks for many years. Of cast iron or aluminum, it's too heavy for toting except by car, pack horse or possibly by canoe. Nevertheless, it's a remarkable utensil. Essentially a kettle, it has three short legs and a rimmed cover; there are several sizes. No flames are involved. The oven is set over a pad of hot coals and more coals are heaped on the cover. The legs keep the bottom of the oven from sitting directly on the coals, thus avoiding scorching, and the cover's rim keeps coals in place. Any recipe that can be baked in a reflector can be duplicated in a Dutch oven. Granted, it's a little trickier to use since the food is not visible, but the cover can be lifted periodically without appreciable loss of heat. Ingredients such as biscuit dough can be placed directly in the bottom of the oven, or in a pie plate. The Dutch oven doubles as a kettle, and is particularly well adapted to slow simmering for stews or soups. It's the perfect utensil for bean-hole beans.

Dutch Oven

For camp stoves, either gas- or propane-fired, there's a folding box oven that fits atop the burner. An interior baffle system distributes heat evenly and there's a temperature gauge on the door. Baking in it is not unlike using a kitchen-range oven. Hot apple pie is possible in camp.

Nor has the backpacker been left out of the baking scene. There is now a nine-inch-diameter oven, three-and-a-half inches deep, which fits on most backpacker's stoves. Weighing slightly more than one pound, it turns out baked goods and meats in one- and two-man quantities. Here the advantage of carrying two or more of the tiny stoves becomes apparent. While one stove simmers a one-pot stew, the other produces biscuits.

Accessory Utensils

For carrying and storing water in a fixed camp, it's difficult to improve on a pair of ten- or twelve-quart galvanized pails. Set on a campfire grid to heat, one serves for

dishwashing, the other for rinsing. For drinking water there are collapsible polyethylene jugs in two-and-a-half- and five-gallon sizes, and polyurethane-coated
nylon bags. The beauty of these is that they are light and fold for transport.

For stirring and serving, "barbecue sets" generally have wooden handles that
are too long to carry in a pack, though they can be cut down to the right size. The
truth is, if you need handles longer than sixteen to eighteen inches, your cookfire is
too big. Most outfitters offer better sets, one including a spatula, a fork and a
kitchen knife, none of which is longer than fourteen inches. Such sets usually
include a compartmented bag for carrying. They're ideally suited for hunting,
fishing and canoe trips and for fixed camps.

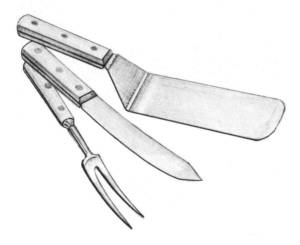

Basic Cooking Utensil Set

Finding suitable mixing bowls for camp use is sometimes a problem. Borrow an
idea from Minnesota guides and acquire a set of "dish-ups," nesting aluminum
bowls. If you can't locate such a set, use pudding pans, which also nest and double
nicely as soup or cereal bowls.

Don't forget that most basic of all tools—the can opener. If yours is new, try it at
home before taking to the woods, to be sure it works. (It's not a bad idea to carry
two.) Even if you leave a can opener behind, all is not lost. Any can may be opened
with an axe or hatchet. Simply apply the heel of the blade to the edge of the can's
top and bear down. Do this once more, at right angles to the first cut, then lift the
four quarters. A lock-blade or sheath knife will also do. These are strictly for
emergencies, however.

A good knife is essential to camp cooking. Some outdoor chefs get along nicely
with a pocket or sheath knife for paring potatoes, slicing meat or peeling onions.
The famed Rapala® knife has a slender and beautifully flexible blade in a choice

of four-, six-, seven-and-a-half- and nine-inch lengths. While it's primarily a filet knife, it's a good choice for camp cooking since it is protected with a sheath.

At a park-type campground you'll find most fireplaces equipped with a grate. In the backcountry, however, there are few such niceties. Carry some sort of a metal grid (unless you're planning to cook entirely on a stove). A discarded refrigerator shelf, set on stones, is quite stable and large enough for an assortment of pots and pans. Better yet is a grid with folding legs that prop it no higher than eight to ten inches above the ground so that the fire can be kept reasonably small. There are also legless backpacker's models, about four inches wide and fifteen inches long, weighing a mere six ounces and meant to be set atop stones. Unfortunately, they're a bit unstable. If you use a grid of any sort, carry it in a cloth bag to avoid spreading soot throughout your outfit.

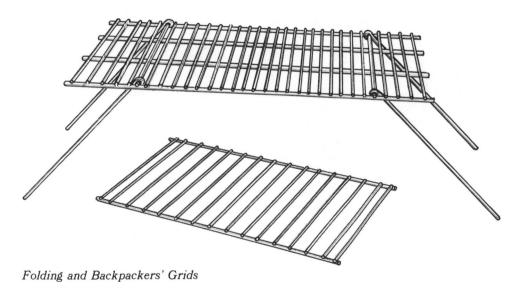

Folding and Backpackers' Grids

Table Settings

The standard table setting in a lumbercamp used to be a metal plate, a one-pint tin cup, a soup spoon, a knife and a fork. Soup was eaten from the plate which was then wiped with bread or a biscuit to accommodate the main course—invariably meat, potatoes and vegetables, or a hearty stew. Dessert, usually pie, was eaten from the same plate. The soup spoon also served to stir coffee or tea. Except for "pass the potatoes," the entire meal was eaten in absolute silence. It wasn't gracious dining but it expedited feeding the crew and the subsequent clean-up by the "cookee." Camp dining needn't be this unsociable but the fewer utensils and table items you use, the quicker you can clean up afterward.

Backpackers usually provide themselves with the ultimate in lightweight and double-duty tableware, often nothing more than a pocket knife, a plastic spoon and a cup. Under less spartan conditions, tableware can be embellished some-what with a three-piece knife-fork-spoon set of stainless steel and a plastic cup and plate. If side dishes are served, use those little plastic bowls (one-pound size) in which soft margarine is sold; you can also store leftovers in them. Whatever you do, don't opt for paper plates, which are fine for picnics but next to useless in camp. Since they tend to grow soggy, it's difficult to dispose of them by burning.

CAMPFIRE COOKING

There are still far-flung places where firewood is so plentiful that its only function is to grow, die and form a new layer of humus. Whenever you have access to such fuel supplies and when conditions permit an open fire, the aroma of wood smoke can be adrenaline to a tired spirit.

If your campsite has no fireplace, gather enough rocks to form a circle or U, roughly eighteen to twenty-four inches across. Scrape away all flammable ground debris for several feet around, building the fireplace on mineral soil or a ledge. One note of caution: avoid using rocks taken from the shallows of a stream or lake. These often contain pockets of moisture which, when heated, turn to steam. Such rocks have been known to explode violently. If strong winds blow, rig a tarpaulin as a windbreak to keep the fire burning at a reasonable rate.

There's no great mystique about fire building. You'll need tinder, kindling and

firewood. White-birch bark is the finest of all tinders because it will ignite readily even when wet. Don't peel live trees, however. There's usually an ample supply on the ground among fallen trees. Lacking birch bark, you can improvise with paper, or you can whittle a heap of shavings from a stick of dry softwood. Dry kindling isn't always easy to find, especially after a three-day rain. Seek out a dry stub, preferably a softwood that has been dead for some years but is still standing. With your axe, cut off the outer layers of wood. You'll find the interior is bone dry. The dried underlimbs of softwoods also make good kindling and are easily broken from the trunk. Probably the best of all kindlings in the North is cedar, in the South, "fat pine" which is highly resinous. White pine, common in the North, is also quite resinous. Naturally, not all campsites provide perfect firewood. You'll have to compromise. Generally, softwoods are best for kindling, hardwoods for cooking.

Split kindling fairly fine, no thicker than three-quarters of an inch. Place it loosely over the tinder so that the latter won't be crushed as it burns. Most beginners, seeking to protect an infant flame, light their campfires on the lee side. You'll have better luck on the windward side where the breeze will blow the flame into the fuel rather than away from it. Once the kindling is burning briskly, add three or more sticks of fuel wood. Stack firewood on the fire so that air can circulate freely under it, thus helping to create an updraft. Keep your cook fire small. An overly hearty blaze scorches food, drives you out of working range and may get out of hand.

The secret to campfire cooking lies in flame control. Rather than allowing your fire to burn briskly at the center of the fireplace, spread the fire out so that it will heat pots and pans anywhere on the grid. There is no need for flames to envelop your pots. For frying, flames create a hazard if they lick up and over the rim of the skillet to ignite the grease. Rake a bed of coals aside and set the skillet on these. If you lack coals, you can place the fry pan over low flames.

Don't underrate a cook fire. Its BTU output is considerable, so it is important to time the cooking of various dishes. Foods that take the longest time go on first and those needing less follow at intervals. For example, take a dinner of fresh-caught trout, biscuits and coffee. The biscuits and coffee will require about twenty minutes, possibly a little longer. Trout fry up in three to five minutes if they're small. So, after the biscuits have risen and started to brown, and while the coffee is settling, put on the trout. If your timing is correct all three will be ready simultaneously. The technique is the same for more complex meals.

The approach to cooking varies with different foods. For example, a steak broiled directly on hot coals is toothsome indeed, but not the gritty bits of scorched wood that stick to the meat. Shake the steak or brush off any charcoal bits that may cling. If this doesn't appeal to you, lay the steaks out on the grid over a moderate fire. As they cook, drops of melted fat will fall into the flames, causing a flare-up. If you start with too brisk a fire, the melting fats will create a conflagration!

When you're finished with a campfire, drown it—literally. Roll each charred stick over, wetting the undersides. Pour on water until the ashes run like thin, gray mud. L.L. advocated placing your hand in the fire pit before leaving it. That's how strongly he felt about fire hazards.

When breaking camp, clean all unburned debris from the fireplace. Some outdoorsmen insist that a fireplace be dismantled and the rocks distributed to leave the site "natural." This makes little sense. On the contrary, a circle of blackened stones can touch off intriguing conjectures. Who passed this way before me? What tales were told by firelight? There's a kinship among those who pause at wild campsites, however many years may separate them.

Bean-Hole Beans

Perhaps the ultimate in wood-fire cooking is the baking of bean-hole beans. Two processes are involved: readying the fire, and preparing the beans.

For the bean hole, dig a pit about two-and-a-half feet deep and some eighteen inches in diameter. Build a brisk fire of hardwood in this, filling the pit to the rim. You may have to replenish the fire once or twice to accumulate red-hot coals to a depth of about twelve inches. When the flames have died down and while the coals are still glowing red, remove about half of them. A long-handled spade is the ideal tool for this. Next, lower your bean pot or kettle into the pit, setting it directly on the bed of coals. Return those that you removed, packing them around the kettle, then fill the hole with soil, packing it firmly. Make sure no smoke escapes. This assures a tight seal. Some six to eight hours later, dig up the kettle carefully so that your spade does not disturb the lid. Ideally, a bean feed should be set up early in the morning. It's then safe to leave camp for a day's fishing or hiking, the delicacy awaiting your return for supper. Bake a batch of cornbread in your reflector oven just before you exhume the beans. The two go together delightfully.

Obviously, bean-hole beans are feasible only at a fixed camp. At a summer cabin or rural home, you can build a permanent bean hole. Dig it about three feet deep and two feet in diameter, then line it with fieldstones, using masonry to secure them in place. Without a stone lining, the sides of the hole will soon fall in.

The preparation of the beans starts the night before. Put about two pounds of dried beans to soak overnight in a kettle large enough to accommodate at least three inches of water over the beans. If the kettle is too small, the beans, as they swell, will climb over the side. Any type of bean will do—California or Michigan pea, red kidney, yellow eye, soldier or navy.

Come morning, while the bean hole is firing up, change the water in the beans, then simmer them until the skins crack and begin to curl, usually in about forty-five minutes. Some cooks add a teaspoon of baking soda during the simmering—as any bean-conscious New Englander will explain, "to remove the snappers." With or without the soda, pour off the water after simmering.

Recipes vary considerably but the following one is popular. The ingredients include:

½ pound of salt pork
1 large onion
¾ cup of molasses
3 tablespoons of brown sugar
1 teaspoon of dry mustard
1 teaspoon of salt

In some parts of the country, a tomato flavor is added to baked beans with tomato paste or sauce. However, at least one notable Maine outdoor cook holds this addition in some contempt. "Anyone who adds tomatoes to baked beans," he insists, "would push his grandmother downstairs!"

If you follow the nontomato recipe, mix the molasses, brown sugar, salt and mustard in one to one-and-a-half cups of hot water, stirring well until the salt and sugar have dissolved. In the bottom of the pot or kettle, lay three slices of salt pork, three-eighths to one-half inch thick. Add a layer of beans, two to four inches deep. Over these place onion slices and more salt pork, then more beans, building up the layers until the pot is full. Pour in the molasses-and-brown-sugar syrup and add hot water to just below the level of the beans.

Because it distributes heat evenly, one of the best bean-hole kettles is the ten- or twelve-inch diameter cast-iron Dutch oven. However, any type of pot will do. It should be equipped with a bail to facilitate lifting from the bean hole. Whatever type you choose, seal the edges of the lid (the tighter this fits, the better) with aluminum foil to prevent dirt from slipping into the beans. When placing the pot in the hole, be sure the bail is upright. This makes it easier to lift out the kettle with a potholder, forked stick or by hooking an axe under the bail. Most important of all, excavate carefully so as not to disturb the lid.

STOVES

Today's camp stoves are remarkably efficient and easy to use. Add to this the retreating supply of firewood along popular hiking and canoeing routes, and you have good reason for carrying a stove. To prevent denuding forests adjacent to heavily used recreational areas, regulations may restrict, or even forbid, open fires. For winter campers, compact stoves make quick meals possible in inclement weather.

There's a great variety of camp stoves, each suited to a specific need. Obviously, a backpacker is limited to one of the many compact, single-burner models which range from one to three-and-a-half pounds. Traveling with a partner, one such stove may be sufficient, but two will provide quicker and more complete meals. Efficiency, and the amount of fuel consumed, must also be considered, as

well as where the stove will be used. For example, water boils at a lower temperature at high altitudes, about one degree for every five hundred feet above sea
level. It would seem, then, that food cooks more quickly in the mountains than at
the seashore. Just the opposite is true. Liquids boil at increasingly lower temperatures as altitude increases and atmospheric pressure drops. As a result, cooking at
high altitude is slower because the temperature is lower, and you'll need an
efficient stove and possibly extra fuel.

By way of contrast, at a fixed camp accessible by car, boat or even by plane, you
can take advantage of the efficiency of multiple-burner stoves, even a three-
burner model. With such a stove the cook can unlimber table fare to match that
eaten at home. However, such stoves are bulky and can weigh up to fifteen
pounds. This is no problem in the cargo deck of a 4 x 4 vehicle but it is certainly
out of the question for a backpacker and a doubtful possibility for canoe trippers
likely to encounter portages. In other words, the stove must fit the trip.

Among the many camp stoves, whether multiple-burner or single, there's a
choice of fuels: kerosene, naphtha, white gasoline, butane, propane and alcohol.
Their potential heat output is illustrated in the following chart:

Fuel	BTU Output per Gallon*
Kerosene	132,500
Naphtha	121,000
White Gasoline	119,200
Butane	101,000
Propane	91,800
Alcohol	64,400

* A BTU is a British Thermal Unit, equivalent to the heat required to raise one pound of water one
degree Fahrenheit.

At a glance it might seem that a kerosene-fueled stove must be the most efficient. Not true. Many white-gas stoves will outheat kerosene models. Burner
design makes the difference.

Although kerosene camp stoves continue to be offered (most are imported),
kerosene is not popular. Being less volatile than other liquid fuels it is difficult to
ignite, it's inclined to be smoky and odorous, and, being an oil, the odor clings to
the hands while more volatile gasolines evaporate almost immediately.

Naphtha and white gasoline, for all practical purposes, are identical. White
gasoline may be difficult to find in some areas but naphtha, marketed commercially as Coleman® and Blazo® fuels, is readily available in the United States and
Canada. Both Coleman® and Blazo® fuels burn cleaner than white gas and are
less likely to clog tiny orifices. Also they contain additives that make lighting
easier, as well as rust inhibitors. All liquid fuels work well in warm weather, but
when temperatures plunge, naphtha-fueled stoves outperform others. The disadvantages of naphtha are twofold, though minor: first, fueling must be done with

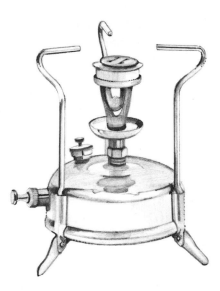

Kerosene Stove

great care. Due to its high volatility, keep naphtha at a distance from open flames, lighted cigarettes or any source of sparks when fueling your stove. Use a strainer funnel to avoid spillage. Second, the stove must be preheated or "primed," usually by burning a small amount of fuel in a priming pan at the base of the burner until the latter is well heated, generally a matter of a couple of minutes. One exception to the priming requirement applies to multiple-burner stoves whose fuel tanks are equipped with a pump. This builds up pressure in the tank which, in turn, forces the fuel into the burners where it may be lighted without delay.

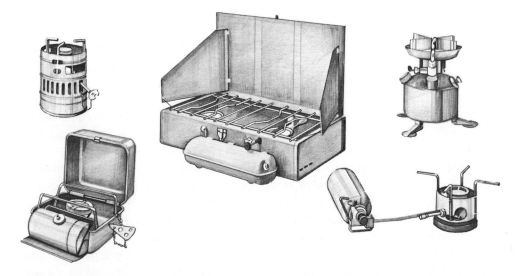

A Selection of Common White-Gas Stoves

Butane and propane, both petroleum derivatives, are similar with one notable exception. Butane will not vaporize at sea level at temperatures below 32 degrees Fahrenheit, whereas propane remains efficient down to 43.8 degrees below zero. Under pressure in their containers both are liquids, vaporizing as they escape and expanding some 270 times as vapor.

 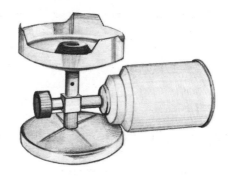

Butane Stoves

Virtually all butane-fired stoves are of the one-burner type. Refueling calls for simply pushing or screwing in the butane canister. Lighting is even easier. Turn on the control knob, apply a match and you have a hot, blue flame, ready to go to work. Some care is required, however, when inserting the canister. Be sure it is properly sealed and firmly locked to avoid the escape of highly volatile gas.

One reminder. As a butane container empties, it will cool and reduce the stove's efficiency almost to the point where it may require twice the normal burning time to cook a meal.

With regard to propane and butane, two other problems arise. Empty containers must be disposed of, which means you'll have to carry them out as well as in. Also the packaging of butane varies. Although contents have been standardized at nine-and-a-half ounces, one type of stove requires that the canister be pushed into it, a needle puncturing the top of the container through which the fuel is fed into the burner. Another type of stove requires that the canister be screwed into a socket. The two types of canisters are, obviously, not interchangeable. Thus it's necessary that you buy butane in containers that will fit your specific stove.

If you don't mind toting out the empties, butane stoves are ideal for warm-weather camping, and are certainly less complex and simpler to light than gasoline stoves. Burning time for the canisters averages about three hours. Butane stoves aren't generally recommended for cold-weather use, however, because the fuel won't vaporize at temperatures below 32 degrees Fahrenheit. (Its successful use by the 1963 American Mount Everest Expedition was due to the high altitude. Air pressure at high altitude is considerably less than at sea level so the butane vaporized despite the low temperatures.)

Like butane, propane (also known as "bottle gas" or "LP gas") is liquefied under pressure within a steel container. At 60 degrees, propane's pressure is about 117 pounds per square inch. Under normal summer conditions, this pressure will not become excessive, but if exposed to unusually high temperatures—storage in a car trunk under a hot sun, for example—a tiny safety valve built into each container will pop, allowing gaseous propane to escape.

A propane stove is also simple to operate. You open a single valve, apply a match and get an instant blue flame burning at between 1,800 and 2,000 degrees Fahrenheit. Pressure is automatic. No pumping or priming is needed.

Propane is generally used with larger camp stoves, two and three-burner units. The most easily portable models are fueled by fourteen or sixteen-ounce disposable steel cylinders that weigh more than their contents. Since threads are interchangeable, cylinders are easily replaced in any stove regardless of brand. Also, the cylinders have self-sealing valves so that a partially full cylinder can be removed. Slight leaks have been known to occur, however. You can expect about six hours of burning from a single cylinder, so that the operating cost is relatively high. Then, too, since the cylinders are virtually indestructible, they must be carried out when emptied.

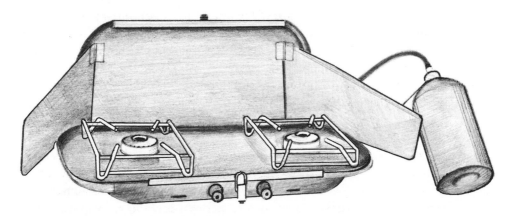

A Common Two-Burner Propane Stove

At permanent campsites, far greater economy is effected by using a stove rigged with a bulk tank, its capacity ranging from four to twenty pounds; the gas is fed into the stove through a flexible hose. Such tanks are not portable and must be refilled by a dealer. With the tare weight—i.e., the weight of the empty container—stamped on the side or top, you can determine the amount of propane remaining by weighing the tank. This is how a dealer determines the amount of propane he puts in. (He allows space for vaporization to avoid having the safety valve pop when the tank is warmed.)

You may run into the terms "low pressure" and "high pressure." Disposable cylinders are considered high pressure, since the vapor flows from them at a pressure dictated by ambient temperature—as already noted, 117 pounds per square inch at 60 degrees. The stove burners used with these cylinders are designed to burn efficiently under such pressures. With bulk tanks, a regulator is inserted in the hose between the tank and the stove. The regulator reduces pressure to the stove to six ounces per square inch; the burners are at their best under this pressure. The two systems may not be interchangeable.

If you choose disposable cylinders, setting up a propane camp-stove outfit can be fairly inexpensive at the outset. But your initial savings may be misleading because you must take into account the constantly recurring cost of cylinders. For occasional use, a cylinder stove is convenient and worthwhile, but if you're a fervent camper, out every weekend and during your vacation, the more expensive bulk-tank outfit is an economy in the long run. Stoves and tanks rarely wear out. You'll buy only gas, not throwaway cylinders.

A multiple-burner gasoline stove can easily be converted to propane. A simple converter replaces the gasoline tank and the generator so that either a cylinder or a bulk tank can be attached. The gasoline unit can readily be restored, too, since the stove is not altered in any manner.

The last of the liquid camp-stove fuels, alcohol, has gained little acceptance, except among boaters. Because it has a low volatility, it is relatively safe to use aboard small power boats. Very early portable camp stoves, those in use at the turn of the century, were frequently fueled with alcohol but as the chart on page 156 indicates, other fuels are more efficient.

Once you've appraised the various fuels, give some thought to the features and characteristics of specific stoves. Stability is one factor to be considered. Obviously, if you're planning on a two-burner gasoline- or propane-fired stove, this is not a problem. Whether you set it on a campground picnic table or even on the ground, the size (usually about twelve by twenty-four inches) and the weight of one of these stoves make it inherently stable. You needn't worry that it will tip over. The smaller, single-burner stoves are another matter. They may have bases as small as three-and-a-half inches in diameter, so that perching a six-quart kettle atop one of them can create a precarious situation. However, if you set up such a stove on a firm, flat surface and use a kettle or pot designed for it, you should have no problems.

Efficiency among the multiple-burner gasoline and propane stoves is generally unquestioned when you stick to well-known brands. Burner output generally runs from 10,000 to 14,000 BTUs. The stoves are also equipped with windscreens, usually formed by the cover at the back and winglike panels at each side. Propane stoves, having no moving parts except for the control valve (this rarely wears out), are the most reliable. Gasoline models can be somewhat less so. They are equipped with a "generator," a tubular compartment that runs from the fuel tank over the primary burner. It is, actually, a heating chamber that vaporizes the air/gasoline mixture before feeding it into the primary and secondary burners. In time, the generator may become clogged and will have to be replaced, a simple chore requiring only a small wrench or pliers. One cause of this clogging is the burning of leaded gasoline. The additives in this fuel will cause clogging. So use it only for emergencies. If you stick to Coleman® or Blazo® fuel, the chances are that your generator will last for years. Nevertheless, it's wise to carry a spare. Tape it to the inside of the stove so that you won't mislay it—but place it away from the burners, or the heat will melt the plastic control knob. To avoid interruptions while cooking, fill the tank before each use. Wipe all spillage dry before lighting the stove.

The efficiency and ease of use among the little single-burner backpackers' stoves vary. The butane models are "instant" lighting. The gasoline models must be primed and preheated. Some require that you open the valve and cup the tank in your hands. This warms the fuel, causing it to expand and run into a priming pan at the base of the burner. When the pan is nearly full, the valve is closed and the priming fluid lighted. This heats the burner and, just before the priming fluid burns out, the valve is reopened, igniting the burner. The process may seem lengthy but it usually requires no more than a couple of minutes. Some minor problems may develop. In very cold weather, cupping the tank may chill your hands severely before the necessary fuel expansion takes place; on a warm day, the cupping process may be unnecessary since the fuel is already well warmed. Placing the stove in direct sunlight may increase heat enough to cause the fluid to expand into the priming pan. This is slow at best. So carry an eyedropper or a plastic straw with which to squeeze fuel directly into the priming pan. A dab of Sterno® heat tabs or priming paste (developed for this purpose) can be substituted for priming fuel.

Other types of single-burner stoves are equipped with a pressure pump, much like that on the larger two-burner gasoline stoves. With these, priming is still required, but not cupping. Pressure in the tank will cause fuel to seep into the priming pan. Generally, among gasoline stoves, the pump-equipped models are easier and quicker to light. (For some of the stoves lacking a pump, there is a miniature one available that replaces the cap on the gas tank.)

Virtually all new backpackers' stoves have a self-cleaning feature. Simply turning the control valve to and fro while the stove is burning will clear out the tiny orifice that feeds fuel to the burner.

No matter what type of gasoline stove you may decide on, two accessories are virtual necessities—a fuel bottle and a pouring funnel. Since it's not always practical to carry conventional gallon-size fuel containers, spun-aluminum bottles are pretty much standard, in pint and quart sizes. These should be equipped with a pouring spout to eliminate the quick surging of fuel as air enters the canister while pouring. As for a funnel, one equipped with a felt strainer will eliminate tiny bits of debris that might otherwise find their way into the tank. Such a funnel is only about three inches long and weighs barely two ounces, certainly not a burden even in an overcrowded pack.

In comparing the many single-burner stoves designed for backpackers (there's no reason why they can't be used by others, including fishermen, hunters and even car-campers), look for an indication of the time required to boil one quart of water. These ratings, of course, apply to tests made under ideal conditions, perhaps even in a laboratory, and are not valid under adverse conditions—high winds or extreme cold. Generally, despite the favorable ratings for butane and propane stoves, those that burn white gas or naphtha will surpass the efficiency of butane and propane models. As a preliminary choice, butane and propane are excellent for summer use, especially where simplicity of operation is sought. However, if you want a stove that will pour out the heat when you need it in cold or windy weather, choose a white-gas (or naphtha) model.

COOKING IN A TENT

Even with today's fire-retardant tents, the danger of fire in a tent has not been completely eliminated. A burning stove, placed too close to the wall or tipped over, can ignite even flame-retardant fabric.

There is a second danger: carbon monoxide, odorless and deadly. Tests have shown that small backpackers' stoves, even when used in uncoated nylon tents with vents partially open, give off enough carbon monoxide to cause dizziness, headaches and nausea. Moreover, when pots are set closely atop the burners, the carbon monoxide developed is greater than when pots are raised an inch or more above the burners. Such amounts of carbon monoxide are not necessarily lethal at low altitudes, though they could be at elevations where oxygen decreases.

Whenever possible, cook out of doors. Rig a tarp for a windbreak. If weather drives you into your tent, minimize the use of the stove as much as possible. Ventilate—almost to the point of discomfort. Be sure your stove is set firmly on the ground, well away from fabric. Pay strict attention to your chores as you cook. Refuel your stove outside, no matter how uncomfortable the process may be. Don't risk having flammable fumes in your shelter.

LIGHTS AND LANTERNS

Some sort of a lantern is necessary at any fixed camp. If your camp stove burns white gas or naphtha, it makes sense to use these fuels in your lantern. If you select a butane stove, there are one or two butane-fueled lanterns. While lighting such lanterns with a paper match is not difficult, a wooden match eases the chore considerably. It's not necessary to shove the lighted match all the way inside the globe. Inserting only the flame will do. Pushing the match in too far may puncture the mantle. For lanterns that require generators, carry a spare. Always fuel and check your lantern in the morning before you leave camp for a day's fishing or hiking. Try it out then, too. It's easier to fuel or to replace a generator by daylight. Carry extra mantles.

In most cases, a single-mantle lantern is more than adequate and, of course, your chances of broken mantles are halved. If size and weight are considerations, there are models that stand about nine inches high and run as light as thirty ounces. On the other hand, a two-mantle lantern illuminates a campsite better—if yours is a large party. When set on a table, keep the handle turned down. It can become hot enough to cause severe burns if left erect for more than a few minutes. If the lantern is hung up, don't touch the bail until it has cooled or use some sort of padding to protect your hands.

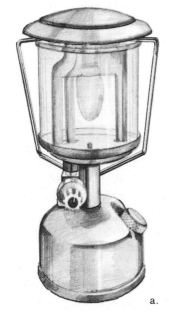

a.   b.

Two Types of Portable Lanterns a. *Thirty-Ounce White-Gas Lantern* b. *Twenty-four-Ounce Butane Lantern*

Gasoline lanterns give off considerable heat and are sometimes used as heaters, particularly during wet weather. It has already been pointed out that gasoline stoves produce carbon monoxide. So do the lanterns. Use caution. Under no circumstances leave one lighted while all occupants in the tent are asleep, even if it's turned down to "night-light" level.

Propane lanterns are indicated if you use a propane stove, although this is not an inflexible rule. These lanterns light as easily as do the stoves and they give off more than adequate light, though nowhere as brilliant as gasoline lanterns. Some operate from fourteen- to sixteen-ounce cylinders. However, these will last no longer than a prolonged evening, seldom more than five to six hours—expensive lighting.

For a fixed camp it makes more sense to operate propane lanterns from the stove's bulk tank. There are all sorts of hose combinations and connections available to rig these. When deciding how much lantern fuel to take along, the season is an important consideration. In June and early July, the months of the longest days, you use minimal fuel. However, during a hunting trip in November, remember that it grows dark in the North at about 4 P.M. Plan on extra lantern fuel.

Many backpackers regard the candle lantern as the ultimate in simplicity. It's also reliable. You can always light a candle. Standing about six inches high, with a bail for hanging, it has a cylindrical globe that can be rotated into the casing to protect it during travel. It's not a powerful light but you can read by it before dozing off to sleep. Designed for tent use, it is definitely not a trail light.

Whether at a fixed camp, on a canoe trip or along a canoe route, each member of the party should carry a flashlight. If you have your own light, you can come and go without disturbing others by "borrowing" the community camp lantern. Most two-cell (size D) flashlights are more than adequate for camp use. If you'd like something a bit lighter and more compact, there are some ABS plastic-encased mini-lights that are barely five-and-a-half inches long and that weigh slightly over three ounces. Powered by a pair of AA batteries, they direct a strong beam while providing a wide arc of light. The life of the batteries on such lights, however, is considerably less than that of size D batteries.

In buying a flashlight, avoid the type that projects a lengthy beam. These, especially when equipped with larger bulbs for added intensity, drain batteries rapidly. For camp use, you need be concerned only with what lies a few feet ahead of you. Don't burden yourself with lights that are more appropriate for search and rescue missions.

If you anticipate any night hiking or after-dark camp chores, consider a head-lamp. The light unit itself—a bulb and reflector—is worn on the head with an elastic band, while the batteries, four D-size cells, are carried in a belt pack.

When buying batteries choose the alkaline type rather than carbon-zinc batteries; they last longer. You may want to consider lithium cells, generally available in C and D sizes. A single lithium cell of 2.8 volts is equal to two ordinary cells of 1.5 volts each. Lithium cells cut down on weight, provide prolonged voltage and survive cold weather very well. There's a hitch, however. You will have to replace one of the cells with a "dummy" since only one lithium cell should be used in a two-cell light. Also, the cost of lithium cells is quite high.

SOME OUTDOOR-COOKING TIPS

Learning to cook out of doors is usually a do-it-yourself project. Stick to familiar or easy recipes to begin with. You'll find that your skills improve as you go along. However, if you get the chance to observe a skilled woods cook in action, jump at the opportunity. Camp cooks are an ingenious breed and they are generally somewhat extroverted, eager to display and share their culinary wisdom. The following are a few tips observed around cookfires and camp stoves.

The midsection of an overturned canoe, rinsed and dried, doubles nicely as a pastry board. (This won't work if the surface is hot.) For a rolling pin, use a round bottle. A bottle can also be used as a potato masher.

To keep slab bacon from becoming moldy, wrap it in cheesecloth that's been wet with vinegar.

If you want to brighten the darkened interior of aluminum pots and kettles, heat a weak solution of water and vinegar, or cream of tartar, in it.

When storing your camp ice chest for long periods, sprinkle a small amount of regular grind coffee in it. This will prevent any musty odor. Don't use instant coffee. It will absorb moisture and turn into a gooey mess.

Scrambled eggs go farther if bread crumbs are added, a good idea when the eggs are running short.

Rub fat trimmings or a strip of bacon over a broiler to keep meats from sticking to it. Incidentally, don't broil meats or cook other foods directly on a discarded refrigerator or stove shelf. Some of these are cadmium-plated and may cause illness through poisoning.

Bacon grease is more flavorsome than cooking oil for frying. Save bacon fat in a small can with a snug-fitting lid.

Stew dried fruits during the supper preparations. They'll then be ready for breakfast.

All in all, skilled outdoor cooking can make for a fun occasion. So can the eating.

Chapter 8

Woods Tools: On Warming Yourself Twice

Henry David Thoreau, referring to the stumps he had pulled from his garden, wrote: "they warmed me twice—once while I was splitting them, and again when they were on the fire." Obviously an idyllic life in the woods involves hard work, especially the cutting of firewood; even with modern tools, your firewood will warm you twice. But choosing the right high-quality tool, and using it correctly, will minimize your initial overheating.

Cutting wood for a trailside campfire differs considerably from working up a sizable woodpile at a backcountry cabin or rural home. At home, you'll need tools that approximate those used by loggers—a chain saw, a full-size axe, a splitting maul and wedges, possibly a peavey, perhaps a sawbuck. But along a hiking trail or a canoe route or even at a nonwilderness campsite, you can get along nicely with nothing more than a light axe and a folding saw. If you're backpacking, ski touring or planning to use a stove, you might even dispense with the axe. Fit the tool to the trip.

The one thing you should always carry is a knife. It's the key implement for backwoods travel, not for cutting firewood, of course, but for dozens of other necessary chores.

AXES IN GENERAL

The best axes and hatchets are fitted with handles or "helves" of tough and resilient second-growth hickory. Axe handles take a beating. The resilience of hickory absorbs the shock of each blow, a shock that would otherwise be transmitted to your hands, arms and shoulders. Avoid axes rigged with steel handles. They will jar your eyeteeth loose.

Beware of a wooden handle that is painted. It's probably of inferior wood, the paint covering the defects. What's more, a painted surface will raise a crop of blisters unless you wear gloves. Check the grain of the handle at the knob end. This should run vertically or nearly so to reduce the chance of splitting.

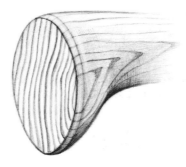

Proper Endgrain in an Axe Handle

The "hang" of an axe is critical. Place it in profile on a flat surface—a store counter, for example—with only the bit (the cutting edge) and the knob touching. The bit should rest approximately at its midpoint or slightly back of this. Next, sight along the cutting edge toward the handle. Your line of sight should bisect the handle exactly. If not, the handle is warped or improperly seated in the axe head.

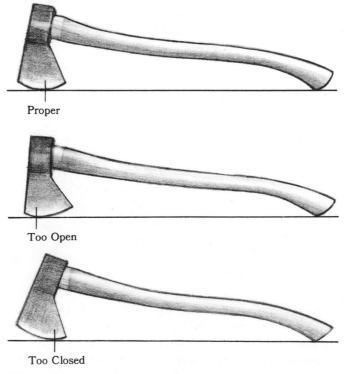

Proper

Too Open

Too Closed

Proper Axe Hang

This may seem a petty matter; after all, an axe is hardly a precision instrument. However, a poorly hung axe or one with a warped handle has a habit of missing its mark. That's not only inefficient; it's downright dangerous.

There are several types of axes: the hatchet, the Hudson Bay axe, the pole, the double-bit, the cedar—plus a host of others now rarely used. The double-bit is the professional's tool, one edge usually honed for chopping, the other for splitting; it's not recommended for recreational use. The cedar axe has an extra wide bit, best adapted to cutting softwood such as cedar. Most of us in the woods for recreation are concerned basically with the first three: the hatchet, the Hudson Bay and the pole axe.

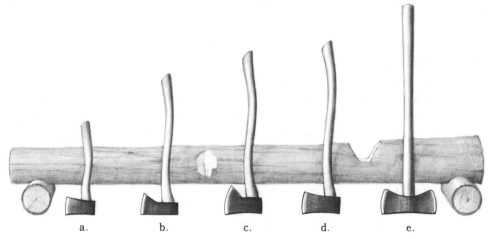

Types of Axes a. *Hatchet* b. *Hudson Bay* c. *Cedar* d. *Pole* e. *Double-Bit*

The Hatchet

Many woodsmen scorn the hatchet, with some justification. Because it's light-weight—usually about two pounds—it has to be wielded forcefully for an effective bite. The short handle, frequently under sixteen inches, prompts the user to swing it with one hand, thus lessening control. Should the bit glance, the one-hand grip often can't prevent it from seeking out a kneecap or an ankle. And the short handle compounds this danger by requiring that you stand (or even worse, kneel) close to your target. You'll work harder cutting or splitting wood with a hatchet than you will with a full-size axe.

The Hudson Bay Axe

A better choice than the hatchet is the Hudson Bay axe. Its head weighs one-and-three-quarter pounds, give or take a few ounces, and its handle is twenty to twenty-two inches long. A Hudson Bay axe generally weighs little more than a hatchet. Yet the longer handle gives your swing a wider arc. With this added momentum, the blade cuts more deeply with each stroke. The longer handle calls for a two-hand grip for better control. Best of all, you can stand safely away from your target. For light work at a fixed camp or during a canoe trip, the Hudson Bay is a fine choice.

The Pole Axe

This model derives its name from its flat-top hammer head or "pole." It is not restricted to cutting poles or saplings, and is, in fact, a heavy-duty tool. For the same reasons that a Hudson Bay axe is superior to a hatchet, the pole axe is the best of the three for heavy work. The pole axe is ideal for cutting hardwood, since its relatively narrow bit bites well into tough fibers. Weights run two-and-a-half, three and three-and-a-half pounds. The two-and-a-half pounder is widely accepted for recreational camping and on extended canoe trips, while the three-and-a-half pound style is better suited to working up a woodpile for cabin or home heating. Most pole axes have handles of about twenty-eight inches.

The extra weight of a full-size pole axe is anathema if your weight restrictions are severe. For backpacking or ski touring, a big axe is out of the question. However, on trips where you can tolerate the extra heft, it's well worthwhile. A pole axe will make the chips fly and, for splitting, it will cleave all but the most stubborn bolt of hardwood.

Whether you choose the hatchet, the Hudson Bay or the pole axe, you'll ease your chores if you let the tool do the work. Don't drive the axe head into the wood so hard that it sends shock waves up your arms to your shoulders. If you work so hard that you grunt, you're overdoing it. Simply raise the axe in a moderate rhythmic swing and allow the weight of the head and its downward momentum to take over. You merely guide it. Not only is this more efficient, it's also safer.

Brush Hooks

Sometimes referred to as a "bush" or "clearing" axe, the brush hook is a combination of machete and axe that has been around for many years. It has a sword-type handle, designed so that the blade can be swung like a hatchet or used with an upward pull to cut brush. It's not a wood-gathering tool, though it can serve as one in a pinch. The brush hook is at its best for trail clearing, and is a good tool for canoe tripping into areas where portages may have become overgrown. It's also effective for clearing brush around a cabin or rural home. An axe can be used for these chores, of course, but there's the ever-present risk of driving the bit into the ground, and nicking it on stones. The brush hook's cutting edge does not extend the full length of the blade so that driving it into the ground probably won't injure the edge. Also, on the opposite side, a sicklelike hook calls for an upward pull, eliminating all danger of contact with rocks.

CAMPING SAWS

Lightweight saws that fold (as opposed to the heavy-duty saws necessary for major wood cutting) are ideal on the trail, along canoe routes or for occasional use at a summer cabin. These small saws require no brawn and, with the exception that you can't split wood with them, accomplish just about any other woodcutting chore. Moreover, they are safer than an axe or a hatchet; many campers forego the latter in favor of a saw.

In the past, the problem with camping saws was that when packed their exposed teeth chewed through knapsacks and tents. Homemade sheaths were devised, made of a piece of garden hose split lengthwise, or of wood. Both types invariably broke apart or split.

The folding camp saw has eliminated the need for a sheath. The blade fits into one section of the triangular aluminum frame, which, in turn, folds into a fully self-enclosed unit barely twenty-four inches long. Aluminum is not usually a good frame material since its flexibility tends to cause the blade to wobble when in use. However, the folding camp saw's frame is girderlike, providing more than ample rigidity. It's important to keep the blade taut, and the folding camp saw does this by means of a thumb screw. The blade is much like that used by pulpwood cutters before the advent of the chainsaw, having four cutting teeth interspersed with a raker tooth, known as "four-teeth-and-a-raker." This cutting edge combination

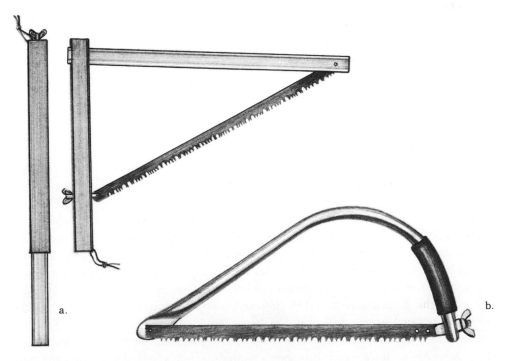

Camp Saws a. *Folding Saw* b. *Bow Saw*

makes the sawdust fly. For every four teeth biting through fibers, there's a raker to withdraw the sawdust. The folding camp saw is the lightest and most compact of camp saws and, although it's not designed for heavy work, it will efficiently cut bolts or logs up to three or four inches thick.

There are also oval-framed bow saws with the same type of blades, usually twenty-four inches or so long—though they run up to forty-two inches for heavy work. These have a cantilever-action locking device that, combined with the steel frame's rigidity, keeps the blade taut. They do not fold and some sort of a sheath should be devised. Oval-framed bow saws are not as compact as the folding camp model, but they will handle larger logs more effectively.

Saw teeth tend to become dull in time, which makes for hard work and poor production. They can be sharpened but it's a job for an expert saw filer. The cutting teeth must not only be sharpened but "set"—alternatingly bent to one side then to the other to produce a saw kerf slightly wider than the thickness of the blade. However, the cost of filing and setting a saw is likely to be greater than replacing it. Many campers buy a new blade at the start of each season.

Protect your blade against rusting or pitting, which slows cutting. Some of today's blades are coated with an industrial-type Teflon®, but this wears off in time. If you store your saw for any extended period, particularly in a place where it may be exposed to moisture, coat the blade lightly with oil.

KNIVES

In *Hunting—Fishing and Camping,* L.L. made few references to knives, but he did suggest that a deer be dressed out "with a jackknife"; and when he built a fire, he added "pine whittlings" to his tinder. During his many years in the woods, L.L. also used his knife to dress out salmon, ducks and trout, as well as deer. He peeled potatoes by the campfire and he cut many a length of rope for guy lines. Knife use is generally so prosaic that few of us give it a second thought. One thing is certain—you'll need a knife every day. Take one along.

Many of us buy knives on the strength of looks alone. Although a knife is a simple tool, there's more to one than meets the eye. Take the matter of steel, for example.

Carbon steel is an alloy—iron to which iron carbide (carbon) has been added, rendering the metal malleable yet sufficiently hard. When new, carbon steel may have a bright, shiny finish but it will soon turn a dull gray. This is in no way detrimental to the knife. Also, the metal will stain, but again, this does no harm. Carbon steel is often favored because it is easy to sharpen and holds an edge well. Probably the best grade is "1095 carbon," which contains .95 percent carbon (almost one percent).

Stainless steel is also an alloy—iron to which nickel, chromium or other metals have been added. While stainless steel has been used in knives for many years, it was often considered difficult to sharpen. Some claimed it was also more brittle than carbon steel. However, the newest stainless-steel knives are no more difficult to sharpen than carbon steel ones, nor are they any more brittle. There are numerous grades of stainless steel, the most common being the 440 series, which includes several subdivisions such as 440A, 440B, 440C. However, significant differences in manufacturers' processes for tempering and heat treating make it difficult to generalize about the characteristics of any specific type. Moreover, a consumer may find it difficult to identify the exact grade of steel used in a particular knife.

Probably the most accurate indication of knife quality—how easily it will sharpen and how well it will hold an edge—is the steel's hardness, or Rockwell rating. If too soft, steel will readily take an edge but soon dulls; too hard, and it resists a sharpening stone and may even be so brittle as to break easily. Before being made into a blade, steel is tested in a Rockwell machine by placing the metal under a diamond-pointed drill-like device which is then lowered under ten kilograms of pressure. The indentation is then noted and the process repeated with one-hundred-and-fifty kilograms of pressure. Based on a metallurgist's "C" scale, the difference between the two readings results in a rating of hardness. A reading of 56 to 59 is considered acceptable for knives, give or take a point or so. Knives with ratings below 56 don't hold an edge well. Anything above 59 is very difficult to sharpen.

Controversy has been longstanding among outdoorsmen, some of whom insist on carbon steel because it's easy to sharpen; and others who prefer stainless steel and its stain- and rust-resistant qualities. It comes down to a matter of personal preference. Carbon advocates don't mind "touching up" the edges of their knives occasionally and are not concerned about the dull gray finish carbon blades take on. (It can be sanded clear if desired.) Stainless steel users don't mind the slight extra work required to sharpen their blades, since the need is less frequent.

Part of the knife-making process, of course, is grinding the edge. A full hollow-ground blade in profile resembles a very thin needle with little backing, resulting in a blade generally too delicate for outdoor purposes. A semihollow-ground blade has some of the backing removed but enough remains to stabilize the cutting edge against undue pressure. Flat-ground blades taper directly from the thickest point of the blade to the cutting edge. Flat-ground blades are a good all-around choice. Generally stronger and somewhat heavier than either the hollow or semihollow type, they withstand rugged use. More difficult to sharpen, since the angle of the original grind must be maintained, they are not well suited to precise, delicate work.

The materials that go into knife handles are varied indeed. One of the least expensive is rosewood, which is tough, fine-grained and able to resist damage from repeated washings and exposure to detergents—providing the wood has been suitably finished. In more expensive knives, oak, ebony and staghorn are also used. Natural materials, despite their beauty, are generally not quite as durable as synthetics. Wood may crack or split; staghorn is expensive and easily damaged.

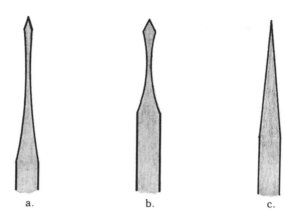

Blade Grinds   a. *Semi-Hollow*   b. *Hollow*   c. *Flat*

Among the synthetics that are widely used are Delrin® plastic and Micarta® —an epoxy-linen laminate. Both are durable and can be fashioned into attractive-looking knives. They can also be "textured" to provide a better grip when wet.

In the recreational outdoors there is little need for heavy, thick blades. Skillful knife handling calls for deft and delicate finger work, impossible with a large blade and a hefty handle. Choose a short, slender blade; anything over five inches is awkward to use. Nor does the blade need to exceed three-quarters of an inch in width.

The shape of the blade is a matter of function and personal taste. One of the most popular shapes for both folding and sheath knives is the clip, including two of its variations, the California clip and the B clip. Both are slender with a sharp point—ideal for close, delicate work. A trapper will usually choose such a blade; a big-game hunter, on the other hand, requires a heftier blade.

The drop-point or spear blade is somewhat sturdier than the clip, being wider and thicker. Hunters like it because of its ruggedness, but its uses are by no means limited to dressing game. The sheep-foot blade is favored by sailors and gardeners. With a relatively straight edge, plus a point, it's also handy for almost any camp chore. The Spey blade resembles a surgeon's scalpel and is generally short, likely to be used by farmers and stockmen. This is probably the least practical blade for general purposes, although it's handy when included in a folding knife with one or two other types of blades.

Filet Knife

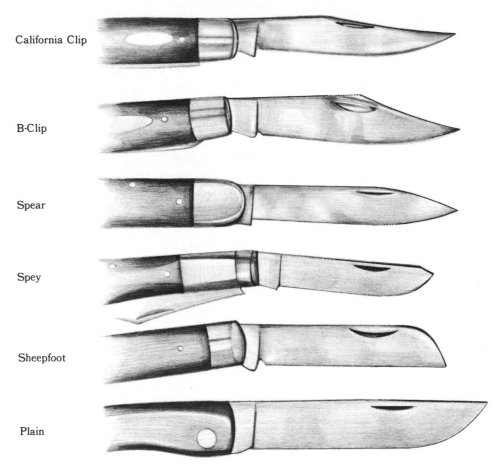

California Clip

B-Clip

Spear

Spey

Sheepfoot

Plain

Common Blade Types

The plain blade—for lack of a better name—is less common than the clip or spear, yet its fairly thick backing makes it particularly sturdy. Designed for heavy work, it is a little clumsy for skinning and whittling. For preparing fish, the long, slender—and quite flexible—filet blade is unbeatable. Unlike most other blades, the filet type is always made of stainless steel and, for outdoor use, is manufactured as a sheath knife.

Folding Knives

Although a sheath knife may seem more "woodsy," the folding or pocket knife has grown tremendously popular. And for good reason. It offers a combination of up to three blades and these are always protected when not in use. You can tuck a folding knife into your pants pocket or wear it in a sheath at the belt. Its blades can handle just about any chore that can be expected of a knife, even the most delicate probing and cutting.

Buying a folding knife calls for some knowledge of its construction. Folding knives generally consist of a spring (single- or double-end, depending on the number of blades) that forms the backbone of the knife, the blade(s) and two side scales that sandwich the spring/blade section. The entire assembly is held together with a number of rivetlike pins, the end pins usually doubling as blade pivots. Decorative side covers may be added to cover the scales, and bolsters may cap the ends of the knife for extra durability and balance. A safety feature in many of the better folding knives designed for outdoorsmen is a lock-blade—that is, one that will lock itself automatically when open so that it cannot snap shut accidentally. The larger models of these lock-back knives, known as "folding hunters," are as strong and safe as sheath knives.

Check the scales and the bolsters. If you find the slightest looseness, discard the knife. The material in the scales of better knives should be brass, nickel or stainless steel; Micarta® is also used on lightweight knives. Less expensive knives usually have carbon or plated-steel scales. As for the bolsters, the best are made of brass; though nickel, silver and stainless steel are fairly common. Less expensive knives may have bolsters of thin metal, which will easily rust or dent.

Open and close the blade(s) several times. There should be no wobble. Test the spring, too. The blade should snap firmly shut and should lock securely in place when opened. Look at the back of the knife. The spring and scales should fit together cleanly, and have a tight, smoothly polished finish.

If the knife is equipped with a lanyard loop, be sure this is secure and not likely

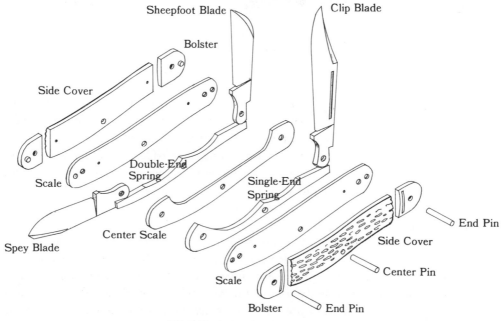

Three-Blade Stockman Knife

Parts of a Folding Knife

to work loose with time. If you prefer to use a lanyard there's still better provision on some knives—a brass grommet running entirely through the knife at one end. But be sure that a knife secured with a lanyard is what you really want. The lanyard may prove to be a nuisance, especially if it is short and limits your reach. Most experienced knife users choose to carry a folding knife in a belt sheath or in a pocket, preferably one secured with a buttoned flap. If you're working on or around boats, however, a lanyard may prevent your losing the knife overboard.

Swiss Army Knives

Among the folding models is the versatile Swiss Army knife, a veritable miniature tool kit. The knife, which comes in many styles, may include one or more blades (serviceable but not superior), a nail file, scissors, screwdriver (regular and/or Phillips), tweezers, bottle and can openers, disgorger (for fishermen), reamer (for pipe smokers), corkscrew, magnifying glass and even a minute wood or metal saw.

How practical is such a knife? The list of minor repairs possible with a Swiss Army knife goes on ad infinitum. A fisherman can repair a reel, a cross-country skier his bindings; a hunter can adjust his gunsights; a camper can tinker with his stove. While the knife has great appeal to the gadget-minded, it is more than a gadget.

Sheath Knives

All folding knives have one minor drawback. You need two hands with which to open them. On a bitter winter day when your fingers are numbed by the cold, you may prefer a sheath knife. It's ready to use the moment you withdraw it. Whether there is actually any need for such speed is questionable, but nonetheless, the handiness of the sheath knife is an asset. It will do anything that's possible with a folding model. Generally, too, sheath knives are more durable and easier to clean. Their main disadvantage is that you are limited to a single blade.

Most sheath knives are equipped with a finger guard, or hilt, a metal protrusion just above the blade that prevents your fingers from slipping to the blade's edge. Some sheath knives lack this guard and you can cut a finger if you're careless. However, skilled whittlers may look on the guard as a nuisance. Here again, personal taste rules.

The blades and handles of sheath knives can be evaluated in much the same way as those of folding knives. However, there are some special features to look for. The grind should be smooth and clean, of course. Note the manner in which the blade is attached to the handle. The blade's shaft—or tang—should extend the full length of the handle's interior and be firmly secured to the pommel or butt of the handle. The guard, or hilt, should be free of any play.

Choose the sheath carefully, too. Some sheaths house only the blade, the handle

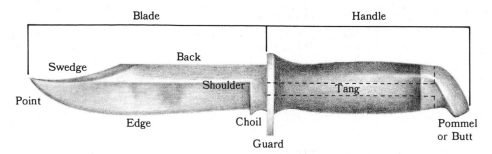

Parts of a Sheath Knife

held in place by a leather loop and a snap. Should the snap pop open you could lose the knife. One good alternative is the full-length Scandinavian-type sheath that houses the handle as well. Whatever you select, make sure the knife fits firmly into the sheath, much like a handgun fits into its holster.

SHARPENING YOUR WOODS TOOLS

The Axe

A dull axe is dangerous. It's more likely to glance. Nor does it bite as deeply as a sharp edge. It's a fallacy, too, that a dull axe is more efficient for splitting. A sharp bit parts the grain better initially and, as the head drives into the bolt, it more readily cuts through knots and sections of cross-grain.

The simplest tool for sharpening an axe is a flat file. Lock the head in a bench vise or prop it against a small bolt of wood, edge up, locking it into position by placing your foot on the handle. Holding the file at about a fifteen-degree angle to the bit, apply pressure and stroke the file into the bit, following its contours. Make only forward strokes to avoid a "rolled edge." No wetting is necessary.

For a truly fine edge, touch it up with a dual-grit hand stone, one side coarse, the other fine. Keeping the stone wet (woodsmen spit on theirs), apply light pressure in a circular motion, first with the coarse side, then the fine. Touch up the edge of the axe after each use to maintain a deep-biting bit.

By far the easiest way to sharpen an axe is with a grindstone. If you're lucky enough to have access to one, turn the stone so that it runs into the bit (toward the eye) and move the axe from side to side across the face of the stone. Maintain the original bevel as much as possible, flopping the axe occasionally to grind both sides evenly. Some axemen grind this bevel down flat for deeper penetration but this may weaken the backing, resulting in a break or chip. It's important that the grindstone be kept wet during the process to avoid overheating. Under no circumstances use a high-speed grinding wheel. This will overheat the metal and draw the temper, ruining the axe.

In time your axe head may loosen, perhaps even fly off. A quick cure is to soak the head in water overnight to swell the wood fibers. This is a short-lived remedy. Once dried again, the handle will be looser than ever. A permanent cure calls for driving an additional wedge into the handle within the eye of the axe. Hardware stores and many outfitters carry such wedges.

Even experts break or split a handle now and then. If the wood is not shattered, winding the handle with tape will fix it temporarily. However, a split handle cannot be trusted for long. It's best to replace it.

Cut the handle off close to the head. Since the front of the eye is larger than the back you may be able to drive the remnant of the handle out. If it proves balky, bury the bit in moist earth, leaving the eye above the ground. Build a small fire over the axe head and allow it to burn a few minutes. (Burying the bit keeps it cool.) This will char the wood and cause the eye to expand slightly. Driving out the wood remnants should then be easy. Instead of a fire, you can use a small propane blowtorch. Handle the axe head gingerly. It will be hot.

Inserting the new handle is a whittle-and-fit process. With a rasp or knife, trim the handle until it fits into the rear of the eye, tapping it in until it sticks and curly shavings begin to form. Withdraw the handle and apply the rasp or knife to these "high spots." You'll probably need several tries. Check the hang of the handle as you progress, trimming to compensate if it appears out of alignment. Inserted fully, the handle will protrude an inch or two beyond the front eye. Saw it off flush and insert a small wedge.

An axe is too important—and dangerous—a tool to be left about casually. Don't leave it out at night, especially in the rain. Moisture will raise the grain of the handle and roughen it—if a porcupine doesn't dine on it first! Bring your axe inside at night, and keep a sheath on the head at all times when you're not using it.

The Knife

Keeping a knife sharp is no great chore, so there is no need for short-cuts. A power grinder is fast but it will ruin the edge in a few seconds by overheating it. A grindstone doesn't pose this danger but it's too coarse for a fine edge. A file is not much better. Only a suitable knife stone will do the job right.

If you're meticulous about your tools, consider acquiring a pair of Washita stones. These are made from novaculite, a fine, granular silica rock, which is mined near Hot Springs, Arkansas. The novaculite stone comes in four grades. Washita Grade 1 is relatively coarse to produce a quick-cutting edge. A better choice for the initial honing is the Soft Arkansas grade, followed by a finish polishing with a Hard Arkansas stone. Honing kits, designed especially for knives, usually include two grades. The fourth grade is the Black Hard Arkansas stone, generally too hard for knife honing and better adapted to straight-edge razors and surgical instruments. While synthetic stones should be kept wet (water will do), Washita stones require that the surface be oiled. Kits generally include suitable oil.

Less expensive are the synthetic stones, one side medium-coarse for an abused blade, the other a fine grit with which to apply a polished edge. On the trail you're probably better off with a synthetic stone, the pocket type with dual-grit surfaces; a kit can take up too much space. However, at your cabin or at home, the Washita stones will improve any edge attained at trailside.

Different stones call for slightly different methods of sharpening. With a pocket stone, wet it first and then apply the blade at about a fifteen-degree angle, moving the blade in a circular motion. Flop it occasionally. If the knife's edge is slightly ragged or nicked, start with the coarse grit. Once the edge becomes fairly sharp, use the fine-grit side. A Washita stone calls for two or three drops of oil. Draw the knife's edge toward you across the surface of the stone, from the hilt to the point, as if you are trying to cut a thin slice from the stone. Flop the blade and repeat, this time pushing the blade away from you. If you have a two-stone kit, start with the coarser one, working up to the fine grit.

FIXED-CAMP TOOLS

When you're traveling afoot or by canoe, woods tools are necessarily restricted to those that are lightweight and easily carried. Generally, you'll need only enough firewood for cooking and possibly for an evening campfire. You can usually glean a wood supply within a few hundred feet of camp and light tools are adequate to cut it.

At a fixed camp, it's another matter. You don't want to spend excessive time gathering quick-burning wood that needs constant replenishing. Some serious woodcutting may be in order. At a summer cabin (possibly occupied for November's deer hunt) or for heating your home, working up a woodpile takes on the aspects of professional logging if it's done efficiently and in sufficient quantity to supply your needs. To work up the best grades of firewood, ones that will cast great heat for hours at a time, you'll need tools not unlike those of woodsmen. This sort of wood garnering involves handling logs, not mere armloads of dry branches, and there's no way to avoid hard work. However, you can ease the chore considerably by using the proper tools.

Saws

Loggers no longer use them, but there are steel-framed bow saws up to forty-two inches long, capable of cutting a foot-thick log with their "four-teeth-and-a-raker" blades. These are difficult to use. Unless the frame is held absolutely vertical as you draw it back and forth the blade will "run"—that is, it will curve to the side, cutting a saucerlike kerf that will soon lead to binding, locking the blade firmly in the wood. As hand-powered saws go, this is a highly efficient tool but it requires considerable skill, increasingly so as the logs grow larger in diameter. On small logs and poles, up to five or six inches, these saws are adequate.

The one-man cross-cut saw is easier to use, although it too requires some skill—not difficult to acquire. It resembles a carpenter's hand saw, though considerably larger and with an enlarged version of the "four-teeth-and-a-raker" cutting edge. (By attaching a second handle, you can convert it to a two-man saw.) If you've ever attended a sportsmen's show where lumberjacks put on cutting competitions you've seen the sawdust pile up in a matter of minutes. Two men, using a cross-cut saw, can cut an amazing amount of wood, but it requires coordination. When one cutter doesn't do his part, his partner usually isn't shy about proclaiming: "If you're going to ride this thing, don't drag your feet!" Whether one or two men use a cross-cut, the secret to efficient cutting lies in simply drawing the blade back and forth rhythmically and smoothly, without bearing down unduly, letting the saw's weight drive the teeth into the wood fibers. For efficiency, there's no questioning the merits of a chain saw. Working up a few cords with a bow or cross-cut saw is good therapy, but if you'd rather be fishing or hiking, the chain saw will save you hours of work. However, it's also tiring—physically and psychologically. There's extra weight to handle, as well as vibration and noise. What's more, guarding against accidents, you'll work under some stress.

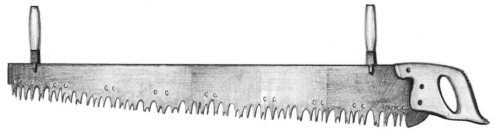

Crosscut Saw

For cutting only one or two cords of wood annually, renting a chain saw is more economical than buying. But if you have your own woodlot, or access to one, a chain saw is a good investment. Owning one jointly with a friend or relative cuts each person's cost. Working together, too, speeds cutting, handling, splitting and stacking. If you decide to buy and are serious about woodcutting, choose one with a sixteen inch or longer bar, and adequate horsepower.

Sawbucks, Peaveys and Log Rests

Traditionally, those who cut firewood have rigged their own sawbucks or sawhorses. Four 2 by 4's—two crossed at each end—with castoff boards for spreaders, and they were in business. For bucking four-foot cordwood, a sawbuck is indispensable. When bow saws and even the old-time wood-frame bucksaw were in use, a sawbuck lasted almost forever. With the coming of the chain saw, the sawbuck started to take a beating. Even with care, the chain frequently zips into one of the spreaders and eventually these have to be replaced.

Where storage space is at a premium, or if you have little inclination toward building your own, folding sawbucks of hardwood are available, generally designed so that either twenty-four- or sixteen-inch wood can be bucked conveniently. Some cutters prefer to "work up" (cut to desired length) firewood "at the stump" (in the woods). The folding sawbuck is ideal for this, since it's easily carried either by hand or in the trunk of a car.

Not all logs can be lifted up onto a sawbuck, of course. Some may be too long, in which case they'll have to be rolled up onto a "skid" (another log). For this the most useful tool is the peavey. In the parlance of old-time loggers, this is a "mooley cow," although no one today seems to know why. It's also known as a log wrench and in some areas as a cant dog. Actually, the peavey (invented by Joseph Peavey in 1858 at Stillwater, Maine) and the cant dog are not completely alike. Each consists of a rock-maple handle, the popular length being about three-and-a-half feet, along with a heavy metal bottom ferrule to which is attached a swinging curved hook hinged on a pin. The hook is known as a "dog." Below this point, the two tools differ. The peavey, designed for use on river drives, has a pointed spike, whereas the cant dog has a pronounced lip for use strictly on land. For all practical purposes, the peavey is just as effective on land and, in fact, has largely replaced the cant dog. The handle affords tremendous leverage so that one man can roll a log that he could not possibly move otherwise.

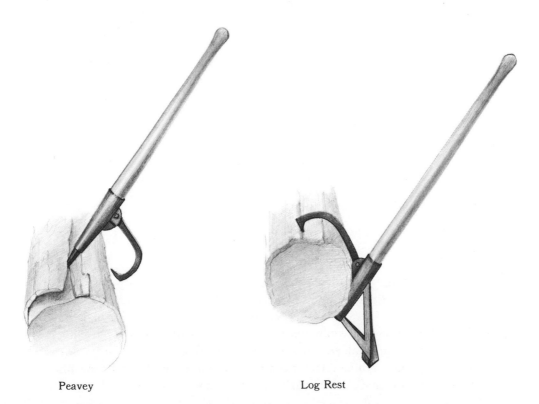

Peavey   Log Rest

Whenever a tree is felled and limbed, it does not always lie in a position con-venient for bucking into shorter lengths. You're going to have to roll it to one side or the other, possibly up onto a skid to lift the log partially off the ground. This is the prime function of a peavey. It is also used for prying a log from a pile. In doing this, always work from one end of the pile, never in front of it, to avoid being struck by a log that might roll free.

Although not a necessity, a woodsman's "log rest" comes in handy. This is actually a peavey to which a triangular bracket has been welded, opposite the dog. You grip the log as you would with a regular peavey and roll it. As the log-rest's handle reaches the ground, the bracket lifts the log some eight inches. You can make one or more cuts, then repeat the lift. The tool is especially helpful when you're cutting tree-length logs that might otherwise be difficult to position con-veniently for bucking.

Mauls, Wedges and Sledges

The chopper's maul resembles a sledge hammer except that one side of the head has an axelike blade. This need not be kept as sharp as an axe bit, but an occasional honing will make your work easier. The maul is at its best when splitting green or frozen logs. Considering that a maul has a thirty-two-inch handle (as compared to the twenty-eight-inch helve on an axe), it provides for a wide arc when it is swung. This, combined with its weight (six to nine pounds), results in a powerful blow. Start your split at the small end of the log, gradually working back to the thicker end. In many instances, a single blow will split a short log. As with an axe, the trick to using a maul is to allow the weight of the head to do the work. You merely swing and aim it.

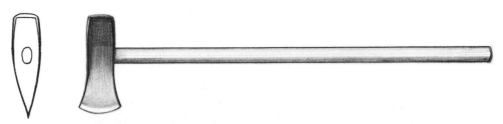

Splitting Maul

There are varying methods for working up firewood. Some people prefer to split logs before bucking them to length; hence they use the maul. Other cutters prefer bucking their logs to length—twelve, sixteen or twenty-four inches. Once these bolts are frozen, or even when they are green, they can be split with some ease with a three-and-a-half-pound axe (even more easily with a maul), especially if the wood is straight-grained. However, in a random woodpile, bolts are likely to contain twisted fiber knots and gnarls that resist splitting.

A steel wedge and a sledge hammer will usually handle this chore. And, of course, so will a maul. Using a wedge and a hammer offers some advantage in that the wedge can be placed and driven wherever the grain is most susceptible to splitting. It's difficult to hit such a spot precisely with a maul. Place the bolt upright on a chopping block, tap the wedge in with a sledge or maul until it bites firmly, then drive it in. Quite often, a single wedge will make the split. Occasionally, if the wood is badly gnarled, and the split balks, a second wedge may be needed (this is rare when wood is frozen). Such wedges, eight to twelve inches in length, weigh four to six pounds. A note of caution is in order when using wedges. In time, the head of the wedge becomes distorted, its edges rolling over. When hitting such a head with a sledge, tiny bits of steel may fly at bullet velocity. Wear safety glasses.

Whether you split with a maul or wedges, learn to "read the grain." Examine each log or bolt to determine where the grain is most susceptible to splitting. Avoid knots and limb stubs when possible. Split around or to one side of these. Quite often, a split will start, then balk, the log halves clinging together tenaciously. This may be caused by twisted grain, a knot or a bend in the grain. Try to figure out where your wedge, or a blow from the maul, will be most effective. The ability to read the grain comes with experience. No textbook can teach it. It's a matter of trial and error at first, and then of not repeating the error.

FIREWOOD

If you have your own woodlot, your fuel supply is assured. If not, you may have to buy from a wood dealer. He may offer "fitted" wood—cut to length and split, or he may sell you four-foot, eight-foot or even tree-length logs. Naturally, fitted wood is the most costly.

The unit of measure is a cord—a stack four feet high, four feet wide and eight feet long, theoretically 128 cubic feet of wood. Since firewood can't be stacked solidly, you'll probably get only about 80 cubic feet. When buying by the cord be sure you understand the dealer's definition. While a full cord is four by four by eight feet, a "face" cord is something else. It will be four feet high and eight feet long but its depth or width may be only twelve, sixteen or twenty-four inches. Thus a face cord of two-foot wood is really only half a full cord.

Ideally, the heavier species of firewood, such as oak and hickory, should be seasoned two years; lighter species, such as maple, one year. Bear in mind that little seasoning occurs outdoors during the winter, at least when temperatures are well below freezing. Whatever moisture remains when cold weather sets in turns to ice crystals, which will not thaw until warm weather returns.

Seasoning is best done in a roofed-over woodshed with open sides, the wood loosely stacked. The more loosely it is piled, the better the air will circulate through it, carrying off moisture. If you must stack it in the open, build your rows (these are known as "ricks") on skids, poles laid on the ground to elevate the bottom layers of wood away from the earth's moisture. Rain will slow seasoning. You have a choice of covering the top of your wood ricks with strips of tarpaper or other waterproof material weighted down with stones (which will slow seasoning slightly) or you can leave it open to the weather, hoping there will be enough sunshine.

The following chart may serve as a guide to weight, heat value and seasoning time. There are a number of variables affecting the latter—exposure to wind, sun and rain or the way the wood is split and stacked.

		Weight per Cord Seasoned (Pounds)	Heat Value BTUs (Millions)
Very Heavy Woods		3,890	26.8
Apple	Hop Hornbeam		
Black Birch	Locust		
Dogwood	White Oak		
Hickory	Blue Beech		
Heavy Woods		3,400	23.4
White Ash	Sugar Maple		
Beech (American)	Red Oak		
Yellow Birch			
Medium-Weight Woods		2,880	19.9
Black Ash	Soft Maple		
White Birch	Norway Pine		
Gray Birch	Pitch Pine		
Black Cherry	Tamarack		
Elm			
Lightweight Woods		2,100	14.5
Aspen (Poplar)	Willow		
Basswood	White Pine		
Butternut	White Cedar		
Pin Cherry	Balsam Fir		
Hemlock	Spruce		

(*Source:* Maine Forest Service)

All wood produces creosote, a major hazard in any wood-burning system: it is smoke carrying oils, acids and tars into the stovepipe and chimney flue. This buildup is alarmingly accelerated when you burn green wood. A creosote accumulation may not be noticed for some time. Then, without your knowing, a spark may set the creosote afire and it may smoulder for hours. Suddenly it erupts into a roaring blaze, shooting flames into the sky like a giant blowtorch.

You can avoid a chimney fire in three ways. First, burn only well-seasoned wood; second, clean your stovepipe several times during the winter, and your chimney at least once a year (there are a number of chimney brushes designed for do-it-yourselfers); third, at least once a day—and this is an easy precaution—let the fire in your stove burn hot for fifteen to twenty minutes with the stove control and stovepipe damper open. If you're burning wood not fully seasoned you'll want to leave the damper open longer. This will burn out whatever creosote has built up. Needless to say, the last process assumes that your stovepipe has been cleaned before you adopt this method.

Finally, if you're about to install your first wood stove, consult your fire department about possible local regulations and for advice on proper installation.

Chapter 9
Winter Travel: Cross-Country On Skis and Snowshoes

Winter brings a new dimension to the outdoors. What were rough trails during the summer become smoothed passageways into the hinterlands. Marshes and swamplands, virtually impassable in August, are broad highways to solitude and serenity. The winter sky seems to hover closer to the ground, whether gray or deep blue, and the play of shadows creates dramatic effects on the snow. Wildlife is easier to approach. Before your eyes, a grouse erupts from its snowy den into which it plunged earlier to escape the cold. A deer lopes with grace, its tail high as it plunges belly-deep with each jump. Chickadees, immune to the cold, light on the birches but a few feet away. A fox trots assuredly across the far side of a clearing, headed for a rabbit swamp and his dinner. Snowy surfaces tell a hundred stories. You have only to step into a pair of skis or snowshoes to be able to read them.

There's more to winter travel afoot than nature study, of course. Day trips on cross-country skis or snowshoes, with a picnic lunch carried in a small pack, are not only superb exercise but a chance to explore backcountry areas almost impossible to reach during the summer. Then there's the adventure of pitting yourself against the cold, defying winter in an overnight camp-out, your tent pitched in a dense stand of softwoods to screen you from arctic winds. On skis, there's the camaraderie of sharing trails with others. Or if you're competitively inclined, you'll have no difficulty signing up for races almost anywhere there is snow. However you choose to enjoy the winter outdoors, you have a choice between cross-country skis or snowshoes.

CROSS-COUNTRY SKIS

Cross-country skiing may be a relatively new sport in America, but it's actually one of the oldest in the world. In the Oslo Ski Museum you can see the Ovrebo Ski, found in a Norwegian marsh. It dates from about 2000 B.C. The Norwegian military equipped scouts with skis as early as A.D. 1200, and during the early days of World War II, Finnish ski troops raised havoc with the Russians. In this country, as early as the mid-1800s, John A. "Snowshoe" Thompson regularly carried mail across the Sierras, a distance of ninety miles. Despite his nickname, he used homemade eleven-foot skis.

Today, cross-country—or Nordic—skiing is strictly for fun, enjoyed by millions. It's easier to master than the Alpine, or downhill variety. However, an understanding of the technique is needed when buying an outfit. Travel on touring skis (the terms "cross-country" and "touring" have come to be used interchangeably) is simply an extension of walking, a series of natural motions. Two basic moves are involved, the "kick" and the "glide." The kick occurs as you push down with one ski, causing it to "bite" or grip the snow surface for purchase. At the same time, you slide the other ski forward, initially with little or no weight on it. This is the glide. As the glide progresses, weight is shifted from the kick ski to the glide ski. Moving forward, the glide ski becomes the kick ski. The secret is to attain as long a glide as possible without a marked loss of momentum.

Skier During Glide Phase

As opposed to a walking stance, bend your body slightly at the waist, flexing your knees just a mite. The forward bend of the body at the waist helps direct pressure to the kick ski and provides balance for the glide.

Using the poles is equally simple. Just swing your arms in a military march manner with the poles angled to the rear. As you bring your kick ski forward, exert a backward thrust with the opposite pole. You're skiing. It's that easy.

Cross-country ski design seems to be in a continuous state of development. Seldom does a year pass without the introduction of new construction methods and redesigned running surfaces. If you first try to acquaint yourself with all of the current, and proposed, developments, you'll bog down and never get around to buying skis. Don't wait for next year's "new models." Today's are superb and it's not likely that touted improvements will make a great difference.

The two areas of concern are performance and durability. The latter is pretty well assured if you pick the right ski for the right job and stick with well-established brands. As for performance, it helps to have a working knowledge of design and materials.

There are three groups of cross-country skiers to whom manufacturers cater: racers, recreational skiers and ski mountaineers. Whichever category you fit into determines the type of ski outfit to buy. If you're competitively inclined, you'll want racing skis. They are stiff, light and narrow, designed for use on a prepared track. However, until you get used to them, racing models are rather unstable, and in deep, fluffy snow they do not provide the flotation of wider skis. Racing skis, at their best on packed trails, are not a good choice for touring.

You'll find the greatest variety of skis among those designed for recreational skiing. They are somewhat wider than the racing models and therefore more stable. Granted, they are slightly heavier, but often this is only a matter of ounces. For most skiers the weight differential is hardly worth considering.

Ski mountaineers have special requirements. To sustain heavy loads and hard use, their skis must be rugged; they must turn well on downhill runs; and they must provide maximum flotation in deep snow. These are the heaviest of cross-country skis, but this added weight makes them more reliable in a demanding and unusually rugged environment.

Obviously, then, there are no "all-purpose" cross-country skis. True, you might successfully attempt a mountain trek on light touring skis but it's not recommended. And you might enter a race with a pair of touring skis but don't count on taking home any trophies. Choose skis that best fit your specific requirements.

There are a few rather open-ended guidelines to help you. If you have a strong physique and like to eat up the miles, you'll want a stiff ski that will give you the longest possible glide. If you're a beginner or simply interested in a leisurely day on the trail, a softer ski will perform better for you. If you're heavier than average, or if you intend to carry a pack, you'll need skis that won't collapse during the glide phase of your stride. Older children and young adults generally ski vigorously, so they may require somewhat stiff skis.

Types of Skis

All-wood skis are rapidly being replaced by fiberglass and fiberglass-reinforced models. Yet wood has a strong aesthetic appeal to many skiers. Well-crafted skis of rich-grained hickory or birch have a beauty that cannot be matched by fiberglass or plastic. Fine wooden skis are made of laminated hardwoods such as hickory, beech and birch, each selected for its strength or flex characteristics; sometimes as many as thirty laminations go into a single ski. The inner core may be made up of softer and more flexible woods such as poplar, spruce or balsa. Each layer is made separately, then glued, cut and placed in a mold for bonding. Obviously, the process is time-consuming and labor-intensive. At this writing, wooden skis are priced about the same as fiberglass models, but it's only a matter of time before the costs of materials and construction will make them more expensive than fiberglass. The demand for fiberglass skis will continue to accelerate, and for good reason. They are generally lighter, stronger, more durable and require less maintenance.

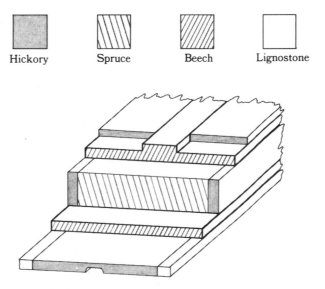

Hickory   Spruce   Beech   Lignostone

A Wood Touring Ski

Although fiberglass skis are built with a core of wood, foam or plastic, the fiberglass is the major structural element, either surrounding or sandwiching the core. The result is one of three basic types of construction: sandwich, torsion box or injection molding. Sandwich construction, the most popular, is used in numerous lightweight but durable skis. Torsion-box construction is somewhat more complex, and hence costlier, producing a slightly heavier but more rugged ski. For the moment, injection molding is the newest process. Foam is injected into a preassembled hollow ski shell, which is then temperature-treated and cured to

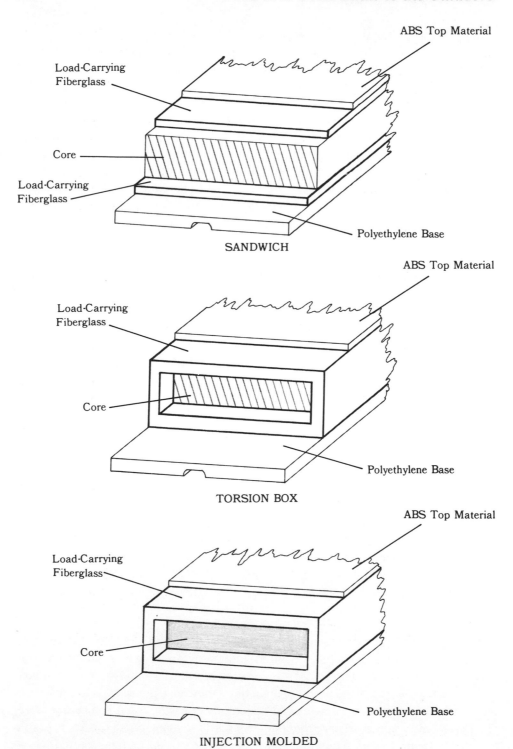

Fiberglass Ski Construction

achieve proper foam density. This is not as expensive as other methods of ski construction and results in a lightweight, durable ski. The finished product among all three types generally has ABS tops and polyethylene (such as P-tex® , Fastex® , and Kofix®) bases. The ABS is long-lasting and light. The polyethylene is water resistant, easy to wax and glides well. It is also remarkably rugged and can be quickly repaired with a polyethylene candle and a piece of sandpaper.

Each of the three constructions has slight advantages and shortcomings but these are of importance primarily to the technician and to the advanced racer. Actually, the type of construction isn't as important as the manufacturer's skill. The best advice is to select one of the popular brands turned out by reputable makers. Then inspect it for visual imperfections. Separations, bubbles or dry spots in the fiberglass layers are signs of weak construction. Eliminating an obviously imperfect ski is but one step, however. You'll also want to know how your skis will behave once they're on the snowfields. Performance is determined by camber, flex and sidecut.

Camber

Camber is the built-in "spring" that causes a pair of skis to arch up when laid on the floor. Only the tips and tails will touch. Camber varies. Some skis are "soft," flattening out easily under your weight. Others are fairly stiff, requiring that you push down firmly to flatten them. Still others are so rigid that it's virtually impossible to depress the arch.

Your weight, combined with your skiing technique, determines the required degree of camber. What you need is a ski that's flexible enough so that the area under your foot makes firm contact with the snow surface during the kick phase, yet maintains its arch during the glide. If the camber is too soft, with the entire length resting constantly on the snow, you'll have a ski that performs the kick well, but won't glide efficiently. If the camber is too rigid, your skis may glide beautifully but you'll get little purchase when you kick.

To check on correct camber use the paper test. It can be done in a ski shop or in your own home. Lay the skis flat on a smooth, uncarpeted floor. Slide a piece of paper under the center section of the skis. Now stand on both skis with your

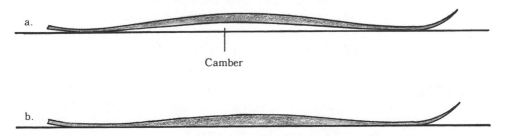

Ski Camber: a. *Glide Phase* b. *Kick Phase*

weight evenly distributed and the tips of your shoes near the balance point of each ski. Have a salesperson or friend try to slide the paper out from under the skis. If the skis have the proper amount of camber the paper will slide out with only slight resistance. Now slip the paper back under the skis, and stand on them again, shifting all your weight onto one foot. The paper should be pinched tightly between the ski and the floor.

For the skier of average build and technique, correct camber will usually be present in skis that have been carefully selected for type (racing, recreational or mountaineering) and proper length. For those who are heavier or lighter than average, and for those who ski more or less aggressively, some adjustment may be necessary. More aggressive skiers generally develop a stronger kick and need a ski with stiffer camber. Racers, for example, choose long, stiffly cambered skis to achieve maximum glide. Beginners and occasional recreational skiers will likely have a less pronounced kick and require skis with softer camber. Generally speaking, stiff skis perform better in wet and packed snow while softly cambered skis are best for touring and mountaineering in untracked and freshly fallen snow.

Tip Flex and Torsional Stiffness

The ski tip's ability to flex affects performance. Checking this flex is easy. With one hand, hold the ski with its top side facing you. With the other, pull the tip toward you. If the ski tip bends easily, you have a "soft" tip; if there is marked resistance to your pull, it's a "stiff" tip. Stiff tips make for easier turning in unpacked snow—though they will also cause your skis to wander if the snow is packed and the terrain uneven. For skiing on well-prepared trails, such as those at ski touring centers, a soft tip is a better choice; your skis will conform more readily to terrain changes and will track straighter. The degree of rise varies among tips, too. A longer-rising tip is preferred for off-trail skiing, since it enhances flotation and carves through the snow better, whereas a shorter tip is generally chosen for racing and trail touring.

Torsional rigidity is the lateral flexibility of a ski. To determine this, twist the tip of the ski in one direction and the waist (the boot area) in the other. Torsionally stiff skis adapt better to ski mountaineering and off-trail touring because they turn well, and "edge" efficiently in both new and hard-packed snow. And, for the beginner, they provide greater lateral stability. For racing and touring on established trails, you'll want a ski with greater torsional flexibility; ruts will not grasp it as easily, minimizing your chances of being pulled out of the track.

Sidecut

The width of cross-country skis is measured at three points: at the shoulder (just back of the tip), at the waist and at the heel. The degree of taper at the waist relative to the shoulder and the heel is called "sidecut." Theoretically, the greater the sidecut, the more easily a ski will turn. Not surprisingly, since cross-country skiing originated in Scandinavia and since many such skis are still manufactured in Europe, specifications have metric designations. Hence, skis designed for mountaineering may have a sidecut of 62 mm, 53 mm and 57 mm (shoulder, waist, heel). Such a pronounced sidecut greatly enhances control for descending steep terrain. Racing skis, on the other hand, may have no sidecut (called "parallel cut"), since their use is generally confined to straighter, prepared tracks.

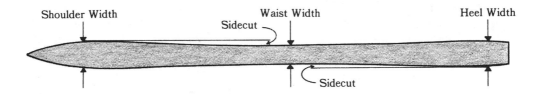

Sidecut

In recent years, the sidecut theory has become controversial. Some Austrian manufacturers now turn out skis with little or no sidecut. The Norwegians, on the other hand, design a number of their skis with pronounced sidecut for general recreational touring. For off-trail use, on mountainous or hilly terrain, where extended downhill runs are likely, some degree of sidecut is undoubtedly helpful. However, if your skiing will be confined to prepared trails, sidecut is not necessary. For mixed skiing, a ski with slight sidecut will provide the best all-around performance.

Selecting a Ski

Cross-country skis encompass four basic uses—touring and light touring (heretofore referred to as "recreational"), racing and mountaineering. Specific combinations of sidecut (if any), tip flex, torsional rigidity and camber are built in according to the intended use of the skis. However, the easiest way to differentiate the types is by waist width.

Touring models are fairly wide at the waist, ranging from 50 to 57 mm, and generally have a pronounced sidecut of 5 to 10 mm, and stiff tips and tails. Torsionally, they're quite flexible. The extra width lends stability, and the ample sidecut the ability to turn well. The soft torsional flex allows them to ride firmly over varying terrain, while the soft camber permits a good bite in unpacked snow. Touring skis are probably the best choice for those who want to venture off trails or into the wilderness. They're a good choice, too, if you're a beginner or if you plan to use them only occasionally.

Light touring skis are the most popular of all. They tend to be narrower (49 to 50 mm) at the waist and are correspondingly lighter than touring models. Sidecut varies, sometimes up to 7 mm. The camber is livelier (stiffer) than that of the touring models, to accommodate advanced or trail-oriented skiers. Yet their moderately stiff tips and tails make them responsive enough for turning in un-packed or crusty snow.

No cross-country ski is as narrow or as light as the racing model. They have a waist width of 44 to 47 mm and weigh as little as 2½ pounds. There's little or no sidecut, tip and tail flex is soft, while camber is usually stiff, to capitalize on the racer's strong kick while increasing his glide. Within the racing category, there are two styles—one for competition and the other for training. The competition model is not recommended for anything other than actual racing; because it is built with a "double camber," a skier must have a highly developed kick to make it perform well. The training model, heavier and more closely approximating the feel of a light-touring ski, is used to some extent by aspiring racers and recrea-tional skiers of advanced expertise. Neither model, however, is as durable as the touring types.

Mountaineering skis are basically beefed-up touring models; in appearance they fall midway between Nordic and Alpine skis. Width varies greatly (one model is as wide as 80 mm and is designed for powder) but sidecut is invariably quite pronounced (6 to 12 mm); both camber and flex are fairly stiff, to support a skier with a pack and to enhance maneuverability on steep and uneven terrain. High torsional rigidity increases edge control on hard-packed snow. Mountaineering skis are primarily for backcountry winter camping and for expeditionary use in the mountains. Metal edges are often attached.

Length

Traditionally, length was determined by raising one hand over your head, the correct length ski touching its tip at your wrist. This is a good starting point. However, remember that ski camber is related to ski length. If you're heavier, or lighter, than an average person of your height, you may want to choose a slightly longer, or shorter, ski for a better kick and glide.

A longer ski will generally give you greater speed and stability than a short one, and many racers increase their ski length by up to 5 cm. However, a long ski is more difficult to turn. Shorter skis are often preferred by mountaineers who need extra maneuverability. Beginners, too, find short skis easier to handle. But they probably have more drawbacks than advantages. Short skis tend to "nose-dive" in unpacked snow unless the tips are unusually soft. Under the added weight of a pack they may not afford sufficient flotation. On the whole, if you're inclined toward a shorter ski, it's advisable to stay within 5 cm of the length you would normally choose.

Ski Bases

No-Wax Skis

The choice between waxed skis and no-wax ones is normally a choice between peak performance and convenience. Properly waxed skis produce a tight kick and a swift, clean glide. They'll outclimb and outrun no-wax skis on all snow conditions except when the temperature hovers around 32 to 34°F. On the other hand, a pair of the waxless type almost always outperforms improperly waxed skis.

If you're a beginner or just an occasional skier, and not particularly enamored with getting from Point A to Point B in near-record time, waxless skis can provide delightful days on the snow with a minimum of fuss. You simply step into the bindings and go. Waxless skis are a logical choice if there are children in a family of skiers. Few youngsters have the patience to apply wax.

There are two basic waxless skis, one with a patterned surface and the other with mohair inserts. Patterned bases such as steps, fishscales, diamonds or other geometric designs are made by cutting into the ski's base, or by adding to it. Although somewhat noisy on hard-packed snow, they're the most popular. The second type has mohair (usually imitation) strips inserted into grooves of varying lengths, the hair bristles pointing toward the heel so that they grip the snow during the kick. These bristles "flow" with the ski during the glide, producing little, if any, friction. In fact, many consider this type of bottom the most effective on crust or hardpacked snow. (It was on a pair of mohair-bottom skis that Bill Koch won a silver medal in the 1976 Olympics.)

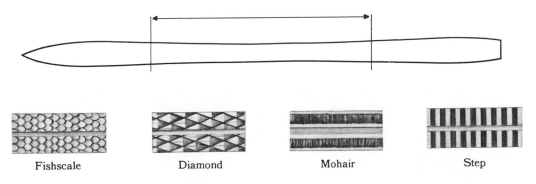

Fishscale   Diamond   Mohair   Step

Waxless Ski Bases

With any type of waxless ski, the application of a "glider" wax to the tips and tail steps up performance. Glider wax, also referred to as "speed" wax, enhances the glide by reducing friction. Usually this needs to be applied only three or four times a season. An occasional spraying of silicone over the kick section will minimize the buildup of snow, ice, wax or dirt which will slow your skis.

Most of the recent developments in cross-country skis have been in waxless bases. One manufacturer has even come up with a chemical base in the ski's kick zone that reacts automatically to changing snow conditions. There is, in fact, an overabundance of varying base surfaces, some unproven, others highly specialized. This is why it makes sense to stick with a type of base known to be effective. Also, talk to friends who have tried various waxless skis. Better yet, rent an outfit at a touring center and test the skis for grip during a climb and for a smooth downhill glide. Some waxless skis provide superb grip for the kick, yet glide poorly or fetch up when turning. If your rental skis don't perform as well as you feel they should, try another type.

Wax Skis

If it's performance you're seeking, there's no alternative to waxing. Considerable mystique surrounds the waxing of skis, little of it justified. While some skiers may seem to make occult ceremonies out of the application and corking process, it's really not that complicated. It's mainly a matter of familiarizing yourself with various waxes and following the directions printed on the containers.

Wax must match snow conditions. For new snow—cold and crisp—a hard wax is required, since the sharp crystals easily penetrate the wax surface. For old snow, or for warm days, a softer wax or "klister" is needed so that the smooth rounded crystals can bite into it. The same wax will not work well for both types of snow.

Before these final waxes are applied to wooden skis, the running surfaces must be protected against water and moisture. Unprepared wood will likely freeze, impeding the action of the skis, and possibly even damaging them. Also, wax will not stick to water or ice. Wooden skis, therefore, require the application of an impregnating compound to seal the surface. This may be sprayed or painted on, usually necessary only about once a season. A tar base may also be used. This is heated and rubbed into the wood.

Fiberglass ski bases are very porous, especially when new, and should be treated with a thin layer of melted paraffin. This is best done when the skis are warm so that the paraffin will penetrate the base before hardening.

From this point we get to the final waxes—called "grip" or "kicker" waxes. For snow that may range from freshly fallen wet to powdery or fluffy, there are no fewer than ten waxes of varying degrees of hardness. They come in sticks that are crayoned to the bottom of your skis. Then, for old snow—granular, soggy, even crusty or icy—there are about five softer or "klister" waxes. These come in tubes similar to toothpaste. For the sake of simplicity, most recreational skiers carry only three hard (Red, Blue and Green) and three klister (also Red, Blue and Green). Which of these is best on a given day is determined largely by the temperature. Both the hard and the klister waxes are color-coded, the warm colors for warmer conditions or old snow, the cold colors for colder conditions and fresh snow. Thus, using a thermometer and the color-coded waxing chart, which includes temperature ratings, you should arrive at precisely the correct wax to use.

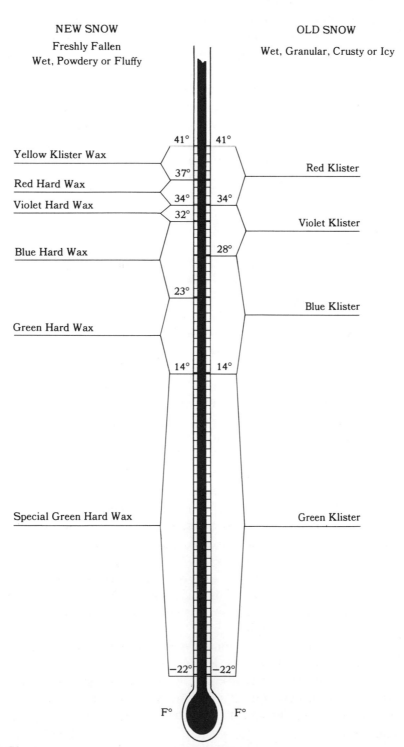

NEW SNOW
Freshly Fallen
Wet, Powdery or Fluffy

OLD SNOW
Wet, Granular, Crusty or Icy

41°   41°

Yellow Klister Wax

Red Klister

37°

Red Hard Wax

34°   34°

Violet Hard Wax

32°

Violet Klister

Blue Hard Wax

28°

Blue Klister

23°

Green Hard Wax

14°   14°

Special Green Hard Wax

Green Klister

−22°   −22°

F°   F°

Waxing Chart

Final waxes should be applied to the middle 60 to 80 cm (2 to 2½ ft.) of your skis—the section extending about 30 to 40 cm (12 to 16 in.) ahead and behind the spot underneath the ball of your foot. For beginners who buy waxable skis, more and more touring centers recommend waxing the entire ski the first couple of times you use it. This gives you the kind of grip necessary to make your first few times on skis more enjoyable. Then as you progress and develop your kick, you can begin to use less wax until, by the end of four or five days, only that middle 60 to 80 cm needs to be covered.

Snow conditions and the temperature may change during the day, calling for a change in wax. If the weather turns warmer, you can simply apply a warmer (softer) wax over the cold one. However, if the temperature drops noticeably, a cold wax is required. But you can't apply a cold (harder) wax over a warm one.

One ski representative likens the waxing process to making a peanut butter and jelly sandwich. Think of the warmer, softer wax as the jelly. You wouldn't try to spread peanut butter on top of jelly. You always spread the peanut butter first. Skis are the same. If you want to apply a colder, harder wax, you'll have to remove the warm wax first. Experienced skiers carry a soft cloth with which to wipe away any moisture, and a small scraper resembling a putty knife with which to remove wax. They also carry a cork block just large enough to fit in the palm of the hand. With this they smooth freshly applied wax. Thus, with these tools and an assortment of hard waxes and klisters, you can "fine tune" your skis to fit any snow conditions.

There's an even simpler approach—the two-wax system. While this may not suit the expert who is bent on extracting every possible bit of performance from his skis, it is a godsend to the recreational skier. The wax comes in two colors. At temperatures below 32°F (0°C) apply the Gold wax; at higher temperatures, the Silver. These waxes perform well over a wide range of snow conditions. The secret to greatest effectiveness lies in the application of thin layers. Use minimum amounts, then cork the surface well. If you still don't get sufficient bite for your kick step, apply another thin layer, but this time don't cork the wax so much. You don't attain a better grip for your kick by changing waxes, but rather by increasing the thickness.

Then there's the glider or speed wax, already mentioned, which can be applied to the tips and tails to increase speed during the glide phase. Glider wax is not a necessity, but rather, an option. This wax is color-coded, too, but any one of the middle-range waxes will do nicely.

If you decide to use a glider wax, apply it before the kick wax. First scrape the base clean, then apply the glider wax, leaving about 60 to 80 cm at the center of the ski unwaxed. Heat the glider wax slightly with a waxing torch or iron, then cork it smooth. Most ski outfitters offer such torches and, often, they are provided at ski centers. Once the glider wax is suitably smoothed, you're ready to apply the kicker wax.

Boots

In buying a cross-country outfit it is natural to focus attention on the skis, but proper boots are actually of greater importance. Unless your feet are comfortable, well-supported and able to control the skis, the latter are almost worthless even if they are the best you can possibly afford. In short, if your budget is tight, cut corners on other equipment but buy quality boots.

A cross-country ski boot is not unlike a running shoe in that it must be flexible yet supportive. It should be torsionally rigid yet flex sufficiently across the ball of the foot to permit forward and backward flexing. With sufficient width and length to allow for heavy wool socks and liner socks, there should be a quarter-inch space at the toes so that your foot can move forward slightly as you kick and glide.

Most ski boots are sized under the European/Norwegian "Paris Point system." The following chart illustrates the comparable sizes in both metric and American size designations.

Boot Size Conversion Chart—Metric to U.S. Sizes

Metric	35	36	37	38	39	40	41	42	43	44	45	46	47	48	49	50
Women	4½	5	5½-6	6½-7	7½-8	8-8½	9	9½-10								
Men				5-5½	6-6½	7-7½	8-8½	8½-9	9½	10	10½	11	11½-12	12-12½	12½-13	14

Even without such a chart, determining the correct European boot size is easy. Measure the length of your bare feet in centimeters. Add 1.5 centimeters, then multiply the results by 1.5. This will give you your European boot size including wool socks.

The uppers of quality ski boots are of full-grain leather which, unlike less expensive split leathers, is durable and breathable while conforming to your foot for full support. Ski-boot leather is usually silicone-impregnated for water resistance. Fabric uppers of nylon and Gore-Tex® are used on some racing and light-touring boots but, while they're durable, lightweight and breathable, they're a poor second to leather for warmth and lateral support.

If it's water repellency and snow protection you're after wear gaiters. These can range anywhere from six to sixteen inches high, to match the depth of snow in which you expect to ski. Some models fit snugly around your boot; others completely encase it. They can be adjusted with elastic drawstrings and/or Velcro® closures.

Check the boot's heel counter. The stitching should be neat and sturdy; the heel cup inside the boot should be smooth and fit your heel comfortably. Look for a padded collar that fits snugly enough around your ankle and instep to keep out snow. (A bellows tongue also helps.) A warm, moisture-absorbent insole is worthwhile.

During the late 1960s newer construction techniques evolved. Manufacturers moved away from the costly stitching of uppers to outsoles in favor of lighter and more water-resistant injection molding. This automated process also allows for the establishment of standardized sole and binding widths. That means that a skier will now find it easier to interchange and mix boots and bindings from different manufacturers. Today, with the exception of heavy mountaineering boots, all have vulcanized or injection molded outsoles, approximately 75 mm (Nordic Norm) or 50 mm (Racing Norm) in width. The Nordic Norm is most commonly used, on all touring and light-touring boots and bindings. The Racing Norm, being narrower, requires a better technique on the part of the skier. Because it provides a more precise control over the tracing of skis, it is preferred by experts who ski on prepared tracks.

Gaiters

Boot designs are classified, like skis, according to their intended use—racing, light touring, touring, and mountaineering. Racing boots are cut below the ankle, resembling running shoes, with uppers, usually unlined and unpadded, of nylon or lightweight leather such as goatskin. Most have 50-mm wide soles although some may be as narrow as 38mm (Adidas Norm). Light-touring boots are similar to racing models, but are cut slightly higher and often lined and padded. Touring and mountain boots are cut above the ankle for support and warmth, the uppers usually well padded and lined. Many types of mountain boots provide for double lacing to enhance support and water resistance. Outsoles may be stitched or molded to the uppers and the heels grooved to accommodate cable bindings.

The Three Basic Types of Cross-Country Ski Boots: a. *Racing* b. *Touring* c. *Mountaineering*

Bindings

Bindings and boots must match. If you select a three-pin type Nordic Norm boot, be sure you buy a three-pin Nordic Norm binding. For recreational skiing the toe, or "rat-trap" model is best. This is secured to the forward edge, or front lip, of the boot's outsole, allowing your feet a freer swing during the kick phase of your stride. While you'll have to bend over and lock toe bindings in place with your hands, you can release several models with the tip of your ski pole. Protruding upward from the binding's foot plate are three pins that automatically insert into three matching holes in the boot sole. Since some foot plates have only two pins (and some, like the Adidas Norm, are specially lipped), be sure that your bindings and boots match in this respect. Be sure, too, that your boots fit snugly into the toe irons with no side-to-side slippage. Once the forward lip of the sole is firmly locked into the binding and the three pins recessed into the sole, what appears at first glance to be a rather flimsy sort of binding is actually superbly efficient. In addition, toe bindings are supplied with a heel plate that is attached to the ski under the boot heel. This minimizes lateral play, aids in turning and discourages snow build-up.

For heavy-duty use, such as mountaineering or skiing on steep slopes, you'll need cable bindings, which provide extra support and edge control. There are two slightly different types—one that closes around the heel, and one that clamps shut in front of the toe—but both operate on the same principle. An adjustable, spring-loaded cable encircles the heel of the boot (hence the groove in the heel), thus wedging the boot toe into a stationary toe plate. Cable bindings are heavier and

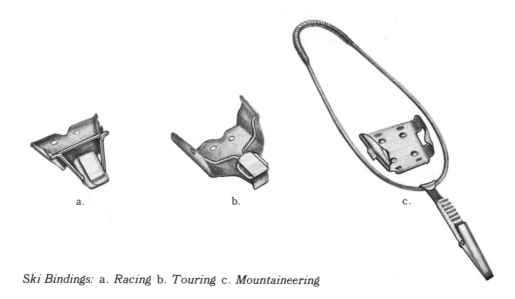

Ski Bindings: a. *Racing* b. *Touring* c. *Mountaineering*

sturdier than toe bindings, and can be used with insulated leather and rubber-top/leather-bottom boots as well as touring and mountaineering boots.

Depending on the type of bindings you choose it's a good idea to take along a repair/parts kit. For the standard Nordic and Racing Norm bindings a screwdriver and an extra bail are sufficient. Bails—the wire loops that hold the toes of your boots against the binding pins—can pop off and become lost during a fall. For cable bindings a screwdriver, a pair of pliers and an extra cable are worth carrying.

Poles

Most cross-country ski poles are of either tonkin or fiberglass-reinforced plastic. Tonkin poles, extremely lively and flexible, are fairly inexpensive. But, since tonkin is a bamboolike natural material, quality varies. If you want tonkin, select the better quality (and usually more expensive) poles. Otherwise look into the fiberglass type. Generally tapered from grip to tip, these are stronger and lighter and somewhat stiffer.

Poles are designed for various uses, too. Racers and light-touring skiers usually prefer stiff poles for added thrust when pushing on hard-packed snow. Among these, fiberglass is the most common, but newer materials, such as carbon fiber, are appearing. They weigh as little as 100 grams with the shafts 15 to 16 mm in diameter; some are tapered for competition skiing. Touring skiers and mountaineers generally select slightly less rigid poles, with a beefier, more cylindrical shaft, 16 to 17 mm in diameter for added strength.

"Baskets" vary, too. These are the appendages at the bottom of the pole to keep it from sinking unduly into deep snow. The old-style round basket has been replaced by more aerodynamically shaped baskets made in countless different geometric patterns. On a packed surface, for example, the newer asymmetrical baskets provide the same flotation as circular baskets but are easier to pull out of the snow and less inclined to catch in crust or branches.

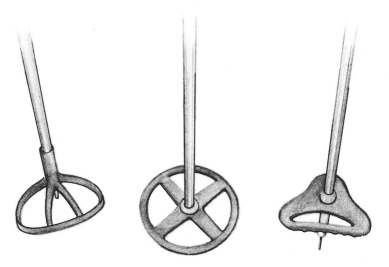

Several Types of Ski-Pole Baskets

Poles should have adjustable wrist straps so that they can be worn over several different gloves or mittens, according to the weather. Pole length runs from 100 to 160 cm, in 5 cm increments, the proper length reaching a point about two inches below the top of your shoulders. Racers and light tourers may prefer slightly longer poles for added thrust, mountaineers somewhat shorter ones so that they can lean forward more easily for downhill runs on steep slopes.

SNOWSHOEING

The origin of snowshoes is veiled in the antiquity of ten thousand snowstorms. It is believed they were in use in Asia well over two thousand years ago and, chances are, they came to North America via the land bridge thought to have existed between Siberia and Alaska's Aleutian Islands. Living far north of the tree line where wind packed the snow, the Eskimos had little use for snowshoes. For the woodland Indians, however, the snowshoe was a necessity and it was among them that various forms evolved, the basic designs only slightly altered today.

Throughout the North, snowshoes are still used extensively among trappers, timber cruisers, game wardens and other professional woodsmen. However, most of today's snowshoers are those who have discovered the joys of an afternoon trek into snowy serenity. Winter campers, too, tote their packs into the backcountry on webbed feet. Mountaineers use them to reach alpine peaks. Rabbit and wildcat hunters would flounder helplessly without them. Ice fishermen hike to remote ponds. Or, more prosaically, some folks park their car by the roadside and snow-shoe to their summer cottage, perhaps to shovel the snow load from the roof, or merely to see how the building is wintering.

Snowshoeing is good exercise, either at a leisurely pace or when you're eating up the miles. Unlike skiing, technique is easy to acquire; it takes only a matter of minutes to learn the basics. Don't worry if you develop *mal de raquette* (French for "pain of the snowshoe") during your first jaunt or two. Undue straddling and excessively long strides stretch muscles and leg joints, resulting in pain in the hips, thighs, and sometimes in the knees. However, muscles and ligaments become attuned after a few hours and you become immune—until next year's first trip.

Mal de raquette cannot be avoided altogether but you can alleviate it somewhat. Avoid excessive straddling. Lengthen your stride a little so that one snowshoe is lifted over the other, its inner side passing close to your ankle. Place it in the snow so that its tail is only slightly to one side of the other snowshoe. Reach forward instead of straddling.

The tail of a snowshoe is meant to be dragged, not lifted. Raise the toe only enough to clear the snow. Anything higher is wasted effort. Rhythm is important. Swing your arms in an even beat with your strides, leaning forward slightly.

Two or more persons snowshoeing abreast may seem companionable, but it's a great waste of energy since each has to break trail. Practical snowshoeing is a single-file form of travel. The second person steps, not in the leader's tracks, but in between them so that a smooth, well-beaten "float" or "beat" is packed down for those who follow, or for the return trip. Every few minutes, the leader falls back to the end of the line and the second person then breaks trail. On well-packed snow, snowshoeing is relatively easy and enjoyable, but in deep, soft snow, you'll earn every inch, so swap frequently.

On hard-crusted slopes where snowshoes get little purchase, metal crampons can be attached directly under the foot. These bite into the crust to keep the snowshoes from slipping. But where there is an inch or two of fresh snow over the crust, the crampons may cause the snow to "ball" under the foot, creating consid-erable discomfort.

Be cautious about "bridging." This occurs when the toe and the tail of the snowshoe rest firmly on snow, but the center section is suspended over a depres-sion. With short snowshoes, such as the Bear Paw models, the danger is not as great as with the longer Pickerel type which might break under your unsupported weight. Incidentally, an old pair of snowshoes, resurrected from the attic, is best left there, or cross-mounted over the fireplace for decorative effect. Even supple ash frames dry out and become brittle with age.

Look ahead along the trail as you travel, not down at your snowshoes. Choose as level a path as possible, avoiding steep pitches or thick brush. A fifty-foot detour consumes less energy than prying your way through an alder run. Frozen streambeds are natural snowshoe routes but are safe only if the ice is consistently firm. Wherever side streams enter, the ice will be thinner, often barely strong enough to support their snow cover. This is also true of inlets and outlets along lake shores. If you must cross ice that is suspect, loosen your harnesses so that you can quickly shed your snowshoes in the event you break through. Walk at least thirty to forty feet apart from other members of your party and carry a ten- to twelve-foot pole. This will support you in case of a plunge into icy waters and can be used to effect a rescue. Generally, such crossings should be considered foolhardy, to be attempted only in an emergency or when no other route is possible.

Snowshoeing is at its best when enjoyed in a leisurely manner. Snowshoes are slow. Trying to hurry, especially in light, deep snow, is quickly tiring. On packed surfaces, the pace can be stepped up a little. Short spurts of up to four miles per hour are possible but this approaches a racing pace. Five-mile runs in slightly over thirty minutes are not unusual in races conducted by French-Canadian snowshoe clubs. However, these are run on hard-packed snow by athletes in top shape competing on lightweight (generally undersized) snowshoes that flap in the wind as they run. Under more realistic conditions, when you are likely to be carrying a thirty-five-pound pack in loose snow, eight to ten miles per day is probably average for a snowshoer in sound physical condition.

SNOWSHOES

Snowshoes have been improvised, sometimes crudely, sometimes cleverly. In the National Museum of Canada there is an ancient example of native ingenuity, a snowshoe made of branches for a frame, and twisted bark for the filling. During World War II, two German prisoners-of-war escaped from a labor camp deep in the Maine woods, on snowshoes contrived with scrap boards. It took game wardens and border patrolmen almost three days to overtake and recapture them.

You'll have little need to improvise in recreational snowshoeing, however. There's ample choice among sturdy and durable models. Although aluminum-framed snowshoes are justly gaining acceptance, white-ash frames still dominate. White ash is among the lightest of the durable hardwoods, straight-grained, resilient, and little inclined to split or sliver once it's finished and sealed. It lends itself well to steaming and bending, then holds a given shape indefinitely. Other woods have been used, notably hickory and oak, but these are not as easily worked and are heavier than ash.

Frame stock is cut to dimension, then planed for a smooth finish and, finally, it is steamed to make it pliable. The frame is then bent to shape with cross-pieces mortised into position. Locked in a form, the frame is dried slowly to prevent subsequent warping. Filling or lacing, plus several coats of waterproof varnish, make up the final steps.

For lacing, early snowshoe makers used moose or caribou hide cut into narrow strips. For obvious reasons, these have been replaced by cowhide. Thoroughly soaked, it is laced into an intricate pattern that distributes weight evenly along the frame and cross-members. As the filling dries, it shrinks, becoming taut enough to hold weight with little give.

The center section that bears the bulk of the weight is usually laced with heavier, wider strips, from three-eighths to five-eighths inch wide, as compared to the lighter lacing, often three-sixteenths of an inch, used in the toe and tail sections. Some makers use heavy lacing throughout but, so far as strength and durability are concerned, the lighter fore and aft lacing is more than adequate and cuts down on weight.

Cowhide lacing stretches when wet, however. To offset this, manufacturers have come up with various processes, usually trade secrets, which guarantee a "no-sag" filling. Nonetheless, sagging will occur if you fail to keep the webbing properly varnished or if you walk for some time in slush; the latter is definitely in the category of abuse. Known as "loading," wet snow will tend to cling to cowhide. One remedy is to coat the underside with ski wax or silicone.

During the 1960s, nylon-reinforced neoprene was introduced for filling, reducing weight about 20 percent. The material repels dampness, so that stretch and sagging have been virtually eliminated. Nylon/neoprene has another advantage; it does not appeal to the taste of mice and porcupines, which consider cowhide rather toothsome, and ends the need for storing cowhide out of their reach. Nylon/neoprene is not varnished, but if the frames are made of ash they must be recoated occasionally. The problem here is that varnishing the frames without daubing the neoprene is difficult. Any varnish applied to the neoprene tends to remain tacky. Also, because the neoprene is not bonded to the frame as is cowhide, it is inclined to slip slightly along the frame. However, this is no particular detriment to the snowshoes.

Which is the more durable—cowhide or nylon/neoprene? Demand among snowshoers is about fifty-fifty. A group of mountaineers spending the summer on the upper slopes of Mount McKinley used nylon/neoprene shoes almost daily, often on abrasive corn snow. The webbing stood up well. A Maine tree farmer, pruning pines during the winter months, used cowhide-filled snowshoes with which he walked on downed limbs as well as snow. The filling gave out during the second winter of such abuse but, when he relaced his frames, he still chose cowhide rather than nylon-neoprene. Thus, even among experienced snowshoers, the cowhide-neoprene controversy remains unsettled.

Models

There are three basic snowshoes. The similar Maine and Michigan patterns; the Pickerel, also known as the Arctic or Alaska; and the Bear Paw. All others are variations.

The Maine and the Michigan are large snowshoes, wider than most others, with considerable bearing surface. Both have tails for better tracking. Also, the tail's weight tends to lift the toe in deep, fluffy snow so that there is less chance of tripping. The difference between the Maine and the Michigan models lies principally in the toe section. While both have only a slight toe upturn, the Michigan model's toe area has a short, rounded frame forming almost a perfect half-circle. The Maine type has a more elongated toe, tapering more sharply at the front. The shorter fore section of the Michigan snowshoe has been attributed to a timber cruiser's need for standing close to a tree in order to caliper its diameter; this seems unlikely. In fact, there are only slight variations between the two snowshoes and it's doubtful that one can be proven superior to the other.

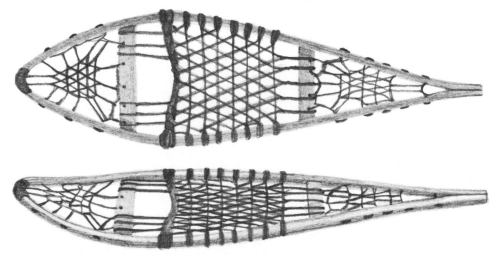

Maine Snowshoe

Both are difficult for beginners to handle. They maneuver poorly in brushy travel and are not well adapted to steep, hilly country, being at their best in open country or on well-brushed trails. No snowshoe offers a greater variety of sizes. The Maine pattern varies from 10 inches wide by 36 inches long to 14 by 48 inches; the Michigan ranges from 12 by 46 inches to 14 by 52 inches. When determining your proper size, bear in mind that the softer and deeper the snow, and the greater your own weight (as well as that of a pack), the more bearing surface you'll need. Women weighing 100 to 125 pounds get along nicely on the 12- by 42-inch model, whereas men, weighing from 150 to 175 pounds or more, may require the 13- by 48-inch or 14- by 48-inch model.

The second type, the Alaska or Pickerel snowshoe, is a long, narrow model, generally available in two sizes: 10 by 48 inches and 10 by 56 inches; some Canadian versions are as long as 60 inches. The toe of all Pickerels has a high upturn, almost 6 inches. It's beautifully suited to open country where snow is likely to be wind-packed. Under these conditions, it is the fastest of all snowshoes. Its narrow width is a boon to beginners, but in order to minimize straddle, a long stride is called for. Thus, a tall person can use this style to best advantage. It's a poor choice for brushy going since the long tail hampers sharp turns. In soft snow, however, the high toe upturn makes it easier to lift the snowshoe without tripping. Of the two models, the 10- by 56-inch model is probably preferable to the shorter 10- by 48-inch style for all-round use, since the speed and buoyancy of this snowshoe derive from its length. Take advantage of it.

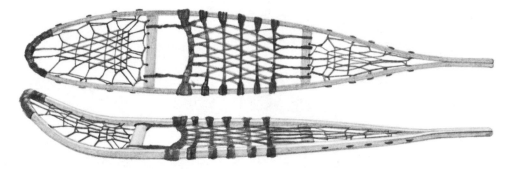

Pickerel Snowshoe

A variation of the Pickerel is the Cross-Country model, but its toe upturn is not as pronounced. It resembles a narrow Bear Paw with a tail added. Its design and size—10 by 46 inches—are well adapted to woods trails, open travel, even traversing hardwood forests where underbrush is not too thick. In fact, it combines some of the advantages of the Pickerel with those of the Bear Paw so that, not surprisingly, it is probably one of the most popular styles sold. While its shorter length (as compared to the Pickerel) does not provide as much flotation, it maneuvers easily.

Finally we come to the Bear Paw model, which has several versions. Some provide enough bearing surface to support 250-pounders, yet they're compact, relatively light and highly maneuverable. Twisting and turning, even in thick brush, poses few problems. The original Bear Paw (even this had variations) is a flat shoe with no toe upturn and, of course, no tail. While the front end is an almost perfect oval, there is a slight taper in width from the midsection to the tail. At one time this model was popular among winter climbers, since the short, flat toe made it easy to kick steps into a steep slope. But because the snowshoer's weight is well forward, and because of the flat toe, this original Bear Paw is inclined to catch under crust, even in loosely packed snow. Few are in use today. It is cited here only for comparison with the more modern, versatile Bear Paws.

Virtually all Bear Paws, except the Green Mountain model, are referred to as "modified." This causes some confusion but, once you examine the two or three other Bear Paws, it's easy to recognize the differences. The oldest of the modified Bear Paws has a sharply tapered toe and heel section and a slight toe upturn, the most popular size being 13 by 33 inches. It's capable of carrying a heavier-than-average man, even with a pack, on a great variety of snow surfaces—and is a notable improvement on the original Bear Paw for general use, whether on a trail, in the open or in brushy country. It adapts fairly well to climbing, too. Despite its width, straddle need not be a problem. You need only to take slightly longer strides.

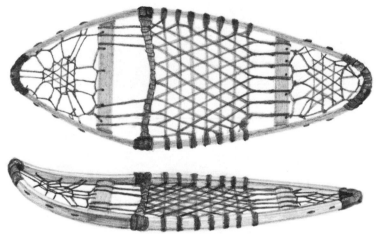

Modified Bear Paw Snowshoe

Another modified Bear Paw is also known as a "Beavertail" or, originally, as the Westover. It closely resembles the foregoing Bear Paw except that a tail has been added. The Beavertail is a compact shoe, much like the earlier modified model. While the tail enhances tracking, it obstructs very little in brushy going. For beginners as well as experienced snowshoers, it's an excellent choice in either the 12- by 34-inch or 14- by 36-inch size, the larger being preferable if you weigh more than 160 pounds, or if you intend to tote a moderately heavy pack. The Beavertail is not generally available with cowhide filling, since the initial model was laced with nylon/neoprene and it continues to be.

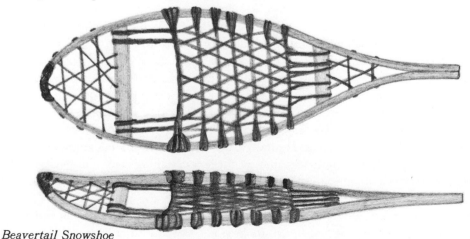

Beavertail Snowshoe

Still another Bear Paw is the Green Mountain model, an almost perfect, elongated oval, 10 by 36 inches, with a moderate toe upturn; you can choose either cowhide or nylon/neoprene filling. While it does not provide the flotation of larger snowshoes, its narrow width appeals to beginners, and justly so, since it is easy to use, even in deep powder. In fact, its popularity is gaining among experienced snowshoers for travel on hilly terrain. The Green Mountain is well-liked among climbers because it will "ski" or slide downhill on packed snow, thus speeding up descents. It has one slight shortcoming. Due to its almost full-width tail section, a fairly long stride is required, the alternative being some degree of straddling.

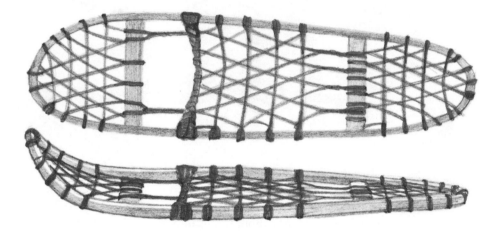

Green Mountain Snowshoe

The Sherpa® snowshoe is shaped much like the Green Mountain model but there the resemblance ends. It has replaced the original Bear Paw model among mountaineers, due to its versatility, especially when traversing steep slopes. And it is rugged. The frame is anodized aluminum, which cuts down somewhat on weight. Better yet, it won't rust or split and never needs varnishing, an almost annual necessity with wood frames. Instead of the traditional filling, a solid unperforated section of nylon/neoprene is laced to the frame with a synthetic material (not identified by the manufacturer) which is claimed to be four times more abrasion resistant than neoprene. The binding is an integral part of the snowshoe, attached to the frame by means of a metal rod that acts as a hinge. Thus there is virtually no lateral play. Under the pivoting harness is a set of metal claws that bite into hard-packed or glazed snow, just about eliminating backsliding or sideslipping. The over-the-boot straps are of the "quick-lacing" type, more easily and more quickly attached than the traditional leather or neoprene harness with its buckle system.

While there are five sizes offered, most outfitters carry only the three smaller versions, 8 by 25 inches, 9 by 30 inches and 9 by 34 inches, which are best adapted to mountain terrain or dense brush. The larger models, 10 by 37 inches and 10 by 44 inches, are best suited to open country or moderate hills when heavy packs are carried.

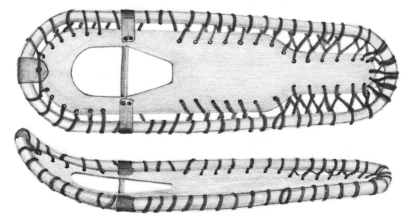

Sherpa® Snowshoe

All-plastic snowshoes have proven quite durable. These have built-in, hinge-type bindings. Made of two sizes, 11¾ by 29 inches and 12½ by 38 inches, they are slightly lighter than ash-framed models and somewhat less costly. They have found little acceptance among serious snowshoers, due to their small size and possibly to some natural resistance toward a new, relatively untried, material. There's no question about it—ash-framed and the new aluminum models are definitely superior but, for casual use by adults or for children, plastic is acceptable.

Snowshoe Selection

There is no all-around showshoe, nor is any one model as specialized as it might seem. True, the Pickerel is at its best in open country, the Maine or Michigan on woodland trails, the modified Bear Paw and Green Mountain in brush, the Sherpa® on a wind-swept alpine slope. No matter which model you choose, there will be days during which you'll wish you'd chosen another style.

Most snowshoers travel a variety of terrain, following woods trails, bush-whacking through frozen swamps, traversing open fields, possibly even climbing a mountain. It's rare, indeed, that a snowshoer confines himself to one set of snow conditions. Even the trapper who spends much time along brush-lined streams frequently crosses open areas or follows woods trails that climb and dip. It's impossible to anticipate all snow conditions and terrain variations. Even a mountaineer who knows that the snow fields at high altitude will probably be hard-packed by the wind may have to plod through deep, fluffy snow where he will sink knee-deep before he reaches the steep slopes.

Therefore, it's best for a beginner to choose a snowshoe with which he'll be reasonably comfortable under varying conditions. If you're about to buy your first pair for recreational use, you can't go far wrong with the modified Bear Paw. A note of caution, however. Whatever style you buy, resist the temptation to choose snowshoes that are too large. You'll gain very little flotation and pay dearly in energy dispensed while maneuvering unnecessary weight.

Determining quality among the ash-framed models is a matter of visual inspection. There are no hidden parts, so that defective material or poor workmanship is readily apparent. Defects in wood, such as knots, splits or slivers, can be seen or felt. One symbol of quality, especially among the rawhide styles, is extra windings at the toe and tail for reinforcement of frame stock that is often thinned and rounded in these areas for a more graceful bend. Whether the filling is cowhide or nylon/neoprene, be sure that it is taut. Nor should you assume that thinner rawhide strips used in the toe and tail sections are less durable than the heavier lacing in the center. There is less weight stress fore and aft, so that light filling is more than adequate; it also cuts down weight. Examine the cross-bars, too, making sure that they are securely mortised into the frame. On the whole, buy one of the well-known brands and you'll find the quality and workmanship good. It's only when you stray to an off-beat brand that a thorough examination is required.

Bindings

Next in importance to the snowshoe itself is the hitch, harness, binding or rigging—call it what you will. Originally, this was a four-foot rawhide strip, looped over the toe of the boot, around the toe bar, criss-crossed under the instep, then wrapped and tied about the ankle, providing a firm but flexible hitch. By today's standards it was far too flexible, resulting in excessive lateral play. Modern leather or nylon/neoprene riggings are easier to attach and remove, they provide greater control and they are far more durable.

One of the most popular of today's hitches is the H-style, consisting of a double strap passing under each side of the toe cord and over the boot toe, a second strap encompassing the heel and a third wrapping the instep. It's easy to adjust and provides good control. The H-style may look complicated, but attaching or removing it is actually a simple process. The toe straps, once adjusted to the boot, are never unbuckled. Only the instep and the heel strap are buckled (or unbuckled). The H-harness is available in leather or neoprene. Leather stretches when wet. As a result your foot may slide forward within the toe loop, thus loosening the entire hitch. During a short trek on dry snow the problem of stretch is not likely to arise, but during a day-long trip, especially in hilly country, some stretch may occur. However, the H-harness is readily adjustable. On the other hand, the problem can be eliminated by using the neoprene H-harness instead, which will not stretch and, once adjusted, will hold securely all day.

Similar to the H-binding is the Howe rigging. The two are similar except that the Howe model has a leather tongue attached to the toe cord under the foot. It

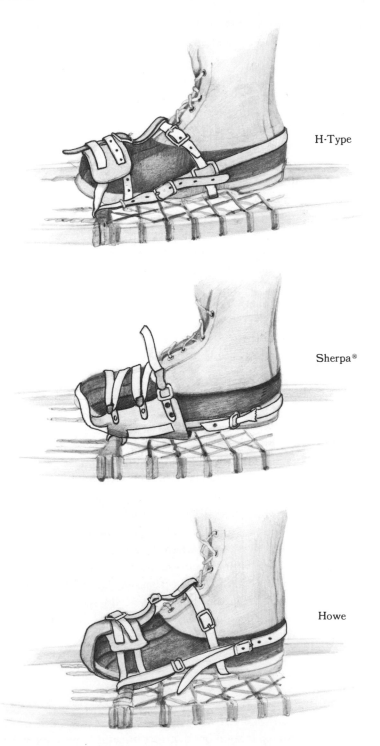

H-Type

Sherpa®

Howe

Snowshoe Bindings

then comes up over the front of the boot toe and attaches to the instep strap. This virtually eliminates fore and aft slippage, a decided advantage during a steep descent.

Perhaps the most advanced of today's snowshoe riggings is the Sherpa® binding, not to be confused with the built-in rod-and-claw harness of the Sherpa® snowshoe. The Sherpa® binding resembles part of a slipper or moccasin with a horizontal strap at the front that prevents the foot from slipping forward. It has the conventional heel strap but it is the lacing system that differs radically. There is no threading or buckling required. Instead two pairs of toe straps are "quick laced" then locked over the instep with a spring-loaded clasp. Putting them on or removing them is a matter of seconds, even while wearing mittens. The system holds securely with little lateral play. Cost is somewhat higher than that of other riggings but, for serious snowshoeing, the Sherpa® is worth investigating.

While excessive lateral play or "wobble" can make for tough going on a favorable snow surface, it has probably been overemphasized. There is nothing wrong with a little play in the matching of a harness to a snowshoe. A firm, unrelenting grip on your feet results in a "lock step," which is efficient on straightaways. However snowshoeing involves turning, too. With slight play in your harness, you can more easily effect a kick turn instead of walking in circles to change directions. Particularly in brush, the kick turn is a time and energy saver. Since the ankle and knees can be turned sideways only so far, being able to "kick" the shoe horizontally in one direction or the other is helpful. So don't fret if there is some lateral freedom. The most popular of all hitches, the H-model, provides this without detriment to overall control.

The matter of traction also deserves some attention. Most beginners need not worry about it. The coarse mesh of snowshoe filling automatically bites into most snow covers, even when they are fairly well packed. However, there are times when a snowshoe will slide, almost uncontrollably. During a January thaw, for instance, it may rain, followed by a quick, hard freeze. The crust that forms often will not support your weight without snowshoes. These, however, slide in all directions. The situation is even worse when the hard freeze is followed by a two- or three-inch fall of light snow which seems to lubricate the icy surface. Then, too, during a steep climb, even on relatively soft snow, the snowshoe tends to slide backward with each step. On hard-packed slopes, this condition is aggravated. Under these conditions, the Sherpa® claw-type rigging or showshoes with crampons are the best solution. If you get caught without crampons, wrap rope around the frames and cross-piece to provide extra traction.

Boots

It's not unusual to see a snowshoer wearing hiking boots, the same ones in which he trudged on summer trails. If such boots are comfortable with extra wool socks for warmth, well and good. However, bear in mind that hard heels such as Vibram®, especially those with crisp, new edges, will soon gnaw through cowhide or neoprene webbing.

The original boot specifically adapted to snowshoeing was the Indian's high-topped moccasin, sometimes known as the "Larrigan," and still available in some parts of the North. In dry, powdery snow the Larrigan works well for those accustomed to it. However, on moist snow it readily wets through. What's more, because the boot lacks an outer sole and heel, it puts a strain on calf muscles and, of course, there is little, if any, arch support. The same can be said for the Eskimo mukluk adapted to Arctic conditions. There are far better boots for snowshoeing today.

Probably the most practical footwear for snowshoeing is the leather-top/rubber-bottom boot. Because it's slightly narrower than most, it fits more readily into a variety of snowshoe bindings. One model is insulated with a full lining of foam with a thick innersole of the same material. Another version has three-eighths inch thick wool felt liners that can be removed for drying. The effectiveness of such liners is vouched for by French-Canadian loggers who worked through the northern Maine and Quebec winters wearing only felt boots and ordinary street rubbers.

Leather boots are adequate for short periods of snowshoeing as long as they've been waterproofed. In deep snow they can be used with overboots or gaiters for extra protection. As with leather-top/rubber-bottom boots, insulated models are pretty much mandatory.

The all-rubber shoe pac is still used by some for snowshoeing but it's self-defeating. Being impervious to moisture, it traps foot perspiration which, in cold weather, leads to chilled feet.

Depending on the style of boot chosen, allow room for at least one pair of wool socks, and preferably two. Some like to add one pair of silk inner socks for added comfort. Also be sure that the boots you buy will fit your snowshoe bindings. Certain types of felt-lined cold-weather boots will not.

Field Repairs

If your snowshoes and bindings are relatively new, it's not likely that you'll have to make repairs afield. However, emergencies do arise so carry a simple repair kit, especially during an extended trek. Include a pocket knife, split copper rivets, a length of nylon/neoprene filling material of nylon cord and a small coil of No. 28 copper wire with which you can repair a split wooden frame. Even one that has been completely broken can be repaired with wire by adding a splint. A piece of leather strap (or neoprene) and a few rivets will repair a binding.

Off-Season Care

Rodents are dedicated gourmets when it comes to cowhide snowshoe filling, and apparently consider the remnants of varnish an appetizer. Keep your snowshoes out of reach, hanging them from fine wire, for example. If the varnish on wood-framed models appears worn, apply two thin coats before storage. If the binding is leather, treat it with a preservative or waterproofing. Neoprene needs no special attention.

Eventually (it may be years depending on the extent of your snowshoeing) the filling may wear through. Some manufacturers repair snowshoes, even brands other than their own, but usually only during slack production periods. So contact them well in advance. If you decide to do this work yourself, snowshoe makers and some outfitters sell ready-cut strips of cowhide or neoprene, usually by the pound. Indicate whether you want the heavier body filling (in the case of cowhide) or the lighter type for the toe and heel sections.

Toboggans, Sleds and "Pulks"

If you're likely to attempt hauling heavy loads—supplying a winter cabin, for instance—a small toboggan is helpful. Tie a twenty-foot length of line to each side of the toboggan's front end, then loop the line over the back of your neck (padded by your collar), running it down through your armpits to the toboggan. Don't attempt pulling any type of sled with a single line held in your hands or run over one shoulder. This will keep you off-balance and make snowshoeing difficult. Attach a snub line at the rear, too, so your partner can keep the rig from running over you during a downhill haul.

Old-time woodsmen used a moose sled, not necessarily designed for hauling a moose carcass, but as a general-purpose toting rig. It was usually homemade with wide wooden runners for good flotation and was pulled by means of a single wooden tow bar. The moose sled was not a truly efficient hauling method. Far better is the modern folding sled, similar in basic design, but only four feet long and weighing about ten pounds. Instead of a tow bar, one or more tow lines are attached. It will carry a greater load than most men can pull for any great distance. Since it folds, it can be stowed in a car trunk.

For cross-country skiers the Norwegians have come up with various fiberglass and plastic shells on runners. Known as "pulks," they are lightweight—and also quite costly. Most models have long handles that you can secure around your waist with a hipbelt so that your arms are free.

Whatever type of sled or toboggan you use, cargo should be completely wrapped in a tarpaulin, not merely covered. It should also be lashed. Spills do occur.

SKIS OR SNOWSHOES?

The choice between skis and snowshoes is often a philosophical one. Skis represent a freedom of spirit, swift flight and a fulfillment of the urge to glide great distances with ease. Snowshoes, on the other hand, have the aura of the Great North Woods about them, bringing to mind the daring and romance of the *coureurs de bois*.

Other factors enter into the choice, of course. Skis are faster than snowshoes—even on flat terrain each stride carries you several feet—and there is the excitement of downhill runs. Obviously, then, in open country or where trails are well defined, skis are a decided advantage.

In thick woodlands, particularly in brush, skis are difficult to maneuver, if not virtually impossible. On snowshoes, especially Bear Paws, you can wind and twist among all sorts of obstacles. Then there's the matter of carrying a pack. A light one poses no obstacle for a skier but a heavy pack raises problems with stability; on snowshoes, balance is easier.

It's possible to travel slowly on skis, of course, so that you can observe nature at first hand. On snowshoes a slow pace is mandatory. You'll see more of your immediate surroundings—the entrance to a red squirrel's nut cache, a partridge budding in a birch tree, a fox skulking at the edge of a rabbit swamp seeking his dinner.

Skis or snowshoes—the choice of one or the other will be governed pretty much by your personal feelings about the outdoors. But either will help you attain your spiritual and physical goal in a snowy world.

Chapter 10

Canoes: Pole, Paddle and Portage

Slipping across the map in a canoe you leave no trail, only flecks of foam in your wake, the panorama shifting with each paddle stroke. Easing along quietly, you're not an intruder. The wilderness accepts you and you become part of it.

Of course, a canoe trip isn't all serenity. Buck a head wind all day and you'll feel pain in muscles you didn't know you had. Run a pitch of wild water, and halfway through you'll wonder where you parted with your sanity. Tote a canoe over a long portage and the carrying yoke will grind into your neck and shoulders, as the black flies devour you and the rain turns the trail into a quagmire. But eventually the sun comes out, the wind goes down, the flies relent, the carry is finished, camp is pitched and there are trout browning in the skillet. While the tough going will not soon be forgotten, you develop memories that will glow increasingly as the years go by.

But the good moments don't just happen. Canoeing fun, whether a white-water weekend or a two-week cruise, results from matching the right equipment to the job. The most expensive outfit is all but worthless if it's not suited to the chore at hand. Nor is there a substitute for the skill that comes from knowing how to handle your canoe in all situations.

CANOES

Most people buying their first canoe generally consider what it's made of—wood/canvas, cedar, aluminum, ABS, fiberglass, polyethylene—and then, its weight. Material as well as size directly governs weight.

Wood/Canvas

The wood/canvas canoe supplanted the surprisingly sturdy birchbark model early in this century, and remained the most popular—in fact, virtually the *only*—canoe until the end of World War II. Its demise resulted from the introduction of aluminum into canoe building, and today most people regard the wood/canvas canoe as obsolete. Relatively few are built in the United States, a somewhat greater number in Canada. Quite a few small shops, usually one- or two-man operations, still turn out the handsome handcrafted canvas canoes, but the total production is slight when compared to that of aluminum, ABS and fiberglass. Nonetheless, there is currently a resurgence of interest in these canoes—reflected not only in the organization, in 1979, of the Wooden Canoe Heritage Association, but also in the restoration of old wooden hulls. Wood/canvas canoes are still the choice of those who appreciate the craftsmanship that goes into them. They insist that "nothing paddles like a canvas canoe." It is a delight to handle, quiet yet responsive. But there are good reasons why wood/canvas canoes are now in limited demand.

Compared to ABS, aluminum, fiberglass and polyethylene canvas is fragile—though wood/canvas canoes once successfully ran many a stretch of wild water in the hands of experts. Minor damage is easy to mend, but more serious crack-ups result in difficult and expensive repairs. Another drawback is the maintenance required. Unless the interior surface is kept well varnished, the hull will absorb moisture, increasing its weight by up to 15 percent. Repainting the exterior may call for the removal of old paint before a new coat is applied, a job that is tedious but less difficult than you might think. Wood/canvas canoes are also expensive, well over twice the cost of other types, due to the great amount of hand labor involved. Even storage can be a problem. A wood/canvas canoe should be stored under cover, and elevated so that ground moisture doesn't initiate rot. Obviously then, anyone who chooses a wood/canvas canoe has reconciled himself to a labor of love. There are those who say it is worth it.

Cedar-Strip Canoes

Cedar-strip canoes are wooden craft, the hull covered with clear fiberglass so that the beauty of the wood is not hidden. The construction differs from wood/canvas canoes in that no ribs are built in. The cedar strips run longitudinally, each bonded to the other. This makes possible a hull shape with a very fine "entry," for speed and ease of paddling; cedar-strip canoes are designed to cut through the water rather than push it aside. Known as "strippers," such canoes are manufactured commercially in small numbers and are all handmade. Many are built in home workshops. They are probably the loveliest of all canoes and owners pamper them, restricting their use to flat water paddling; they are relatively fragile, and easily damaged in white water. Strippers are among the lightest of all canoes.

Aluminum

Although some rather sleek designs with finer cutwaters were introduced in 1980, most aluminum canoes carry their beam well forward and aft so that they push, rather than cut, through the water. This hull design, however, makes the canoe initially more stable and increases its carrying capacity. Well-made aluminum canoes are rugged and most dents can be punched out. Even when left outdoors all year, neither rain nor snow affects them and they will not take on weight with age. Most models are self-righting and respond reasonably well to the paddle. They are rigged with flotation air tanks or foam compartments to render them unsinkable.

Aluminum, however, is not without sin. It is noisy and, when you ram a rock, it tends to cling rather than slide over. It readily conducts heat and cold, which means that you'll need knee pads during the chilly spring run-off, and caution in July when picking up a canoe that's been left overturned in the sun. The self-righting feature is commendable, but if you flip in a high wind you had better make a quick grab or your canoe will go sailing off without you. While the standard-grade aluminum canoes built of metal .050- to .051-inches thick generally compare in weight to those of wood/canvas and are notably sturdy, the .032-inch thick lightweight models are easily damaged in rocky waters. In the seventeen- to eighteen-foot models, rigidity of the hull should be assured by no fewer than three thwarts and, if you're going to take your canoe through white water, by the addition of reinforcing ribs. Most makers offer these either as options or as standard equipment.

ABS

ABS is the acronym for acrylonitrile butadiene styrene, a sandwich material developed by the U. S. Rubber Company under the trade name of Royalex®. (Some canoe manufacturers who use ABS have given it their own brand designation.) Canoeists have dubbed ABS craft "rubber boats" and for good reason. Since the material tends to flex slightly, it is "forgiving," tending to slide over rocks, or bounce off them, with little more than a surface scratch.

During the summer of 1973, an ABS canoe lashed to the pontoons of a small plane flying over the Maine woods broke loose and fell some eight hundred feet. When found a few days later, the only damage was a cracked deck. ABS has earned a reputation for near indestructibility, and one that is probably justified. For all practical purposes, ABS is one of the two most damage-resistant canoe fabrics in use today, polyethylene being the other. True, some people have torn large gashes in the bottom of ABS canoes while running over sharp ledges. But such damage is rare. Badly dented hulls, even those that have literally been bent around a rock, have been restored to their original shape, without cracks or leaks, by the application of heat. A warm flatiron will do the job, but even strong sunlight has been known to smooth out dents and reform the craft to its original contours.

ABS is an extraordinary material, but you should be aware of its limitations. A capsized ABS canoe will float, but just barely. It is not as buoyant as a wooden canoe, and don't expect to climb into a swamped ABS to await rescue, or to hand-paddle it ashore. Also, as pointed out earlier, the material tends to flex, the bottom visibly undulating, which slows its speed. It you feel that flexing inhibits your style of canoeing, jam blocks of styrofoam under the thwarts. This reinforces the bottom and also provides buoyancy in case you swamp. Some canoeists use a styrofoam block as a seat when paddling alone. Again with regard to flexing, a sixteen- or seventeen-foot ABS canoe should be built with at least two thwarts. Many owners have discovered that the single midship thwart often provided is not enough and have added a second one some three feet forward of the stern seat. Finally, when wet, the interior surface of an ABS canoe is slippery, which is disconcerting when you're poling through a set of rapids. Some manufacturers apply a nonskid finish, or you can do it yourself with a can of special spray.

ABS requires little maintenance and can be left outdoors all year—although ABS canoes with wooden gunwales and peaks should be propped to avoid ground moisture. The cost of ABS canoes is roughly half that of wood/canvas.

Fiberglass

Literally dozens of firms have sprung up in recent years to produce fiberglass canoes. Fiberglass is a relatively easy material to work and while some canoe makers use more sophisticated methods, most stick to the basic mold process, bonding fiberglass mat and cloth with a resin. Some wood/canvas builders now substitute fiberglass cloth for canvas. While usually heavier than ABS and some aluminum models, fiberglass canoe weights can be considered reasonable.

The relatively low cost of fiberglass has accounted for much of its popularity. Its toughness, too, makes it attractive. It can be molded easily to produce any type of hull, a wide-beamed "pusher" or a sleek racing model. Minor repairs, even at riverside, are not difficult, although major ones may be costly. Like aluminum, fiberglass can be left out in all sorts of weather, maintenance is virtually nil and with the color built in, repainting is eliminated. Since fiberglass will not float, buoyancy is built in by the use of air chambers or foam compartments, usually installed under the deck at each end.

Many of the best fiberglass canoes have a balsa-wood filler, sandwiched between fiberglass cloth and matting. Strengthened with resin, it's not the flimsy material you used for building model airplanes as a youngster. In fact, sample pieces of this balsa/fiberglass material have withstood hammer blows. Another method for reinforcing fiberglass canoes calls for sandwiching in a polyester-fiber mat that, when saturated with polyester resin, strengthens the floor area while only slightly adding to the canoe's weight. Use care when buying a fiberglass canoe, however. Among the major firms there is no question about craftsmanship and, should defects appear, the manufacturer or dealer will make good on them. But beware of fiberglass canoes offered at unusually low prices. The workmanship may be less than good. Defects in a fiberglass hull are often visible. They may appear as whitish spots or areas where the layers of cloth and mat have separated or where resin has not thoroughly penetrated. Following a severe blow, a bubble or delamination may occur, though as much as forty-eight hours may pass before it shows up.

Kevlar®

The product of the E. I. Du Pont De Nemours Co., this closely resembles fiberglass but is made up of aramid fibers. Canoes made of this relatively new material are not only exceptionally rugged but are the lightest on the market, weighing less than half as much as fiberglass models of the same length and hull design. And yet, Kevlar® can be subjected to tremendous abuse. (Bear in mind, however, that no canoe fabric is indestructible.) Kevlar®, like fiberglass, can be readily molded to conform to almost any hull design. Kevlar® is a superb material for racing canoes and for wilderness tripping where difficult portages are expected. Solo paddlers, too, appreciate its light weight. But it has one drawback. It's expensive.

Polyethylene

A relative newcomer, introduced as a hull material in 1977, polyethylene is probably the toughest of all canoe fabrics, and is currently being used more extensively than any other material. The principal reason is cost. Polyethylene canoe prices are about two-thirds to one-half those of ABS models.

Polyethylene, however, is not without drawbacks. It flexes considerably more than does ABS so that it requires an aluminum inner skeletal reinforcement which some consider a nuisance when loading gear aboard. Also, many look upon this interior frame as unattractive. Like ABS, polyethylene canoes require flotation chambers to prevent their sinking when swamped. And repairs in the field are difficult, if not impossible, often requiring a torch.

Inflatables

Inflatable canoes have considerable appeal. When folded they are quite compact and their weight—twenty to thirty pounds—makes them ideal for toting to remote fishing waters or for storage in today's small-car trunks. The better-quality versions are made of heavy-duty vinyl-coated polyester, or PVC, with multiple air compartments. If one compartment springs a leak, you still have some flotation. Size, and to some degree shape, varies, with lengths usually running six to twelve feet. Such inflatables are sufficiently durable to withstand the punishment of moderate white water, but this durability is limited. Be sure to carry a repair kit. Consider, too, that an inflatable canoe's capacity is relatively small and that it is a slow craft. And, of course, you'll have to inflate it before launching; this is best done with a foot pump.

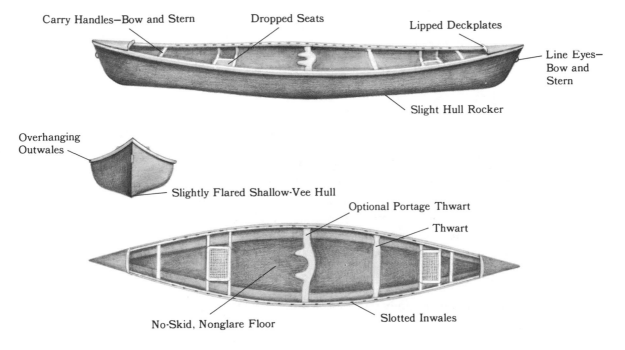

A Recreational Canoe

Canoe Weights

No one enjoys toting a ninety-five-pound canoe over a two-mile portage, nor is it fun to hoist an eighty-five-pounder on top of a car single-handedly. Most of us want a canoe we can juggle with some ease. On the whole, though, canoe weight gets more attention than it deserves. Virtually all canoes in the sixteen- to eighteen-foot range are easily handled by two persons. In fact, most of them can be cartopped or portaged single-handedly once you acquire the knack of lifting them. You can round out your canoe expertise by learning to lift yours alone.

In the meantime, note the chart that follows, indicating the minimum and maximum weights of canoes among the various materials and lengths. The chart includes only those suitable for general recreation, tripping and informal whitewater running. Specialty craft, such as racing models, are not included.

Canoe Weights (pounds)

Type	16'	17'	18'
Wood/Canvas	67 – 76	75 – 82	78 – 88
Wood/Fiberglass	67 – 70	72 – 85	77 – 90
Strippers	50 – 56	56 – 61	56 – 66
Aluminum			
Standard	75 – 82	73 – 91	71 – 91
Lightweight	———	60 – 70	67 – 72
Fiberglass	65 – 85	67 – 95	78 – 107
Kevlar®	40 – 45	52 – 56	52 – 80
ABS	68 – 78	70 – 84	79 – 86
Polyethylene	70 – 75	78 – 81	———

Note that among the sixteen-footers, only two weigh more than eighty pounds; most are in the reasonable sixty-five- to seventy-five-pound range. The seventeen-footers are somewhat heavier, naturally, but a few actually weigh little more than sixteen-foot models.

Why do so many canoes of the same length very so much in weight? It's a matter of materials, hull configuration and construction. Some aluminum canoes are reinforced with extra ribs for bumping and grinding through heavy rapids. These add weight. Some fiberglass canoes have thicker hulls than others. And because some hulls are "fuller," their width carried well forward and aft, more material goes into them.

While weight is certainly an important consideration, it should not be the foremost one. Granted, for carrying to remote waters, you'll want as near a flyweight as you can find. Generally, though, it's wiser to buy a canoe that will do the job you expect of it rather than one that's easy to lift. A canoe's performance is more critical in the water than on land. A few extra pounds can spell the difference between enjoying your canoe and fighting to keep it upright.

Capacity

Designers generally have an inkling of a canoe's capacity while it's still on the drawing board, but there are proven ways of obtaining a more accurate rating. Some rely on a complex mathematical formula. Others use a method that may seem primitive but results in a rating that stands up under scrutiny. With the canoe afloat, fifty-pound sandbags are loaded aboard until six inches of freeboard (the vertical distance between the water and the gunwale) remains. Count the bags. Multiply by fifty. You have the craft's capacity. Simple and practical.

When manufacturers cite capacity, their specifications apply to the canoe only under optimum conditions. Their ratings are only guidelines and do not take into account four-foot waves on a wind-lashed lake or throbbing haystacks at the foot of a white-water pitch. Nor do they know how well the customer can handle a canoe.

There are two things you can do to enhance your new canoe's performance within its rating. First, unless you're paddling under the most ideal conditions—smooth water, no wind, no tumbling rapids—deduct a hundred pounds from the manufacturer's rating.

Second, "trim" your canoe properly. (Trim is a canoe's fore and aft stance in relation to the water's surface). By distributing cargo weight, with the heaviest packs on the bottom along the keel line, you will produce the correct trim. For downstream running in swift though not turbulent water, the bow should be slightly heavier than the stern so the current won't grasp the stern and swing it. In heavy white water, where you may have to pivot and otherwise maneuver quickly, an even trim with the weight centered amidship, or even slightly to the rear of amidship, is preferable. For upstream work, on paddling against the wind, lighten the bow slightly. And don't forget to take into consideration your own weight and that of your partner. Otherwise, you might trim your craft nicely with your gear, only to throw it out of kilter when you step aboard.

The hundred-pound deduction for adverse conditions is not the only precaution you can take. If the wind kicks up so that even a moderate load may be difficult to handle, wait for the wind to go down. On northern lakes, traveling at night after the wind has died down can be a good idea. Sleep by day, paddle by night. And when the rapids seem just a mite too vicious, tote your gear around. You'll be glad, then, for the hundred-pound deduction.

The Keel

Whether or not your canoe should be equipped with a keel depends on the use to which you will put the craft. For open water—large lakes, for example—a keel three-quarters to seven-eighths inch deep will minimize side drift caused by wind. Even for use on a small pond, a keel is a definite asset when fishing. A keelless canoe will swing or drift considerably in a light breeze, and will swerve sharply in a strong blow. At a glance, a keel may not seem to be a great deterrent to drift, but when you consider a three-quarter-inch keel on a seventeen- or eighteen-foot canoe provides close to one-hundred-and-fifty inches of water resistance, the keel's effectiveness becomes readily apparent.

On the other hand, since a keel inhibits pivoting and side pushes, it is a detriment in running water. Where a smooth bottom, minus keel, will set over easily, one with a keel will balk and respond so sluggishly that you may ram the obstruction you're trying to dodge. A river canoe should not be equipped with a keel.

In fact, most canoes come from the factory minus a keel: these days people seem mainly interested in river running, whether flat or white water. A keel can be added to almost any canoe. One notable exception is the aluminum canoe for which a keel is a structural necessity, since it binds the two halves of the craft together. The standard aluminum keel is about seven-eighths inch deep. For river running, some aluminum canoes offer the option of a "shoe keel," or "river keel," which is essentially no keel at all, but rather a faintly bulging plate along the keel line.

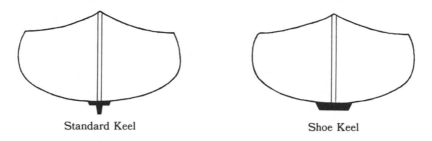

Standard Keel   Shoe Keel

Keels

It's rare, however, that a canoe is confined to lakes or rivers. While lake paddling is enjoyable, the real fun of canoeing is on fast water. If you plan to enjoy both, opt for a keelless canoe. You can live without a keel on a lake, but you can't live with it in quick water.

Seats and Gunwales

A seat may seem a trivial aspect of choosing a canoe but don't forget that you may spend considerable time perched on one, especially during a lengthy cruise. Seats are likely to be of plastic, aluminum, fiberglass, or cane or rawhide lacing in a wood frame. The least durable, but probably the most aesthetically attractive, is the caned type, intricately woven with rattan. This can be expensive to replace. A wood-framed seat laced with rawhide woven like the lacing of a snowshoe has a nice "woodsy" appearance, and the rawhide is durable. Both caned- and rawhide-laced seats should be kept well varnished to protect them against moisture. Plastic seats are durable, but since they are invariably slightly concave, puddles tend to form in them when the spray flies, soaking the seat of your pants. The problem can be partly solved by drilling two or three holes in the seat. Aluminum seats may present the same problem. In addition, they are cold.

At one time, experts derided the use of seats. The early Canadian canoes did not have them, a wide thwart being substituted. Actually, there's no reason why you can't enjoy the comfort of a seat when the sailing is smooth. But when the wind and waves come up, or when you enter wild water, slip to your knees for increased stability and control. A few canoes are purposely designed with lower-set seats for use on choppy lakes and fast water. These will provide some extra stability but they are not a substitute for kneeling when the going gets rough. Beware of canoe seats that are set so low that getting your legs back under them is difficult. In case of a spill, extricating yourself quickly isn't easy. Such seats are known as "bear traps"! Avoid them.

Gunwales are likely to be of wood, plastic or aluminum. A gunwale consists of an inwale that runs inside the hull, and an outwale, running outside. If the inwale is solid, with no drain holes, you'll have the devil's own time draining the canoe. Even when tipped over ashore, some water will remain in it. As for the outwale, it helps to turn away waves and spray if it protrudes somewhat over the outside of the hull. An outwale flush with the hull may seem neat and trim but invites water to slop aboard. A suitable outwale acts much like the spray rail on a power boat, thrusting water aside.

Length, Beam and Tumblehome

If all canoes were designed exactly alike, with the same proportion of beam to length, choosing the right canoe would be a simple matter. The longer the canoe, the greater its stability and carrying capacity. But canoe hulls are not all proportioned alike.

Even considerations of length are not as simple as they might seem at first glance. Learn to differentiate between overall length and waterline length. They are rarely the same. Many manufacturers' specifications include "overall length" or simply "length," measured between the extreme ends of the canoe and, of course, including some above-water overhang of the bow and stern. What really counts is the length when the canoe is loaded to the capacity for which it is designed. This is the waterline length. After all, it's the underwater part of the canoe that will be affected by, and will respond to, the action of water. Waterline lengths will vary among canoes of the same overall length because of varying hull shapes.

Next there is the matter of beam. You might assume that the wider a canoe is in relation to its length, the greater its capacity and stability. Up to a point this is true. But where should you measure a canoe's width for beam? Traditionally, beam has been measured at the gunwales. This is still done, but many expert canoeists now feel that the waterline beam—which may not necessarily be the same width as that at the gunwales—is a more accurate place to measure.

This brings us to "tumblehome," perhaps the most delightful word in canoe terminology. Tumblehome can be seen in profile from either end of the canoe. The canoe's sides bulge outward from the waterline, then slope inward to the gunwales so that at one point its width is greater slightly above the waterline than it is at the gunwales. This is tumblehome and it is built into virtually all canoes with noticeably flat bottoms to provide longitudinal strength. Not all canoes have tumblehome. In some cases, the gunwale width is greater than the width at the waterline, so that the hull flares outward somewhat—hence the term "flare." In rough water, flare thrusts aside spray and waves, keeping the inside of the canoe as dry as possible.

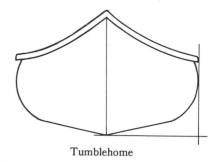
Tumblehome

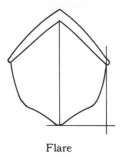
Flare

Hull-Entry Shapes

Depth

Depth, which should be measured amidship, can range from ten to fifteen inches for sixteen- to eighteen-foot canoes. Generally, the greater the depth, the greater the carrying capacity—although this is also influenced by hull shape. You'll find shallow depths in racing models, since there's little need for capacity beyond the weight of the paddlers and a minimum of gear. So-called "recreational canoes" or family-type craft will generally range in depth from twelve to thirteen inches. Canoes with fourteen- to fifteen-inch depth will stay the driest in rough water, since their depth adds considerably to freeboard—the portion of the hull above water. Also, such canoes are often the workhorses, capable of greater loads than shallower-depth craft.

Since high, upswept ends are scorned as wind catchers, one wonders why many of the old fur-trade canoes boasted such elevated stems and sterns. The famed "Canot de Maître," a thirty-six footer with a sixty-six-inch beam and a thirty-two-inch midship depth was fifty-four inches deep at each end. Yet, the canoe was functional, ashore and afloat. These craft were always heavily loaded—supplies and trade goods on the outgoing trip and furs on the return. With such loads, the canoes rode fairly low in the water and were hardly bothered by wind. At night, overturned and propped up by their high ends, they were converted into excellent shelters. Today, however, few of us sleep under our canoes. And, in any case, modern canoes, with their low profiles, provide poor shelter.

Some height is necessary at each end, of course. Even the flat racing models incorporate a small degree of sheer, the upsweep along the gunwale from amidship to each end. Used in heavy white water or during a rough lake crossing, a low-ended canoe could "submarine," or plunge into a wave rather than riding over it. As a result, most canoes used for white water, fishing or cruising incorporate a pronounced sheer. Canoe designers differ regarding bow and stern depth, and there are no hard and fast rules governing it.

Hull Shape

When considering hull shape, some subtle delineations appear, so that canoe features cannot be compared in terms of linear measurements. However, if you look at a canoe hull in profile, it becomes easy to assess the difference. Take "rocker," for example.

Rocker is the upsweep of the keel line from amidship to each end which allows the canoe to balance fore and aft and to pivot readily at its center. Since much of their travel was on rocky, rapids-strewn eastern rivers, many early Indian birch-bark canoe builders included varying degrees of rocker in their craft. Some Passamaquoddy canoes incorporated only a gentler rocker line not unlike that found on many of today's white-water canoes. The Ungava Cree, on the other hand, built in a pronounced rocker, so much so that one of their craft became known as a "crooked canoe." Not even the wildest water fazed these superb canoemen. Their center-pivoting canoes twisted and turned at the stroke of a paddle. While canoes with pronounced rocker handle nicely in turbulent rapids, they become slow "pushers" on flat water, their speed and ease of paddling cut down considerably. Indians were aware of this, of course, and for flat-water travel they developed canoes with a straight keel line.

Now consider the shape of a hull as seen from above. In some canoes, the fullness or width of the midship beam is carried forward and aft so that the hull ends are relatively blunt. This contributes to carrying capacity and initial stability; such canoes will ride up and over waves nicely. When lightly laden they paddle easily, since they sit rather high on the water, but when they're loaded, paddling becomes a tedious chore. Slow canoes that plow through the water, they are affectionately referred to as "river pigs."

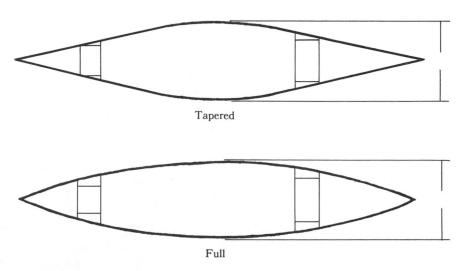

Tapered

Full

Hull Shapes—Overhead View

On the other hand, if the hull tapers sharply fore and aft, some carrying capacity and stability may be lost. But the result is a faster canoe, one that surges ahead with each paddle stroke. Increasingly, modern canoes designed for tripping have adopted a variation of this form. At the waterline, the hull is sharply tapered for easy cutting through the water while, at the gunwale line, the fullness is carried forward, producing a flare—and a drier canoe. This also gives the craft the ability to lift up and over waves.

We next come to symmetry—or the deliberate lack of it. Most canoes are balanced fore and aft: the shape of the stern as seen from above is identical to that of the forward half, in canoe terminology a "balanced symmetry." In contrast, an asymmetrical hull has its maximum beam slightly back of midship so that the stern half of the canoe is more blunt than the forward half. This design aims at the greatest possible hydrodynamic efficiency, engineering jargon for speed with ease of paddling. Such a hull has a fine forward entry, knifing through the water while at the same time allowing displaced water to flow smoothly by the stern with a minimum of disturbance. While racing hulls are most often assymetrical, a few cruising models have also adopted this design.

Bottom shapes vary considerably. This can be seen by looking at a canoe's cross-section in profile, from either end. In the belief that it is the most stable, novices traditionally opt for a flat-bottomed canoe. And there is justification for this. It requires a concerted effort to tip such a craft, especially since the flat bottom is usually carried well to the sides. Almost invariably there is a pronounced tumblehome for longitudinal rigidity. Lightly loaded, the flat-bottom canoe paddles easily and responds well; heavily laden, it plods. When equipped with a keel, it's a reasonably good flat-water craft. Stable and safe, it's generally considered to be a "family canoe." It's also good for fly fishermen who like to stand when casting. But for white water and extensive cruising, you can find more suitable models.

The round-bottom canoe, for example, is faster and, when properly loaded, probably more stable—though it has always had its detractors. Northern guides, accustomed to their big (often twenty footers) flat-bottom craft, looked on the round-bottom model as a "fool killer." This is unjustified prejudice. Most of the big freighters used in the fur trade for lake travel had deeply rounded bottoms. With their tremendous cargoes stowed low in the hull, these canoes were amazingly

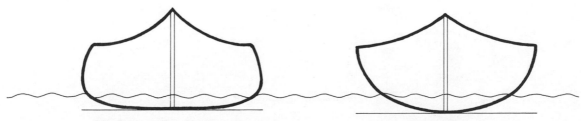

Flat Bottom with Tumblehome   Round Bottom

Hull Shapes—End View

stable and could ride out water that drove other craft ashore. As for such a canoe being "tippy," they were—when only lightly loaded.

The shallow-arch bottom is much like the round bottom, the main difference being that its depth in relation to its width is not as great. It, too, isn't as stable as the flat bottom. But load it properly and you have a seaworthy craft that is fast and responsive.

The shallow-vee bottom is just what its name implies. Seen in profile, it is an obtuse vee, with the apex at the keel line. Generally, the vee flattens amidship. This configuration makes for speed and firm tracking. It helps keep a canoe on course almost as well as does a keel, but without the detrimental effects of a keel when it comes to maneuvering. The shallow vee cuts down a great deal on the bow lift that accompanies each paddle stroke. Instead of bobbing fore and aft, the craft cuts straight ahead. This efficiency has not gone unnoticed among builders of cruising and freighter-type canoes. And, almost invariably, shallow vee canoes incorporate noticeable flare, as opposed to the tumblehome in flat-bottom craft.

The shallow vee lacks some initial stability, but it's probably the best all-around recreational hull design. Empty, it simply is not as stable as the flat-bottom. However, when a shallow-vee canoe starts to tip, it seems to take on what might be called a "secondary stability." It will tip just so far, and then "fetches up."

There are also deep-vee canoes. Quite unstable for general recreational use, they are just about unbeatable in competition. This is the canoe for racers.

WHICH CANOE FOR YOU?

There is no all-around, all-purpose canoe. However, except for racing models and ultra-lightweight craft, most will adapt to a variety of situations. So, when buying a canoe, first consider your primary interest—cruising, white-water running, fishing and hunting, or possibly just lazy paddling on a nearby lake or stream.

Assume that you want a canoe to keep at your cottage at the lake. You and your wife enjoy the outdoors but have no particular desire to take a long, extended trip. You have two children, both good swimmers and old enough to paddle. In your case, aluminum or fiberglass, in the medium-price range, is a good choice. You really have no need for ABS. Shop for a craft in the sixteen-to eighteen-foot range,

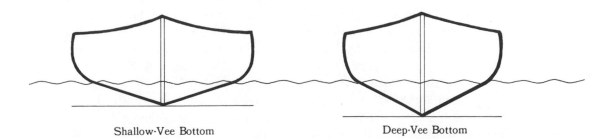

Shallow-Vee Bottom   Deep-Vee Bottom

with a thirty-five- to thirty-six-inch beam, a flat bottom for stability, and a rated capacity of about 650 pounds. A keel will be helpful on the lake. Rocker is unimportant so disregard it. Since there will be times when all four of you may want to go out together, be sure to choose a canoe that can easily hold your combined weight. Yet a pair of youngsters (wearing life jackets, of course) should be able to handle the same canoe on their own. A midship depth of at least twelve inches is called for. A canoe that weighs between sixty-five and seventy-eight pounds can be conveniently lifted in and out of the water, or on top of a car. Check the chart on page 224. None of these qualities will produce a fast canoe nor one that is well-suited to white water but, otherwise, you will have one that comes close to being an "all-purpose" craft. That is to say, it will suit all *your* purposes.

Suppose your favorite sport is fly fishing on ponds and small rivers. You're not interested in extended trips or white-water running. You simply want a canoe that is stable and easy to transport on your car. Choose a thirteen-footer with a forty-inch beam (which is four inches wider than many eighteen-footers). The bottom is flat, the keel line straight. In such a canoe you can even stand to cast and, since it weighs only about sixty pounds, you can single-handedly cartop it if need be. This can be justly termed a "pond canoe," ideal for fishing but not one you'll want to paddle a great distance.

There's a growing interest in solo paddling among those who like to drive their craft at speeds that cause its wake to gurgle and who thrill at the maneuverability of small canoes. For them there are eleven-, twelve- and thirteen-foot craft, weighing thirty-two to forty-four pounds, with beams ranging from thirty-two to thirty-three inches. Some have shallow-vee bottoms.

Perhaps the most notable of all small canoes was the Sairey Gamp built by Henry Rushton in 1883 for "Nessmuk" (the pseudonym of the naturalist George Washington Sears). The canoe, named after a character in Dickens' *Martin Chuzzlewit,* was nine feet long with a beam of twenty-six inches, a center depth of six inches, and it weighed ten-and-a-half pounds! Nessmuk, who weighed only 110 pounds, obviously traveled light during his numerous cruises among the Adirondack lakes. Of the canoe, he wrote: "The Sairey Gamp has only ducked me once in a six weeks' cruise, and that by my own carelessness." You can see the Sairey Gamp today, at the Adirondack Museum at Blue Mountain Lake, New York.

Many of us, of course, feel the call to adventure, an irresistible urge to explore a distant wilderness river, one that may be little more than a winding blue line on the map, bordered by vast empty spaces. If you're going to be out in the wilderness for ten days or more, you'll need a canoe that can freight a substantial outfit, perhaps up to a half ton, through all sorts of water—wild rapids, wave-tossed lakes and swift, though quiet, streams. You'll need a canoe that's tough. ABS fabric is a good choice, ideally in a sixteen- or seventeen-foot length, fifteen inches or so in midship depth, with a shallow-vee bottom, some rocker, flared sides and at least a thirty-four-inch beam. The eighteen-foot model may present some problems in close quarters among rocks that are liberally strewn in a pitch of white water.

The sixteen-footer is a superb white-water canoe, though not when loaded to capacity. With two skilled paddlers aboard, and a minimal amount of gear, it responds beautifully and will stay reasonably dry. If you want to make a specialty of running white water, try a sixteen-and-a-quarter-footer with a twenty-seven-inch gunwale beam, a fifteen-inch depth and a shallow vee-bottom. It has won honors in national white-water competition. The manufacturer warns, however, that it's "for experienced paddlers only."

For flat-water racing, designs differ radically from trip-type and white-water canoes. One favorite is an eighteen-and-a-half-footer with a thirty-three-inch beam, twenty-nine inches at the waterline, a depth of eleven inches, a shallow-arch bottom and a straight keel line. Even without seeing it, those lines are a tip-off. Long, fast and sleek, it's made for one purpose only—winning flat-water races.

To match a canoe to your requirements is not as baffling as it may seem if you have never before run into such terms as "rocker," "shallow vee," "tumblehome" and "flare". When you're ready to buy your first canoe, reread this chapter and make notes on the features you require. It's often suggested that you rent a canoe before buying it. This may mislead you. Many canoe liveries only keep on hand canoes designed for durability rather than for performance. You'd be better off seeking advice from experts.

PADDLES

The old-time formula for length called for a paddle that reached from your toes to your chin for the bow, or from toes to eyes for the stern. Old-time guides wielded long paddles, often six-footers, even six-and-a-half-footers if they anticipated paddling while standing, not an uncommon practice. The longer paddles, they felt, afforded more leverage and a deeper, fuller sweep with the blade. Such long paddles—fine for lake and flat-water paddling—are unwieldly, and inhibit quick maneuvering. Many of today's canoeists prefer shorter paddles, thus cutting down on the wide-arc recovery time in racing and white-water maneuvering. The blades of these paddles run four to five inches shorter than the twenty-six- to twenty-eight-inch blades of the traditional Maine Guide paddles. As a result, you could end up with a paddle that's much too long if you determine length by the old floor-to-chin method. What counts is shaft length. To get a proper fit, sit in a canoe with the paddle blade almost throat-deep in the water. The paddle's grip should then be at shoulder level.

Another requirement among early paddlers was flexibility or "whippiness" in the shaft. They had a point. During a day's travel you'll probably take up to ten thousand strokes. With each of these, a faint shock, hardly perceptible early in the day, will be telegraphed to your arms and shoulders. As the day progresses, you'll become increasingly conscious of it. A maple paddle or, preferably, an ash blade, will absorb much of this shock effect. It seems a trivial matter, until you've put in several hours of hard paddling. Nonetheless, most of today's paddlers seem to prefer laminated paddles that have little, if any, flexibility, but are more durable.

Blade width can stir up controversy. A narrow blade, five to six inches, is easier to draw through the water than one eight inches or wider, but it gives you less purchase, which means more strokes per mile and a slower response by the canoe. The wide blade, on the other hand, drives a canoe faster and brings about a quicker response; it's also more tiring.

Blade widths run from five to ten inches. For racing, paddlers seem to favor blades eight or more inches wide. However, when such blades are used on ex-tended canoe trips, they can be a hindrance. They inhibit quick maneuvering in white water, and on a windy lake they tend to "sail" when caught by the wind and must be feathered. Because of the powerful thrusts they afford, many canoeists stick to the wide blades. On the whole, though, if you're going to paddle all day, mile after mile, five- to eight-inch blades are preferable.

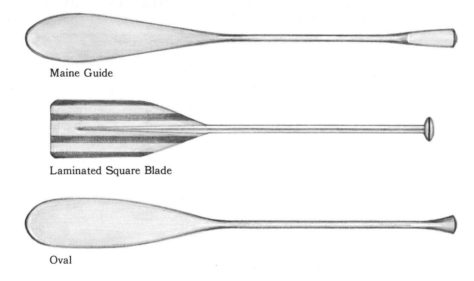

Maine Guide

Laminated Square Blade

Oval

Canoe-Blade Shapes

Blades come in four basic shapes. The oval blade, up to twelve inches wide, is popular. Generally, this has a relatively short overall length, forty-eight to sixty-two inches for quick, powerful strokes. Square blades are common among lamin-ated and fiberglass paddles. The bottom of the blade is cut off square, and often a horizontal piece is fitted across the bottom for reinforcement. The square corners provide a greater bite but they are noisy and not well suited to stealthy paddling. Such blades in a nine-inch width and twenty-two-inch length or thereabouts are adapted to flat-water use, while similar shapes, roughly eight inches wide and twenty-six inches long, are used in white water. Two other shapes, the Beavertail and the Maine Guide, are similar, usually found in one-piece all-wood paddles.

The Beavertail is more nearly oval, while the Maine Guide carries its width farther up the blade. An eight-inch width is typical of both these styles, though narrower models are available. Both offer good purchase and are quiet as well as graceful.

Most laminated paddles are light, a joy to wield and are often available in increments of one or two inches: choosing the right length is not a problem. There is little "whip" in laminated paddles but they are rugged. This isn't to say that you can use them for prying canoes off rocks, nor should they be used for poling. Laminations may include spruce, hickory, mahogany and even cedar, in varying combinations.

A relative newcomer among laminated paddles is the bent-shaft model, in which the blade is angled at about fifteen degrees from the shaft. It is used with the blade angled forward. It was originally devised for flat-water racing, and it still sees very specialized use. The effectiveness of the bent-shaft paddle is best explained by pointing out what happens to a canoe when it is driven by conventional paddles. Initially, blade power is directed downward; then, as the paddle completes its arc through the water, that force is directed upward. This causes the canoe to bob fore and aft, seriously cutting down on speed. With the bent shaft, the blade's arc is modified so that a greater proportion of forward thrust is maintained during the latter part of the stroke; bobbing is reduced. Thus the canoe's momentum is directed on a more level keel. It's with the short, quick strokes of a racing paddler that the bent-shaft blade attains peak efficiency.

Bent-Shaft Paddle

There are also paddles similar to the laminated types with blades of ABS, plastic, fiberglass or Kevlar®, all with aluminum shafts. In some instances, the shaft is covered with a plastic sleeve, and since the shaft is hollow and sealed at both ends, such paddles will float handle up; they are easily spotted in the water for retrieval. But their best features are strength and durability. While they lack

Aluminum/Plastic Paddle

the "whip" of longer, all-wood paddles, their light weight pays off when quick maneuvering is called for, as well as during extended cruising. They are probably less tiring to use than any other type of paddle.

Among the one-piece, all-wood paddles, lengths range from forty-eight to seventy-two inches; the blades usually have the Beavertail or Maine Guide shape. Among these you have a choice of spruce, maple and ash. Spruce is the lightest and least expensive, but tends to be stiff and brittle, and is easily broken by a burly paddler. Maple is heavy but the sturdiest of the three, and, as noted, is quite flexible. Not surprisingly, it's the most expensive. Ash seems to be a good compromise between the stiffness and brittleness of spruce and the weight of maple. But maple and ash paddles must never be left in the hot sun—on the beach after landing, for example—because the blades will warp quickly.

Grips vary. Particularly for racing and white-water running, many of the newer-style paddles are equipped with T-grips. These afford the best lateral control, but until you get used to them, you may experience some wrist discomfort.

Many of the square-blade paddles, most of the Beavertail and some Maine Guide models have an oval knob for a grip. Because you can slide your hand to one side of the grip, still retaining firm control, they are comfortable to use. These oval knobs vary greatly, some being rather broad, others little more than a small fistful of wood. Still another style is found on some Maine Guide-type paddles. The throat—the point at which the shaft joins the grip—broadens to the full width of the grip at the same time flattening out, thus providing additional spring or flexing. The grip is a compromise between the T-grip and the oval knob.

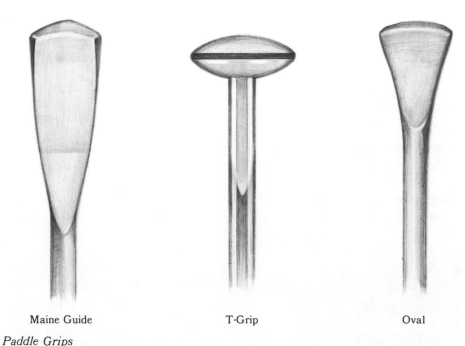

Maine Guide   T-Grip   Oval

Paddle Grips

Obviously then, after looking over the assortment of paddles, you have a wide selection. If the paddle you choose has a wooden shaft, you can build in added years of service and greater durability: soak the paddle in water until the wood's grain is raised, producing a rough surface. Dry the shaft, then sandpaper it until smooth. Next rub in boiled linseed oil. This will be absorbed into the wood fibers, increasing strength and resiliency. Also the finish will protect your hands from blistering. The blade itself does not require this treatment. Instead, apply one or two thin coats of spar varnish. And lastly, there's one hard and fast rule to follow. During a trip, particularly an extended one, always carry at least one spare paddle for every two persons in the party.

THE SETTING POLE

There is increasing interest in poling, enough so that the American Canoe Association sanctions competitions. It's done in a standing position, either solo or with a partner. Generally, a pole will take your canoe where a paddle cannot—up a swift run or through moderate rapids, or along a shallow stream with insufficient depth for the paddle blade. Downstream running is feasible, too.

Poles range from ten to fourteen feet, with the twelve-footers probably most popular, especially among competition polers. In the Northeast longer poles are favored, often fourteen-footers, of maple or ash fitted at one end with a soft-iron "shoe," which affords a firm grip on the bottom. Also available is a twelve-foot, two-piece pole, the bottom end fitted with an aluminum shoe. Pole diameters run between one- and-a-quarter inches and one- and-three-fourths inches, with a weight up to six pounds.

Along waterways of the Ozark region, aluminum poles have come into use in recent years, developed for competition. In their excellent book, *Canoe Poling,* Al, Syl and Frank Beletz suggest a twelve-foot length of aluminum with a one- and-one-eighth-inch diameter. Such a pole weighs between two- and-one-half and two- and three-quarter pounds, less than half the weight of most wooden poles. A tubular aluminum pole should be sealed at each end with a wooden plug so that it will float. Generally, there's no need for a shoe although various types of spikes have been improvised. Whatever you use, avoid long, slender spikes. These will sink too easily into mud and sand and readily lodge in a rocky crevice. A blunt shoe is best.

If you're at ease with a paddle, you'll find that poling is not especially difficult to learn. For your first attempt, choose a shallow lakeshore, sheltered from the wind, poling a course parallel to the shoreline in no more than two feet of water. Stand just back of the center of the canoe (if it's otherwise unladen) so that it's trimmed with the bow only slightly raised. With knees flexed just a bit, face about forty-five degrees off your bow. Now, drop the pole to the bottom just back of your position and as close to the canoe as possible. With both hands thrust the pole backward. Be prepared for a sudden burst of speed. A pole affords far greater purchase than a paddle and your canoe will respond accordingly. As the craft moves forward, continue pressure against the bottom, "climbing the pole" hand over hand until you reach the top. At this point, snap the pole upward with your upper hand, sliding it through your lower hand, so that it clears the water. Then repeat the process, taking another bite on the bottom. At first, your course will be erratic, but with practice you'll learn to alter your thrust in order to steer. Once you've acquired confidence and initial skill along a lakeshore, move into slowly flowing water with a few obstructions; then, as skill improves, into more difficult water.

Poling

Snubbing is actually "applying the brakes." Practice this along the lakeshore, too. While your canoe glides ahead, reverse the pole's position, pointing it forward. Drop the shoe to the bottom as far forward as you can reach and, again, as close to the gunwale as possible. When doing this, brace yourself. Your canoe will come to an abrupt stop. As you move into flowing water with this technique, snubbing cannot be expected to stop your canoe completely if the current is swift or powerful. Instead, each probe against the bottom with your pole increasingly slows the canoe. Don't try to stop too suddenly; you'll be pitched over backward. Once you feel confident enough to tackle more and more difficult water, poling becomes exciting—and highly practical.

Tandem poling can be tricky. Both polers should be of approximately equal skill and fine coordination is required. Here again, practice does it.

SQUARE-STERN CANOES

A square-stern canoe is not a double-ender chopped off to accommodate a transom on which to hang a motor. It is designed, from stem to stern, for outboard use.

Extra ribs reinforce the hull and spray rails are built in along the sides to turn flying spume. Usually there's a keel. All this adds up to greater weight than in paddling canoes.

The hull material in square sterns includes fiberglass, aluminum, wood/canvas, cedar strips, polyethylene or even Kevlar®, although not all of these materials are available in all lengths.

Stability as well as capacity is important. Some of the shorter models have a generous beam, an eleven-footer with a forty-four-inch width, for example. By way of contrast, a popular nineteen-foot model has an identical beam, its stability deriving from its length and flat bottom. Generally, the longer types are easier to paddle when necessary because of their low width-to-length ratio. A seventeen-footer with a thirty-six-inch beam will handle more easily than a twelve-foot model with a forty-four-inch beam.

OUTBOARD MOTORS

When distances are great and time limited, a motor will make an otherwise impossible trip feasible. Also, with a powered canoe you can supply a remote cabin or transport gear to a temporary hunting camp. It will get you to the best fishing grounds quickly and, if you like to troll, you can cover more water with greater ease than with paddles.

Many canoe manufacturers offer a detachable bracket that will fit their canoes, and possibly a number of other brands, though it's doubtful that there exists a universal type that will fit all canoes. There are simply too many variations in canoe construction. Most brackets are rigged with clamps that lock to the gunwales just back of the stern seat.

The bracket should be set low enough to permit the motor's lower housing to submerge fully, even when your canoe is bobbing in rough water. Otherwise, cavitation occurs. The propeller surfaces, sucks in air, the motor races and then, as the propeller drops back into the water, the motor lugs.

Whether a canoe has a keel or not will have little effect on its performance with a motor. What is important is trim. Load the canoe so that the bow is slightly higher than the stern. A bow-heavy canoe, under power, answers the tiller sluggishly, resisting turns, particularly sharp ones.

An outboard-powered double-ender is a highly practical craft. Many canoemen prefer it to the square-stern canoe. With the square stern, the motor's tiller is behind the pilot so that steering requires awkward bending of the arm and wrist. With the side-mounted bracket, the tiller is conveniently at your side. True, a side-mounted motor drives a canoe somewhat less efficiently than one mounted directly astern on the transom. This deficiency, however, is really quite slight. Another problem with the side mount occurs not on the water, but ashore. Once you have unloaded your canoe while it's still afloat, there's no ballast to offset the weight of the motor. Your canoe may flip over. It's always a good rule to remove your motor before you unload, or to beach your canoe first.

When choosing a motor for your canoe, whether it's a square-stern model or a double-ender rigged with a bracket, respect the canoe manufacturer's recommendations. As power is increased beyond them, you soon reach a point of diminishing returns. A canoe is a displacement craft, not a planing hull. No matter how much power you apply, your canoe will not lift and skim along like a speedboat. You merely risk damage to your canoe. It is not built to withstand the stress of excessive power and there's great danger that too much power will flip the craft, particularly if sharp turns are attempted.

A two- to three-horsepower motor is generally more than adequate for a bracket-rigged double-ender. It will propel you at speeds far greater than are possible with paddles. You may be able to use a five-horsepower motor on larger double-enders, eighteen-footers, for example, especially if you plan to buck swift-flowing, heavy water. As for the square-stern's powerhouse, manufacturers of even the big nineteen-footers limit their recommendations to five horsepower—seven and a half at the most.

Modern outboard motors are extremely reliable if properly cared for. Maintain the correct oil/gas mixture, and be sure to keep the lower housing greased. However, breakdowns can occur and, far from home, they can be disconcerting. Carry one or two extra spark plugs correctly gapped; an extra propeller if you'll be traveling far from your base; and a tube of housing grease. If your motor is an older model lacking an automatic clutch, don't forget a supply of shear pins. In a pinch, a 6d or 8d common nail, cut to proper length with wire cutters, can be substituted for a shear pin. Estimate your fuel needs realistically. Before undertaking an extended trip, determine your mileage for a full tank and carry the indicated amount of gasoline (and oil). Bear in mind that you'll get good mileage running downriver whereas bucking a strong current, or against strong wind, you'll use gas at an alarming rate.

Tools are important. Examine your motor for fittings that might require either special tools or special sizes. Some handy tools are pump pliers (their expanding jaws are versatile); both a regular and a Phillips screwdriver; a small set of open-end wrenches; a spark-plug wrench; and a pair of vice-grip pliers.

CANOE ACCESSORIES

Life Vests

Most modern canoes will float, albeit with varying degrees of buoyancy, but this isn't necessarily true of their occupants. Although discussed under the heading of "Canoe Accessories," life jackets (now designated by the Coast Guard as "Personal Flotation Devices") should never be considered optional. In many states they are mandatory, even in canoes, and on all coastal waters under the jurisdiction of the Coast Guard as well. Generally, it is required that PFDs be carried aboard all watercraft, though not that they be worn. However, a life jacket in the bottom of your canoe will do you little good when you flip. Climbing into it while you're in the water is difficult at best, and virtually impossible in rough water.

Heavy white water has incredible suction power, along with waves having the striking force of a pile driver and aerated water that will barely float a Ping-Pong ball. If you spill into such a maelstrom without a PFD, the odds for your survival are slim.

A suitable life jacket, properly fitted, should not impede paddling and, of course, it should keep your head well above the water and protect you from bruises should you strike a rock. It should fit snugly enough so that it cannot slip free over your head, with some sort of a belt or drawstring to secure it in place. While snug fit is important, the PFD must also be large enough to fit over a wool shirt or wet suit. A bright color—yellow, orange or red—will make it easy for rescuers to spot you.

There are three basic models of PFDs. One is the kapok or foam-filled horse-collar type designated by the Coast Guard as "Type II Flotation Devices." These provide excellent flotation but they are bothersome to many canoeists. Durability depends on the type of fill. Kapok-filled models are neither as dependable nor as durable as those filled with foam. Once the plastic tubes containing the kapok are punctured, the fill absorbs water and loses virtually all its buoyancy. Models filled with closed-cell foam will not lose their buoyancy. The major drawback of this type of PFD is that it does not provide much upper-body protection against rocks in heavy water.

A better type of PFD—designated by the Coast Guard as the Type III life jacket—has closed-cell foam for flotation, a nylon shell and a mesh interior. There are usually five to ten layers of foam sandwiched between the shell and the mesh lining. This style is comfortable, restricts paddling less and provides good protec-

  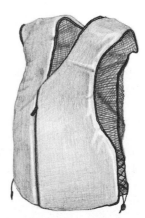

Segmented Tube   Kapok Horsecollar   Closed-Cell Foam

Three Types of PFDs

tion for the upper body. Most models are light, weighing about one-and-three-quarters pounds. The Type III lifejacket also serves as a windbreaker while you're paddling, though it may chafe the underarms slightly during a long haul.

Another Type III PFD is the segmented-tube model. It includes a nylon shell and interior lining, with polyethylene foam tubes between them. It's comfortable, weighs about one pound, does not restrict you when you're paddling and does not chafe the underarms. Despite its minimal bulk it does a good job of keeping you afloat and protecting you in the water.

For any type of PFD, nylon zippers are best, being more durable than metal and easier to slide up and down. And they won't rust.

Seat cushions (Type IV PFDs), though complying with the laws in some states, are not recommended. In quiet water you might be able to cling to one but in the turbulence of white water where you'll need both hands to fend off rocks, a boat cushion is next to useless.

Repair Kits

Occasionally you'll wrap a canoe around a rock and, unless the hull is made of ABS or polyethylene, your loss will be total. However, most canoe damage is not that serious—usually small breaks or tears in the skin that can be repaired at streamside. Carry a repair kit that includes duct tape. This will stick even to damp surfaces until more permanent repairs can be made.

For a wood/canvas canoe the kit should include a tube of Duco® or Ambroid® cement, a piece of cotton fabric (preferably light canvas), a spool of nylon thread and a heavy needle. Lift the edges of the gash slightly. Cut an oval or round patch of fabric somewhat larger than the tear. Work this in so that it lies flat between the canvas and the planking, then daub it liberally with cement. Allow this to dry until it becomes tacky, a matter of a few minutes. Now press down the edges of the canvas, and apply a second patch on the outside, also well daubed with cement. It will dry quickly. If the gash is extensive, sew the two edges together after applying the inner patch. Then apply another patch outside. If you lack a repair kit, all is not lost. Cut patches from a cotton shirt and cement these with spruce pitch heated until it melts. Spruce pitch will hold as well as cement, as will pine or balsam fir pitch.

Aluminum damage is likely to consist of dents. Don't bother about the small ones. They won't seriously affect the canoe's performance. Also, trying to work the aluminum skin back into shape may stretch it, causing some loss of strength. If the dent is major, and one that makes the canoe difficult to manage, you'll have to risk stretching the material. You can pound out such dents by using a boot with a rock in it as a hammer. The rock alone is hard on aluminum. Another method is to float the canoe in shallow water and, while your partner steadies it, stomp on the interior until you've restored a sufficient degree of form to make the canoe usable.

There are rare instances when the aluminum may be punctured. An aluminum repair kit should include an epoxy putty and duct tape. Work the putty into the break with a knife point, then tape both surfaces, inside and out. Lacking putty, use chewing gum. Aluminum canoe manufacturers supply kits for permanent repairs, but since they require the use of an electric drill and rivets, they are not suitable for backcountry use. These are primarily home-repair kits.

A riverside fiberglass patch job is likely to be somewhat crude; try to make do with duct tape until you get home. Bear in mind that an improvised patch will make work more difficult if you intend to restore your canoe to its original gleaming appearance later on. A fiberglass repair kit should include fiberglass cloth in seven-and-a-quarter- or ten-ounce weight, a small supply of quick-curing epoxy or a polyester resin plus a hardening agent, a fine-grit sandpaper, a small paintbrush and duct tape. A tin can will do as a mixing container.

If the break requires more than duct tape to seal it, cut away the jagged edges of fiberglass back to the point where they are solid and firm. Briskly sandpaper the area around the hole, approximately one-and-a-half to two inches. Now apply narrow strips of duct tape on the inside, conforming to the hull's contours in such a manner that they partially cover the damage. Apply a couple of layers of fiberglass cloth over the duct tape, then daub liberally with resin. Fit several layers of the cloth in the hole from the outside, again being generous with the resin. When the hole is filled to its original thickness, apply larger overlapping patches on the outside. Once the resin has set, such a patch will get you home.

Although punctures of the ABS hulls are rare, manufacturers do provide repair kits and instructions. Limited damage can be mended with fiberglass cloth and a suitable epoxy. Some epoxies, however, will not bond well to ABS surfaces. (Among those which have proven effective are: Ren 1250®, Epoxical 606®, Uniroyal OC 2490® and Thermoset 110®.) Epoxybond® putty also works well. Cut away the ragged edges of the break, removing as little of the material as possible. With a knife point, scour the foam sandwich filling around the perimeter of the hole. Sandpaper the vinyl exterior briskly, then wipe clean. Apply the putty, working it into the scoured edges thoroughly, then squeeze these together tightly. Next apply two thicknesses of fiberglass cloth over the break, inside the hull and out.

Some claim that polyethylene hulls are even tougher than those of ABS and the possibility of a puncture even more remote. If this is true, it's a blessing indeed, since polyethylene hulls are virtually impossible to repair in the field. About all you can do is to seal any break with duct tape. Repair kits are available for home repairs but these involve the use of a propane or butane torch, an item not usually carried on canoe trips.

Other items that might be included in a repair kit, no matter what the material of your hull, are a small roll of soft copper wire for patching up broken seats and thwarts (No. 26 or 28), a pair of pliers and a screwdriver.

Portaging and Carrying Yokes

If your canoe has a center thwart and you anticipate only short portages, you can probably do without a carrying yoke. Simply rest the thwart across the back of your neck with a folded wool shirt or sweater for padding. Incidentally, with or without a yoke, a horsecollar-type PFD cushions beautifully. It may seem out of place on a carry but since you have to tote it over anyway, why not enjoy the comfort it affords?

Portage Yoke

For long carries—a half mile or more—a yoke of some sort is useful. A carrying yoke is usually made of hardwood curved to fit around the back of the neck, its sides resting on the shoulders. Another style has cushioned shoulder pads. Some are rigged with clamps that lock to the gunwales, so that they can be removed when not in use. Another model is bolted permanently, and is a substitute for the center thwart. The latter is generally preferable to the clamp-on type because the canoe rides lower and there's no danger of the clamps working loose; nor are there wing nuts to lose.

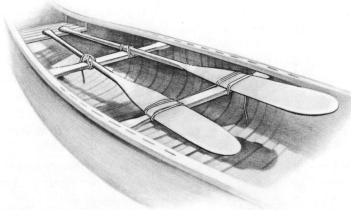

Improvised Yoke

Lacking a ready-made yoke, you can lash two paddles to the center thwart with the blades protruding a few inches forward of it so that, when the canoe is inverted, the flat of the blades rests on your shoulders. Be sure that the paddles are lashed on top of the thwart, not under it, so that the canoe's weight rests on the thwart, not on the lashings, which might give way.

Planning can make portages somewhat easier. Before starting on your trip, eliminate all nonessential gear. Leave behind any item that you're likely to use only once or twice. And, once you're underway, don't carry loose clutter in the canoe. Have everything in a pack, or lashed to one. A pack is easier to tote than an armload of fishing tackle, camera and map cases, binoculars and canteen. Ideally, a portage should require only a single trip across, with one person toting the canoe and a light pack, and his partner going ahead with the rest of the outfit. You may not always be able to achieve such neat organization but it's worth striving for.

Organize your packs. Load one with such relatively light items as the sleeping bags and the tent, which one partner can carry with the canoe. Lash spare paddles in the canoe, in such a manner that it balances well, just a mite stern heavy. (This raises the bow enough so that you can see ahead on the trail.) In another larger pack, or two medium-sized ones, load the grub, cooking gear and miscellaneous items for the second partner to tote across. The person toting the canoe should not carry equipment in his hands, which should be free to help him balance his load as he walks. The person under the remaining packs, however, may possibly carry cased fishing rods, or an axe if it's part of your outfit (be sure it's sheathed). However you arrange your packs, remember that a second trip over a portage does not double the required time. It triples it.

Incidentally, it's wise for the pack toter to walk ahead of the person carrying the canoe. With an axe or hatchet, he can clear fallen limbs or blowdowns. If these cannot be cleared, he can drop his packs and assist with getting the canoe by any obstructions.

Painters and Bailers

Line is indispensable in canoeing. The chief use is probably for painters, with a twenty- to twenty-five-foot length attached to each end of the canoe, essential on river trips, highly recommended on lakes. Canoeists used to carry fifty to one hundred feet of quarter-inch manila rope, for lining a canoe through the rapids and for a dozen other uses around camp. Today, synthetics such as nylon and olefin have replaced manila. They're stronger and, while they stretch under stress, they're more stable than manila, which shrinks when wet, stretches when it dries and eventually rots.

Lining consists of floating the canoe downstream (or pulling it up), controlling it by means of a pair of lines, one attached to each end of the craft. One or more persons handles each line. Sometimes the canoe is lined fully loaded but, in a critical situation involving unusually rough water, the load may be removed to lighten the canoe. In both downstream and upstream lining, the force of the current is used to help steer the canoe. For example, in lining upstream, if you pull the stern closer to shore while you relax the bow line, the canoe will "ferry" toward midstream. The opposite is true if the bow line is taken in and the stern painter let out; the current will ferry the craft toward shore. In this manner the canoe is guided around rocks as it is worked up- or downriver. Lining has limited application. It works well in moderately turbulent water, but if the rapids are violent, you'll risk swamping or flipping your canoe. The technique calls for good judgment and an understanding of the forces of running water. Try lining on an easy set of rips if you're interested in learning how. Upstream lining can be tough work, and may endanger your canoe if you misjudge.

Downstream lining is usually easier since the current does just about all the work. But downstream lining still requires judgment. Relaxing the stern line and pulling in the bow line will edge your canoe toward the center of the stream. Pull in the stern line and the current will set the canoe toward shore. Under the right conditions it's possible to line through a set of rips without getting your feet wet, but don't count on it. Ideal conditions—the right current and a passable assortment of river boulders—are rare. You may have to wade to help guide your canoe.

When you're underway, painters should remain attached to the bow and stern, ready for instant use. Elastic shockcord loops can be used to hold the coiled lines, or if it's not likely that the coils will be needed, they can be stuck to the inside of the canoe with duct tape. Don't just coil the lines loosely on the floor. Inevitably they'll become a tangled mess. It's perilously easy to be dragged under if lines entangle your legs during a capsize.

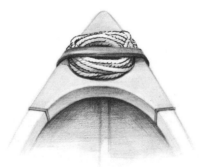

Painters Strapped to the Bow and Stern Deck Plates of a Canoe

No one likes to have water sloshing around in the bilge. What's more it makes for needless extra weight. Carry a bailer. The simplest is a plastic bleach bottle cut to form a scoop. Tie the bailer to a seat or thwart. A sponge also does a good job. With the canoe slightly higher at one end than the other, water will run to the lower end where it can be easily sponged or scooped out without your having to unload.

Deck and Spray Covers

There are times when bailing is not feasible—while traversing a wind-blown lake, for example. Paddling in the rain, too, will result in water accumulating in the bilge. A spray cover can help. It snaps on over the gunwales, running the full length of the canoe, with oval-shaped openings or ports equipped with skirts that tie about the paddlers' waists. These ties should be of the quick-release type in case of a spill. The ports are usually designed so that you can paddle sitting or kneeling and some spray covers include a midship port through which gear can be stowed or removed.

Commercial spray covers are usually of coated nylon and are likely to incorporate a cable that fits around the gunwales and is kept tight by one or more small turnbuckles. In effect, a spray cover converts an open canoe to a covered craft. However, the spray cover has limitations. It is not recommended for heavy white water where the pounding of standing waves or the weight of large volumes of water may pull loose the snaps or turnbuckles.

You can improvise some protection against spray or rain for your cargo simply by draping a tarp over it, tucking the edges under the gunwales to keep the wind from blowing them free. This is, however, a stopgap method. It will keep some water from your gear but bailing will still be required.

In white water, most canoeists try to increase flotation—offsetting the weight of the water that sprays aboard—by wedging air bags, old inner tubes (inflated, of course) and foam blocks under the thwarts. This helps the canoe ride a bit higher.

Knee Pads and Wet Suits

Kneeling is virtually mandatory for running white water. It lowers your center of gravity and it affords better control. However, kneeling is hard on the knees. So wear pads. The better types are cup-shaped to fit the knees, their rubber surfaces giving a firm grip on the canoe floor, while neoprene padding inside cushions the knees. With adjustable straps, they can be snapped into place quickly and removed just as easily. Using a boat cushion as a kneeling pad is not satisfactory. Most cushions are too small to allow for spreading your knees apart.

Wet suits are vital for running white water during the spring runoff when water temperatures are barely above freezing. Being dumped into such chilly froth makes you an instant candidate for hypothermia. The most popular suit is the nylon-backed one-eighth inch foam "Farmer John" type which insulates well against the water's chill yet permits freedom of movement in the canoe.

While no two white-water accidents are exactly alike, there are two rules that apply universally. One: If you spill, always remain upstream of the canoe. Filled with water and hurtling along with the current, a canoe can strike a crushing blow, possibly pinning you to a rock. It's feasible, however, to follow the canoe downstream with one person on each side, trying to guide the craft and keep it in line with the current—but never do this broadside.

Two: Ride the current with your feet forward as much as possible, keeping them as close to the surface as you can. Don't drag them. Conceivably, one foot could become wedged between two rocks, whereupon the force of the water may pull you under. Floating in the foot-forward position, you can fend off rocks.

Cartop Carriers

Lashed on top of a car, a canoe is subjected to air pressure of up to twenty pounds per square foot. In a twenty-five-mile crosswind, side thrust can reach fifty pounds. Additional pressure is exerted upward by air rushing along the top of the car under the inverted canoe. And we all know of the blast of displaced air that strikes us upon meeting a high-speed trailer truck. Obviously, then, a sturdy cartop carrier, supplemented by secure lashings, is called for.

One type of carrier has a roller bar on the back unit. You need lift only one end into place, then roll the canoe into position for lashing. This carrier is ideal for heavier canoes and for more bulky fishing boats.

It's possible, too, to purchase only the four gutter brackets with which to build a carrier to your own specifications. By adding hardwood crossbars you can fashion a carrier of any width, up to that permitted by law. Standard, ready-made carriers are usually sixty inches wide, with optional seventy-eight-inch crossbars for carrying two canoes side by side. A sixty-inch carrier can be widened easily by bolting longer hardwood crossbars to it. Such a carrier can also be rigged with a platform for carrying luggage as well as a canoe.

Gutter-mounted cartop carriers are not always feasible. Many new cars are without a rain gutter, or are equipped with only a partial one. And even if your car is equipped with full-length gutters, there's a limit to the weight they'll support. For example, carrying two canoes on a gutter-mounted carrier may pose no problems on a smooth highway, but when you turn off onto a woods road, jouncing along toward the landing, the gutters will take a severe beating.

Under these conditions, a carrier with rubber "feet" that ride directly on the car's metal roof is preferable. If you fear that the rubber will mar the paint surface, insert a small foam pad between the rubber cup and the car.

Another type of carrying device consists of four solid foam blocks notched to fit snugly over the gunwales. When the canoe is inverted, these rest directly on the car top. Nylon straps for lashing are included in the kit.

Most cartop carriers are equipped with such straps and, providing they are made of nylon and not cotton, they are adequate for the job. There should be two straps lashing the canoe's midship to the carrier. At each end of the canoe, use two lines, angled so that they pull against each other, in an inverted V. Also angle them so that the front lines pull somewhat against those at the rear. This combination prevents the canoe from pivoting on the rack and from sliding forward or backward. Heavy shockcord can be incorporated into this system to maintain constant tension. While nylon straps are suitable for lashing the canoe to the carrier, lines of nylon rope at the bow and stern are more secure.

Once the canoe is lashed on top of the car, there's lots of wasted space overhead. It's logical to secure the paddles in the canoe, of course, but you can also alleviate some of the crowding in the car by stashing bulky, lightweight gear in the canoe—sleeping bags or the tent, for example. However, don't assume that the overturned canoe will protect them from the rain. In fact, water will be drawn in by air spilling over the roof. So wrap your equipment in a waterproof tarp. A nine-by-nine-foot urethane-coated tarp is a perfect size. It weighs only about one pound and can also serve as a wrapper in the canoe to protect your outfit against rain or spray.

GETTING AWAY FROM IT ALL

The most challenging experiences canoeing offers may be white-water running and trips to far places. But there's more. A canoe is the ideal craft for nature watching, whether you're looking for songbirds or wild game. And, of course, photography from a canoe offers you a whole new perspective. Canoeing is one of the few modern sports that allows you an escape from crowds, providing of course, you avoid the popular streams to which so many newcomers seem to gravitate. For serenity, seek out smaller, lesser-known waters. Day trips, with a picnic lunch on a sandbar or in a streamside hemlock grove, are a refreshing change from the usual roadside table.

Chapter 11

Map and Compass: North Is That Way...

In his Fall 1941 catalog, L.L. wrote that he wanted no part of a compass dial that was "cluttered with figures, lines, and ornaments." So he had a manufacturer make up Bean's Maine Woods compass with a dial showing only the four cardinal points—N, S, E and W, along with the intermediary markings: NE, SE, SW and NW. When designing this compass, L.L. apparently thought in terms of deer hunting. He knew that when a hunter enters the deer woods he's not likely to travel very far, certainly not the miles a backpacker will cover. A simple, basic compass is generally adequate.

For any sort of extended travel, however, you'll need a compass that isn't just a toy, one that will do more than assist you out of a ten-acre woodlot. Backpacking trails are sometimes obscure. With fishing pressure so great these days, many fishermen choose to hike to remote ponds, often without benefit of a clearly defined trail. Even canoe trippers run into problems—trying to find a portage along a far shore that "looks all alike," for example.

The farther afield you go the more urgent the need for a precision instrument. Dillon Wallace's classic tale of northwoods tragedy, *The Lure of the Labrador Wild,* is an account of what happened when he and his partner, Leonidas Hubbard, entered the wrong bay at the head of Labrador's Grand Lake. Traveling by canoe, the two were seeking the mouth of the Nascaupee River. Instead, early in July, 1903, they started up the Susan River, became lost trying to go cross-country, and were finally trapped by winter. Hubbard died of starvation. Wallace was rescued by trappers as he waded through deep snow, seeking help for his partner who he thought was still alive at their camp.

You may not be planning to explore Labrador, but, nonetheless, whenever you leave familiar surroundings, always carry a map and compass. This is not to say that if you get lost your compass and map will bring you home by themselves. "The best compass in the world is useless," L.L. wrote in 1942, "if you do not know how to use it." The instruction booklet he supplied with his Maine Woods compass gave detailed instructions on how to use the instrument and how to find your way into the woods but—perhaps by design—it never said a word about how to get back.

A compass has but one function—to point in the direction of magnetic north. Getting home is up to you. Too many of us wait until a panic situation arises before unlimbering a compass. Even when you don't really need them, take out your map and compass, and practicc finding a route or locating yourself on the map. While hiking a well-established trail, occasionally take a compass bearing on a distant landmark—a mountaintop, for example. Actually this can be a fascinating game—and, in fact, there are numerous orienteering clubs throughout the country that hold frequent field trials with map and compass. Avoid the pitfall of faithfully carrying a compass but never using it until, as one guide put it, you're "turned around so bad you're a half-mile from your own tracks."

One final—and critical—point. Believe your compass. As long as the needle swings freely it will point to magnetic north and only to magnetic north. You may be convinced that the needle has gone berserk and is pointing southeast, or elsewhere, but don't be swayed by your hunches. A compass needle has a one-track mind.

There may be minor exceptions but they're easy to recognize and control. A compass held too close to an axe or held waist-high near a large metal belt buckle may deviate, the needle being attracted by the metal. Hence the compass term "deviation." Put your axe aside, at least five or six feet away. There are instances of deviation beyond your control, too. Certain areas containing iron-ore deposits—such as Mount Hale in New Hampshire or Mount Katahdin in Maine—will cause compass needles to act erratically.

COMPASSES

There are five basic types of compasses—the fixed dial, the lensatic, the cruiser, the sighting and the orienteering compass. The fixed-dial compass is the simplest of all, possibly too simple. It consists of a metal or plastic case, often with a folding

Fixed-Dial Compass

cover to protect the crystal, and a center-pivot needle that swings over a compass card permanently affixed to the bottom of the case. Models are also available in lapel pin-on and wristwatch designs. There may be an azimuth scale, with degree demarcations around its perimeter, running from 0 at north, clockwise to 90 degrees at east, 180 at south, 270 at west and back to north completing the 360-degree circle. The azimuth scale is often omitted and only the cardinal points indicated, as in L.L.'s Maine Woods compass. Some fixed-dial compasses have a mechanical "damper," a lever in the side of the case that locks the needle to prevent wear on the pivot bearing when not in use. The lever may also be used to minimize oscillation of the needle when a bearing is taken. However, this technique (known as "damping") makes accurate readings difficult. All in all, though, the fixed-dial compass is adequate only for rough direction-finding, usually without the benefit of a map. It will guide you to a road or a large lake, but it's not to be trusted for precise readings. In view of the low cost of better models, there is little point to buying one.

Far more sophisticated is the lensatic compass in which the dial pivots, its azimuth scale swinging freely around the case. The dial may have a needle superimposed so that the two work as a single unit. Like all compasses, it points to magnetic north so you'll have to make a relatively simple adjustment for declination, as explained on pages 269–71. Perhaps the finest of the lensatic compasses is the U.S. Army version, sometimes known as an "army engineer's compass." There are currently a couple of commercial versions whose quality matches that of the

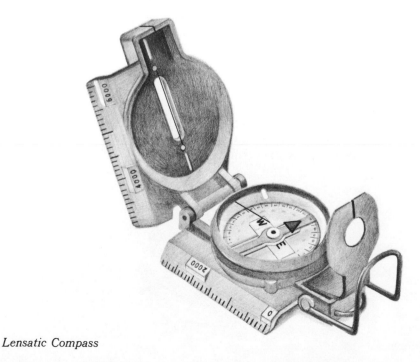

Lensatic Compass

army model. When the cover is lifted, it presents a fine wire sight set in a vertical slot. On the opposite side a small tab lifts open; within it is a tiny magnifying glass. Holding the compass at eye level and sighting the objective through the cover slot, you can at the same time read the magnified bearing on the dial. Because they are liquid filled, most lensatic compasses need no damping device since the liquid minimizes needle oscillation. However, one version of the army compass uses "induction" damping. This model has a copper-lined inner shell that reflects the electric currents caused by the movement of the needle and brings it to rest quickly.

An interesting compass is the cruiser, a professional's instrument used by foresters and timber cruisers. It's unique in that its azimuth scale, on the outer rim of the dial, runs counterclockwise. All other compasses are clockwise. There is also a quadrant scale of 90 degrees each, the northeast and southwest calibrations clockwise, the northwest and southeast, counterclockwise. And, to add to the confusion, the east and west cardinal points are transposed on the inner scale! Although all of this seems to make little sense at first glance, it's actually an ingenious arrangement. On the inside of the open cover is a "lubber's," or orienting line, and, on the opposite rim, a rifle-type sight. You simply sight your objective along the lubber's line, either through the rear sight or with the compass held at the waist. In either position, the north end of the needle gives you your degree bearing. It takes some getting used to, but once you're accustomed to the transposed dials, it's an easy compass to use. The cruiser compass does have drawbacks for recreational use. It's costly, bulky (three-and-a-half inches in diameter), heavy (slightly over a half pound) and, because of the mechanical damper device, it's relatively slow, requiring up to twenty seconds before the needle can be brought to rest.

The sighting compass is more sophisticated and probably one of the most accurate of hand-held instruments. It has an optical sight in the side of the case that magnifies the calibrated dial to half-degree readings. It's compact enough so that

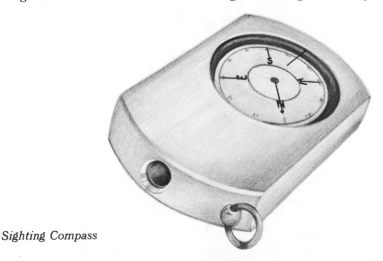

Sighting Compass

you can keep one eye on your objective and the other on the dial reading. Sighting compasses are excellent for hunters and fishermen who are familiar enough with the area they're in so that they need only quick reference bearings. Such compasses are also good for canoeists on open water who want to maintain a straight course in order to reach a particular bay, island or river outlet. Sighting compasses are not well adapted to working with a map.

Virtually all of the foregoing types of compasses have certain drawbacks, be it weight or bulk, poor needle damping, inadequate azimuth scales, high cost—or they're difficult to use with a map. There is a compass, however, that overcomes all these shortcomings—and then some. It's the orienteering model.

The orienteering compass has a rotating transparent plastic base plate that makes it easy to use with a map. The azimuth scale is inscribed on the exterior of the housing—which can be rotated on the base plate—and is in two-degree increments. There are two reasons for this. First, one-degree increments would so crowd the azimuth scale that it would be difficult to read. Second, it's generally accepted that two-degree accuracy is about the best that can be expected from any hand-held compass. This doesn't mean you're going to miss your objective by a country mile. As a matter of fact, a one-degree error will bring you within ninety-four feet of your objective at a distance of one mile. This, of course, assumes that you can walk a perfectly straight line from your known position to your objective—a practical impossibility. Trees, boulders, swamp holes and other natural impediments will cause detours which, in turn, may require new bearings as you travel. Nevertheless you'll find the two-degree increments more than adequate.

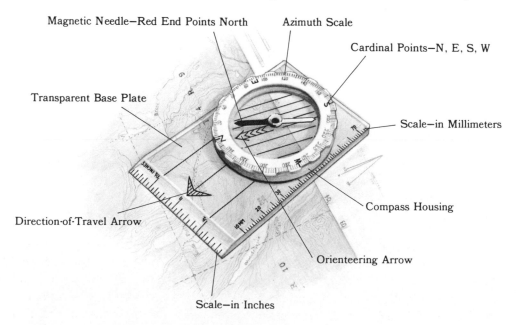

An Orienteering Compass and Its Parts

The orienteering compass is unlike others in several respects. On the base plate there is a direction-of-travel arrow; within the housing, an orienting arrow; and along the edges of the base plate, millimeter and inch scales used in estimating map mileage. Most orienteering compasses are liquid filled, but won't freeze even at 40 degrees below zero. Best of all, the liquid-filled models damp the needle's oscillation in about four seconds, far faster than induction damping. (Don't be alarmed if a bubble appears: this does not affect accuracy.) Some models also provide for a declination adjustment.

Various orienteering compasses offer options that are more than just extra gadgets. One is a magnifying glass built into the base plate. With it you can decipher fine detail on a small-scale map. Some models have luminous cardinal points. Traveling by compass in the dark isn't recommended, but should an emergency arise requiring night travel, the luminous points are helpful. One or two models have a folding cover within which is a sighting mirror and sighting line, the latter much like that on the army engineer's compass. It is probably the most sophisticated of the orienteering compasses. In fact, among many timber cruisers, foresters and other professional woods travelers, this style is replacing the time-honored cruiser compass.

Most orienteering compasses can be carried in the leather cases provided for them; others have lanyards that can be attached to your belt or shirt-pocket flap. All in all, the orienteering compass is a wondrous instrument, especially when you consider that the lightest can weigh as little as one ounce, and the heaviest, a mere three ounces. And it can be tucked into a shirt pocket.

Beyond avoiding physical abuse, compasses require little care except, ironically, when they lie idle. Don't store yours close to electrical wiring or any sort of household transformer—your doorbell system, for example—that may include electromagnetic fields. These could cause your compass needle to reverse its polarity, pointing south instead of north. For the same reason, a compass should never be stored with other magnetic compasses.

FIELD WORK WITH A COMPASS

The word "azimuth" is derived from the Arabic and means, simply, "the way." In other words, an azimuth is a compass bearing, a direction of travel. Since a compass azimuth scale has 360 degrees, you have, in essence, 360 "ways" or directions of travel. Compass work involves determining which one of these is correct.

For example, your state road map indicates a stream about one mile to the southeast, a stream known to offer good trout fishing in its more remote sections. There's a bridge several miles upstream, and another three miles down. You could drive to either of these but in both areas the fishing has been heavy. You want to fish where few anglers take the trouble to go—the midsection of the stream. You could wade or walk the banks from either bridge, of course, but that's a slow, tedious route. So you decide to go cross-country, through the woods, directly to the good fishing grounds. Your compass will take you there, quickly.

Hold your orienteering compass at waist level and turn it so that the direction-of-travel arrow on the base plate is pointed in the direction of the stream. Now, without turning the base plate, rotate the housing until the magnetic needle overlays the orienting arrow within the case. This is known as "orienting" your compass. Next, read the azimuth scale at the point closest to the direction-of-travel arrow. (Some compasses are marked "Read Bearing Here.") Let's assume you obtained a reading of 120 degrees. This is your azimuth, your direction of travel.

However, it's not practical to walk through the woods with one eye on your compass and the other on the footing underneath. Nor can you put your compass away and rely on your judgment as to where your 120-degree course lies. If you do, you're likely to walk in circles. But you couldn't walk a perfectly straight line anyway, because you'll have to detour around obstacles. Once you have obtained your reading, sight along your direction-of-travel arrow to some landmark, as far ahead as possible. It may be a big pine, or a stump, anything that stands out in the woods. Put your compass away and walk to it. Even if you make slight detours en route, you'll still be on course when you arrive at this first landmark.

The chances are that your housing has not been disturbed and that your direction-of-travel arrow is still aligned with your 120-degree azimuth. If by any chance the housing has been turned slightly while the compass was in your pocket, realign the 120-degree azimuth with your direction of travel. Take another look as far ahead as possible along your azimuth, noting a second landmark, perhaps a boulder or a blowdown. Walk to this. It may seem a slow, tedious and complicated process. It is not. In fact, you can probably obtain your bearing at each landmark stop within twenty to thirty seconds. With practice, you'll probably find yourself doing it almost automatically. It's virtually foolproof if you use care in reading your azimuth scale.

Of course, it's possible to reach your destination without repeatedly sighting on landmarks along your route. You can walk with your compass in hand, stopping every few hundred feet (or at shorter intervals) to check your azimuth. Although there is a greater chance for error, this technique will almost certainly get you to that stream.

Many backpackers enjoy "bushwhacking"—traveling without benefit of a trail. It lends an element of adventure to hiking. Let's assume you have just climbed a small mountain via a well-established trail. From the summit you see another mountain some three miles away—but there's no trail to it. You decide to "bushwhack" through the wooded valley below. While the mountain is clearly visible from where you stand, you know that once you enter the intervening woods, your objective will disappear. So, in fact, may the one on which you're now standing. You'll be able to use neither as a visible reference point. Out comes your compass.

Since the other peak appears to be about three miles away, you'll want as accurate an azimuth reading as possible. Place your orienteering compass on a ledge or rock, so that it's firm and level. Turn the base plate until the direction-of-travel arrow points directly at your objective peak. Now orient your compass, turning only the housing (not the plate) until the magnetic needle perfectly over-lays the orienting arrow. You have a bearing of, say, 320 degrees. Make a mental note of it. Better yet, jot it down on a piece of paper. If you forget this azimuth while you're deep in the woods below, unable to see the peak, you'll be in trouble.

Next, sight downhill over your direction-of-travel arrow, seeking out some prominent landmark—a boulder, a copse of juniper, a scraggly wind-blown spruce. Walk to this point. Take another sighting, again being sure your compass is oriented and that your indicated azimuth is still 320 degrees. Seek another land-mark. Repeat the process, carefully, and as often as is necessary.

Mountain terrain is likely to be rough—cliffs, ravines, old rock slides and blow-downs make walking a straight line virtually impossible. Always pick a landmark that you can recognize from either side of your direction of travel. If, by some chance, you lose sight of a landmark, don't cast about in several directions looking for it. Stop. Take another sighting along your 320-degree azimuth, finding a substitute landmark. With careful and frequent readings, you'll attain that far-off peak.

You pause a while on the summit, exhilarated, enjoying the view and the satis-faction of having accomplished some pretty good woodsmanship. It's time to go home and you decide the best route is to go back the way you came, picking up the trail on the first summit. You glance in that direction. Clouds have rolled in! You can see the lower slopes but not the peak! What now? With the peak in sight you could have taken a backsight from your objective to your starting point. Clouds, however, prevent that. The alternative is simple.

Because a complete reversal of your route is actually a complete 180-degree turn, the process for obtaining a backbearing is simple. Your azimuth was 320 degrees. Deduct 180. Your return route then lies along a 140-degree azimuth. Rotate the housing until your direction-of-travel arrow intercepts your azimuth scale at 140 degrees. Orient your compass again—and follow your direction-of-travel arrow, again using the landmark-to-landmark technique. It should take you directly over the same course you have just traveled, and back to the trail you left a few hours ago.

There's a simple formula for obtaining a backbearing. If your original bearing was 180 degrees or more, deduct 180 degrees, just as you did above. If the original bearing was 180 degrees or less add 180 degrees. For instance, if your original bearing was 90 degrees, add 180, which results in 270 degrees, your backbearing.

Another method for determining a complete reversal of your course requires no mathematics. In this case, assume that your original azimuth was 150 degrees, and follow the imaginary diameter line that bisects the azimuth scale to the side directly opposite your original bearing. Your new reading is 330 degrees. Rotate the housing until the 330-degree mark is aligned with your direction-of-travel arrow. All you need to do is orient your compass, and follow your direction-of-travel arrow.

All too often hunters look upon the compass as an emergency instrument. Getting lost in the deer woods is easy if you're careless. But there are uses for a compass, even when you're not lost. Suppose you're alone in the woods and you've just dropped a handsome buck. You field-dress it and guess its weight to be about 175 pounds. That's a lot of deer meat—too much for you to drag out single-handedly. You'll have to go back to camp and enlist your hunting partners. But it's getting late in the day, and you may not be able to return for the deer until the next morning. If you're properly prepared, you'll have a length of nylon rope with you. Hang the buck from a tree limb so that it's clear of the ground, and attach your handkerchief to the animal. Better yet, if you're wearing a bright orange or red rain shirt, use it. Why? For two reasons. First, the human scent may keep a wildcat or bear from helping itself to your meat, though that can't be guaranteed. And second, when you return for the deer, your bright rain shirt will be easy to spot in the woods.

Now sit a few minutes and reconstruct your travels since you left camp. You recall that you set out along an abandoned logging road that ran approximately northwest from the cabin. You hunted along this, slowly, for about two hours, and then entered the woods on your right, or in a roughly northeasterly direction. You estimate that you're probably about three-quarters of a mile from the logging road. Point your compass plate with its direction-of-travel arrow roughly in a southwesterly direction, toward the road. Now orient your compass and take a bearing. You come up with 210 degrees. Make a mental note of this bearing. You'll need to remember it in the morning for the return trip. You can now follow your direction-of-travel arrow back to the road, using the landmark method. At the road, place a marker of some sort, something you'll easily recognize the next morning: possibly a Boy Scout type of trail marker such as two or three rocks piled atop each other. Just be sure that you can find this point without fail when you return. You can now trudge gleefully back to camp to celebrate your luck.

Come daylight the next day, return to your trail marker with your partners. If your course yesterday was 210 degrees, deduct 180 degrees. Your new azimuth—30 degrees. Follow your direction-of-travel arrow, again using landmarks, and you should soon come within a few feet of your deer, your attention drawn to it by the bright rain shirt.

Even if you know the country well, compass precautions pay off. For example, when clouds hang low enough to obscure hilltops or ridges, or when a thick fog settles, even a familiar landscape takes on a dismaying sameness. This is a good day for a compass. Nonemergency use of your compass will almost guarantee that no emergency need for it will arise. A compass renders its best service before you get lost.

MAPS

Among nonprofessional outdoorsmen, the most widely used maps are the quad-rangles, or topographic maps, issued in the United States by the U.S. Geological Survey and in Canada by the Maps and Survey Branch of the Department of Energy, Mines and Resources. Sporting-goods stores and outfitters throughout both countries generally have them in stock for local areas.

Good maps are also available from the U. S. Army Corps of Engineers, the Forest Service, the National Park Service and the Bureau of Land Management. The maps may vary, some being highly detailed for backcountry travel, others being little more than colorful road and trail maps for tourist use. Timberland owners, logging companies, timber management firms, state conservation depart-ments, mountain clubs, outdoor organizations and some county agencies also issue maps, often at low or no cost. Maps of varying usefulness to sportsmen are also available from commercial map publishers and chambers of commerce. However, you should make sure that these are accurate and drawn to scale. Tourist maps, often embellished by leaping fish and water skiers, are of no use to outdoorsmen. (For a list of outdoor organizations and map sources, see Appendix II.)

In the examples of map-and-compass work cited in this chapter, the U. S. Geological Survey quadrangle for the Traveler Mountain area in Maine is used as a reference. A wild section of Maine with few man-made features, it includes a part of Baxter State Park and incorporates a wide variety of map features—mountain peaks, rivers, lakes and ponds. Parts of the map are reproduced for reference as you read.

Scale

Scale is the size relationship between features on a map and those same features on actual terrain. It is usually indicated in the bottom margin of the map at the center, and is often shown in two forms: a ratio such as 1:62,500 or 1:24,000, or as a bar scale. The ratio indicates that 1 inch on the map equals 62,500 inches on terrain, or roughly 1 mile. It's important not to confuse inches with feet. Always use inches with inches, feet with feet. On some maps, kilometers or even meters may be used.

The bar-scale form is much like that used on highway maps. Yet some Geologi-cal Survey quadrangles include three bar scales designating miles, feet and kilo-meters. One end of each bar is subdivided into smaller segments for measuring short distances. Using the scale on the edge of your orienteering compass, or a ruler, you can measure one of these scale segments and "walk" it along your proposed route, counting each "step." Since this method can follow the windings and twistings of a trail or river, it results in a fairly accurate estimate of distance. Using a pair of compasses—the kind you used in your high school geometry

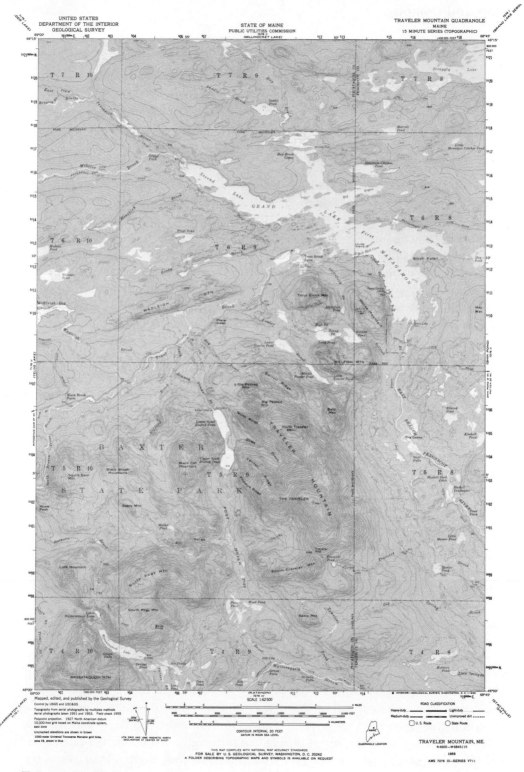

Topographic Map

class—produces even more accurate estimates. There are also mechanical "map measures"—little pocket instruments at the base of which are tiny wheels. Rolled along a trail on the map, they activate a dial needle which, in turn, indicates distance just as a stop watch shows elapsed time.

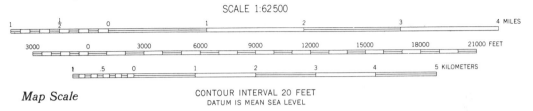

Map Scale

Most orienteering compasses have a bar scale along one or more edges of the base plate. For example, one model is graduated for a 1:24,000 scale along one edge, and a 1:62,500 scale along the other. Superimposed over a map, these base-plate bar scales will give you accurate airline distances but you'll have to make allowances for the bends in a river and the twistings of a foot trail. Also, for foot travel, you'll have to take into account that terrain may include steep grades, uphill and down. Therefore, in using a map's scale to estimate travel distance and time, make allowances for such impediments.

Scale varies among the numerous Geological Survey quadrangles. One type is designated the "7½-minute Series," another, the "15-minute Series"; this is indicated at the top right-hand corner. They refer to the area covered. The entire globe is divided into degrees of latitude and longitude. However, for global navigation, by air or by ship, degrees alone are not sufficient to pinpoint a position accurately. So each degree is divided into 60 minutes, and each minute into 60 seconds, resulting in a relatively fine grid. A 7½-minute quadrangle covers only a small portion of the earth's surface, somewhere between 50 and 70 square miles on a map that measures about 22 by 27 inches. Scaled at 1:24,000, the map still shows considerable detail. On the other hand, a 15-minute quadrangle portrays a much larger area, anywhere from 197 to 282 square miles—yet the resulting map size is only about 17 by 21 inches. Obviously, then, the scale must be smaller— 1:62,500.

There is a good reason why some quadrangles belong to the 7½-minute series and others to the 15-minute group. Urban areas are likely to be depicted on the 7½-minute maps for their enhanced detail since land values are obviously greater than in sparsely settled regions. Something near pinpoint accuracy is required. On the other hand, a map of thinly populated terrain, or of a wilderness region, does not require minute detail. Such areas are depicted in the 15-minute series. What is important to you, however, is not the series but the scale. Always check this in the margin before using a map.

Not all Geological Survey maps fit into the 7½- and 15-minute series. Those that portray Alaska and much of the American West are on a smaller scale, as the following chart indicates:

Series	Scale	One Inch Equals	Area Depicted (in square miles)
7½ minute	1:24,000	2,000 feet	49–70
15-minute	1:62,500	Nearly 1 mile	197–282
Alaska	1:63,360	1 mile	207–281
U. S.	1:250,000	Nearly 4 miles	4,580–8,669
U. S.	1:1,000,000	Nearly 16 miles	73,734–102,759

Contour Lines

Elevations are indicated by contour lines shown in brown, imaginary lines that never deviate from their assigned positions at a given elevation above sea level. On a map's margin (usually below the scale) you'll find the designation "Contour Interval." On the Traveler Mountain quadrangle, this is twenty feet, the vertical distance between each line. Some quadrangles may use a twenty-five-foot contour interval. Depending on this, every fourth or fifth line is somewhat bolder than the others, marking hundred-foot intervals with the actual elevation above sea level printed somewhere along the line. The closer together these lines, the steeper the terrain. Steep or gentle, you'll climb or descend twenty (or twenty-five) feet each time you travel from one contour line to another.

Thus, valleys and peaks are delineated clearly. Depressions or bowls cannot be mistaken for elevations, since the contour lines indicating these have tiny, straight-line appendages attached to the contour line on the downhill side.

In using maps for foot travel, both the scale and contour lines should be considered jointly. For example, use the scale distance as the base of a triangle. With the contour lines, plot the elevation of, let us say, a mountain you plan to climb. The elevation then forms the vertical leg of the triangle. Now, if you recall your high school geometry, you know that the slope must be the triangle's hypotenuse, always longer than either side. And this is your travel route.

For a direct application of this, check the map on page 263, showing a portion of the Traveler Mountain quadrangle. You arrive at the foot of the Horse Mountain fire-lookout trail on the Trout Brook road, about one-half mile west of Grand Lake Matagamon. Your map indicates that the lookout tower is about seven-eighths of a mile almost directly south. In flat country, over a smooth trail, you could probably cover this distance in twenty minutes to a half hour, even under a reasonably hefty pack. But take another look at that trail. Notice the figure "793" at the foot of it. This is the elevation above sea level. Now, note the figure at the lookout tower—"1589." Thus, you will have to climb 796 feet in less than a mile. Another indication of the steep approach is the proximity of the contour lines to one another. Unless you're in superb physical condition, you had better plan on considerably more than a half hour for this jaunt.

Contour lines can also help you determine whether or not a stream can be run safely by canoe. While there are many canoe route guides available, most of them

Horse Mountain Trail

include only the major waterways; many potential canoe runs are not included. In a map appraisal of one of these, count the contour lines that cross the stream between your proposed starting point and the terminus. Multiply these by twenty (or twenty-five, depending on your map's contour-foot interval) and you have the number of feet the stream drops in that section.

As an example of this procedure see the map on page 264, showing Trout Brook between Black Brook Farm and Grand Lake Matagamon on the Traveler Mountain quadrangle. Your scale will tell you that the airline distance is eight-and-a-half miles but, due to the windings of the stream, the actual distance is probably ten or twelve miles. The map depicts the stream as a solid blue double line, indicating a substantial stream despite its humble "brook" designation. At first glance the trip may appear to be pleasant and leisurely, the distance an easy one-day jaunt with time out for some fishing en route. However, take a closer look. Contour lines cross the stream at eleven points—a drop of 220 feet. Divide the total estimated distance into this and you come up with an average drop of eighteen to twenty feet per mile, certainly not a formidable flow. Now, take another look. Of the eleven crossover contour lines, eight of these occur within the upper four miles or so. This presents an average drop of forty feet per mile. Any experienced canoeist will tell you that a drop of thirty to fifty feet per mile means very "sporty" water! But with only three contour lines crossing within six miles or so, the lower section of the stream probably will be smooth sailing. Note, too, that starting at the point marked "The Crossing," the stream flows through relatively flat country—the contour lines are generally far apart until the stream reaches the lake. Trout Brook might be a superb run if the pitch of the water is right, but you had better scout that upper section thoroughly before committing yourself to it!

Widely spaced contour lines crossing a stream generally mean reasonably

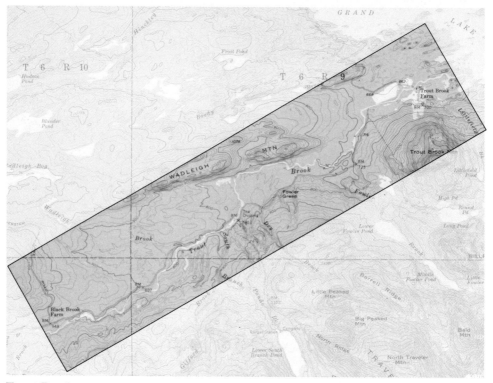

Trout Brook

smooth currents, perhaps with an occasional minor rapid. But it may be that among these widely spaced contours, there occurs a concentration of several at one point. This should warn you of potentially dangerous rapids or even a major waterfall. Contour lines are a help in plotting a river trip but your decision on whether you should attempt it should not be made solely on them.

While poring over a map, you'll often encounter the letters "BM" with a black numeral beside them. These are bench marks, the site of map control points marked permanently by small, round, bronze plaques set in a ledge or in masonry.

Bench Mark Control Point

The number is the elevation above sea level. On the Traveler Gap Trail, to Lower South Branch Pond, there are six such bench marks. Since they are identified on the map with their respective elevations, the location of them along a hiking trail pinpoints your position and your elevation precisely.

Color

Color plays an important part in making maps easier to read. Water—streams, rivers, lakes, swamps and marshes—is shown in blue. On maps scaled at 1:24,000, waterways less than forty feet wide are shown as a single blue line; on those maps scaled at 1:62,500, single lines indicate waterways up to eighty feet wide. Larger rivers are depicted with double lines, spaced to scale and filled in with blue.

A number in the center of a lake or pond indicates its elevation above mean sea level. On some maps, there may be several numbers, particularly on large lakes. These indicate depth. Such maps are useful for navigation, of course, but some fish and game departments issue them for the benefit of fishermen seeking fish that lie at varying depths according to species or season.

Swamps and marshes are easily recognized by their groupings of tiny, tufted markings not unlike—appropriately—grass hummocks.

Major roads are shown as bold red lines; secondary and unimproved roads as black double lines, either solid or dotted. A single dotted black line is a foot trail. A solid overlay of green represents forest; clearings have been left in white. But these color indications are not infallible. Since the map was issued (the date usually appears in the lower right-hand margin), clearings may have grown up into woods or thick brush and forested areas may have been cleared.

On many maps of wilderness areas, townships may lack names, simply because they have not been settled and support no permanent residents. These are indicated by range and township numbers. Ranges (simply a surveyor's designation) usually run six miles wide, north and south. Townships, also six miles wide, run east and west. On the Traveler Mountain quadrangle, ranges 8, 9 and 10 are included, along with townships 4, 5, 6 and 7. Since range and township lines cross each other in checkerboard fashion, they form townships approximately six miles square, or thirty-six square miles in area. And their designations are shown as, for example, T6 R9—township 6 in range 9.

Man-made Features

Obviously, many man-made features cannot be shown to scale. A country church, for instance, appears as a tiny, though clearly visible black block with a cross on one side. Drawn to scale, it would become an indistinguishable dot. Therefore, a standard-size symbol is used for all buildings forty feet square or smaller, while larger structures are drawn to scale. Heavily built-up areas, larger than three-quarters of a square mile, are indicated by a reddish-tint overlay with only streets and important buildings shown.

With regard to man-made features, the date a map was published, or last revised, is important. Many Geological Survey quadrangles have not been updated for more than thirty years, during which time that cabin you're planning to bunk in may have long ago collapsed and the clearing grown up to brush. Don't count on bridges, either, particularly those built by logging companies. Many of them were intended for temporary use, and may have been washed out after they were abandoned. On the other hand, you may discover that roads and camps have been built in what appears on the map to be virgin wilderness. If you're using an old map, check with local residents about possible major changes.

Some one hundred different symbols are used on Geological Survey quadrangles, many of regional interest only—a wire fence in ranch country, for instance, or a fire-lookout tower in forest land. For an explanation of the most commonly used symbols, see the chart on page 267.

AFIELD WITH MAP AND COMPASS

Let's assume that you want to fish Billfish Pond and its outlet stream. (See Traveler Mountain quadrangle insert, page 268). There's a foot trail from the Grand Lake Road, about one mile west of Trout Brook Farm. This runs southeasterly to Round Pond, a distance of about two-and-a-half miles. From that point, however, you'll have to bushwhack another half mile, part of this through a marsh, to reach Billfish Pond. And even then, you'll find yourself on the wrong side to fish the outlet. All in all, the prospect isn't attractive, and you scout the map for a better approach.

You notice that Billfish Pond is only about seven-eighths of a mile from the junction of Grand Lake Road and Eagle Lake Tote Road. Contour lines indicate a steep but short climb. You weigh this against the three-mile hike from the other side and decide on the shorter route.

Now, in order to obtain an azimuth bearing to the pond from your position at the road junction, you know that your map will first have to be "oriented." This means, simply, that it must be so turned that its features—mountains, lakes, roads—correspond directionally with those on the actual terrain. You turn the map so that its north end faces north, lining up your compass needle with the map's north-south meridian lines (these are the lines that form the large grid overlay on the quadrangle). Lake Matagamon is north of you, and to the east you locate the East Branch of the Penobscot River and, roughly southwest, you can see the top of Billfish Mountain. Your map is "oriented."

Since there's no trail to Billfish Pond from this side you'll have to go cross-country through the woods where your objective will be hidden. So you need a compass bearing. Without disturbing the map, place one edge of your

TOPOGRAPHIC MAP SYMBOLS

VARIATIONS WILL BE FOUND ON OLDER MAPS

Primary highway, hard surface	Boundaries: National	
Secondary highway, hard surface	State	
Light-duty road, hard or improved surface	County, parish, municipio	
Unimproved road	Civil township, precinct, town, barrio	
Road under construction, alinement known	Incorporated city, village, town, hamlet	
Proposed road	Reservation, National or State	
Dual highway, dividing strip 25 feet or less	Small park, cemetery, airport, etc.	
Dual highway, dividing strip exceeding 25 feet	Land grant	
Trail	Township or range line, United States land survey	
	Township or range line, approximate location	
Railroad: single track and multiple track	Section line, United States land survey	
Railroads in juxtaposition	Section line, approximate location	
Narrow gage: single track and multiple track	Township line, not United States land survey	
Railroad in street and carline	Section line, not United States land survey	
Bridge: road and railroad	Found corner: section and closing	
Drawbridge: road and railroad	Boundary monument: land grant and other	
Footbridge	Fence or field line	
Tunnel: road and railroad		
Overpass and underpass	Index contour — Intermediate contour	
Small masonry or concrete dam	Supplementary contour — Depression contours	
Dam with lock	Fill — Cut	
Dam with road	Levee — Levee with road	
Canal with lock	Mine dump — Wash	
	Tailings — Tailings pond	
Buildings (dwelling, place of employment, etc.)	Shifting sand or dunes — Intricate surface	
School, church, and cemetery	Sand area — Gravel beach	
Buildings (barn, warehouse, etc.)		
Power transmission line with located metal tower	Perennial streams — Intermittent streams	
Telephone line, pipeline, etc. (labeled as to type)	Elevated aqueduct — Aqueduct tunnel	
Wells other than water (labeled as to type)	Water well and spring — Glacier	
Tanks: oil, water, etc. (labeled only if water)	Small rapids — Small falls	
Located or landmark object; windmill	Large rapids — Large falls	
Open pit, mine, or quarry; prospect	Intermittent lake — Dry lake bed	
Shaft and tunnel entrance	Foreshore flat — Rock or coral reef	
	Sounding, depth curve — Piling or dolphin	
Horizontal and vertical control station:	Exposed wreck — Sunken wreck	
Tablet, spirit level elevation	Rock, bare or awash; dangerous to navigation	
Other recoverable mark, spirit level elevation		
Horizontal control station: tablet, vertical angle elevation	Marsh (swamp) — Submerged marsh	
Any recoverable mark, vertical angle or checked elevation	Wooded marsh — Mangrove	
Vertical control station: tablet, spirit level elevation	Woods or brushwood — Orchard	
Other recoverable mark, spirit level elevation	Vineyard — Scrub	
Spot elevation	Land subject to controlled inundation — Urban area	
Water elevation		

Horizontal and vertical control station values shown:
- Tablet, spirit level elevation: BM △ 5653
- Other recoverable mark, spirit level elevation: △ 5455
- Horizontal control station: tablet, vertical angle elevation: VABM △ 95/9
- Any recoverable mark, vertical angle or checked elevation: △ 3775
- Vertical control station: tablet, spirit level elevation: BM × 957
- Other recoverable mark, spirit level elevation: × 954
- Spot elevation: × 7369   × 7369
- Water elevation: 670   670

Topographic Map Symbols

orienteering-compass base plate so that it connects the outlet of Billfish Pond with the junction of the two roads. The direction-of-travel arrow on the plate is now parallel to your proposed route. Turn the housing (but not the base plate) until the

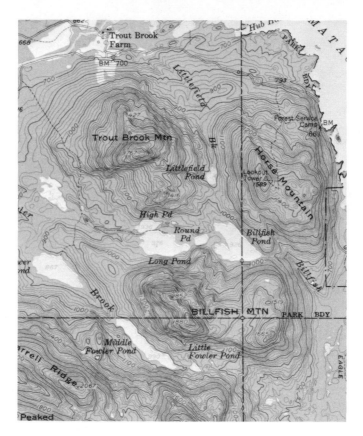

Billfish Pond

orienting arrow in the housing is perfectly overlaid by your compass needle. Your bearing now appears on the azimuth scale where it meets the direction-of-travel arrow—270 degrees. You've read the azimuth scale carefully; you're confident of your course. You're ready to go.

But hold on! If you follow this bearing you'll probably walk by Billfish Pond without even seeing it. As careful as you were in taking your bearing, it is not accurate. You overlooked "declination."

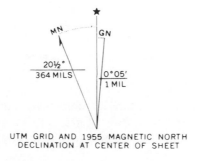

Declination Symbol

Declination

Declination is the difference between magnetic and true north, indicated by an offset V on the bottom margin of Geological Survey quadrangles. Most of us understand that there are two "poles"—magnetic, and geographical or true north. The latter is the top of the world, a specific location where our maps' north-south meridian lines converge.

Magnetic north, on the other hand, is about 1,300 miles from true north, in the general vicinity of Canada's Ellesmere and Bathurst islands, well north and slightly west of Hudson Bay. Unlike true north, magnetic north cannot be pinpointed precisely—being actually a fairly large area. Nor does magnetic north "attract" a compass needle. Rather it is the magnetic fields within the earth that direct the needle.

Obviously then, the needle does not point to true north. However, by coincidence, it does point to both magnetic and true north along an agonic line (also called a "zero-declination" line), which runs roughly from the east coast of Florida, through eastern Georgia, Tennessee, Kentucky, Ohio, Indiana, Michigan, Minnesota and on into Ontario. In areas east of this agonic line, your compass needle will point west of true north; in regions west of the agonic line, the needle is directed east of true north. This is declination.

Look at the Traveler Mountain quadrangle declination symbol. Note that the right leg of the V is marked GN—geographical, or true, north. The left leg, marked

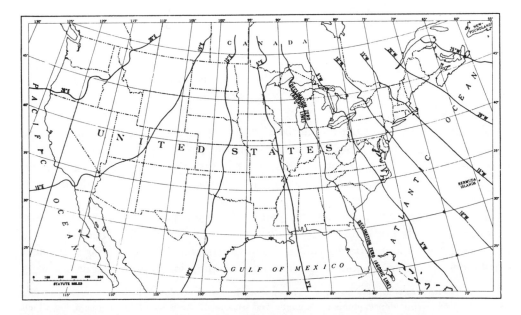

Declination Chart for the United States, 1960. Please note declination changes yearly.

MN for magnetic north, points twenty-and-a-half degrees west of true north. In the Maritime Provinces of Canada, and particularly in Labrador, the declination is even greater. In the Puget Sound area of Washington, the compass needle points some twenty-five degrees east of true north, with an even more pronounced declination in the Canadian Northwest.

Take another look at the declination symbol on the Traveler Mountain quadrangle. There's a thin line dividing the V, at the top of which is a tiny star. This is Polaris, the North Star. Contrary to popular belief, Polaris is not always in true north position. It wanders a little, due to the earth's slight "wobble" as it rotates on its north-south axis. Polaris actually attains a true-north position only twice each night, the precise time varying with the seasons. However, this wandering by the North Star does not affect compass use for nighttime recreational purposes; for all practical purposes, Polaris is close enough to true north.

Canadian maps often use a different system for indicating declination. Small-scale maps (1:250,000), covering vast regions would need several V symbols for accuracy on all parts of the map. Instead, the map is reproduced in miniature on the margin, its vertical sides oriented to true north. Within this marginal map, several isogonic* dotted lines indicate magnetic north. For instance, on the eastern edge of the map, the declination is shown as twenty-one degrees; a center isogonic line indicates twenty degrees; and one on the western edge, nineteen degrees.

Other Canadian maps may have only a simple statement in the margin, to the effect: "Magnetic declination 1966 varies from 16 degrees westerly at the west edge to 18 degrees westerly at the east edge." Declination symbols, whatever their form, are usually dated because magnetic north is slowly shifting. This is important to surveyors but will have little, if any, affect on work with a pocket compass.

Now let's return to the proposed trek to Billfish Pond from the junction of Grand Lake Road and the Eagle Lake Tote Road. You oriented the map according to features around you and then checked this by lining up your compass needle with the north-south margin of the map. You obtained a bearing of 270 degrees—a bearing which is in error.

At any point east of the agonic line (zero-declination line) you must add the declination. Thus since the Traveler Mountain quadrangle declination symbol indicates 20 degrees, your correct bearing for Billfish Pond is not 270 degrees, but 290. West of the agonic line—in the American Rockies, for example—the declination is subtracted.

Failure to account for declination can lead you far astray, even during a relatively short hike. You can stray from a true course as much as fifty feet per degree for every half mile you travel. Billfish Pond is almost a mile away. For very short distances, or when working without a map, declination can be pretty much ig-

---

* Do not confuse "agonic" and "isogonic." The agonic line is the line along which the compass needle, strictly through coincidence, points to magnetic and true north. An isogonic line is one along which the compass needle points only to magnetic north.

nored, but in the case of the trek to Billfish Pond where a map is required, you could miss the pond by more than a thousand feet, possibly fifteen hundred! (Twenty degrees times fifty feet.) During a five-mile hike, you could miss your objective by as much as a mile. Declination is vital.

And it's also confusing. Taking a bearing, then adding or subtracting the declination calls for mathematics every time you take a compass bearing. There's a far simpler and easier method, which calls for a few minutes work at home before you take to the woods. Working on a flat surface, with a straightedge draw your own magnetic north lines across the face of your maps parallel to the magnetic-north leg of the declination symbol. Cover the entire map with these. If you locate these lines one inch apart on the popular 1:62,500 scale maps, it will closely approximate a scale mile, corresponding to an actual mile on terrain (thus making distance estimates easier). With magnetic-north lines superimposed on your map, orienting and obtaining a bearing is not only easier, but it's more accurate.

Let's try the Billfish Pond trek again. This time, place your map on the ground with the pivot or center of your orienteering compass on one of your magnetic-north lines. When the needle comes to rest, turn the map slowly until the compass needle points along the line. It's that simple. Your map is oriented accurately.

Take another reading on Billfish Pond. The edge of your compass base plate should connect your starting point and your objective. The direction-of-travel arrow will indicate your route. Now, rotate the housing (not the plate) until the compass needle overlays the orienteering arrow in the housing. Your bearing will be 290 degrees.

Some compasses, notably the cruiser and other better-quality instruments, incorporate a mechanism that compensates for declination. In other words, the azimuth scale could be adjusted twenty degrees for use on the Traveler Mountain quadrangle; thereafter readings would automatically compensate for declination. However, the most foolproof method, and one that will work with any compass, is to draw in the magnetic-north lines on your map.

Triangulation

Triangulation (also known as "taking cross-bearings" or "resection") will help you locate your position on a map by taking sightings on at least two visible and prominent landmarks—mountain peaks, for example.

You are traversing a large Canadian lake in a canoe, and are looking for the outlet. High winds come up and you are forced ashore on a small island. You examine the map and discover that the lake is dotted with dozens of such islands. On which one are you windbound? To determine a course to the outlet, you must know your present position. Islands tend to look alike, even to blend with the shoreline, and navigation among them can be tricky.

Glancing about, you notice a prominent hill roughly to the northeast, and another to the northwest. You check the map and find that they are unnamed but, because of your map's contour configurations, you can definitely pinpoint them. And, since the hills are approximately ninety degrees apart, they're ideally located for position fixing, or triangulation. You name them Hill 1 and Hill 2.

First you take a backbearing on Hill 1. With the direction-of-travel arrow on your compass plate pointing to yourself, and its other end toward the top of the hill, rotate the housing (but not the plate) until the orienting arrow in the housing is perfectly overlaid by the compass needle as it points north. Read the azimuth scale where it intersects the foot of the direction-of-travel arrow. You have a backbearing—195 degrees.

Let's assume, moreover, that you had not drawn in the magnetic-north lines on your Canadian map. You will, therefore, have to compensate for declination. The declination calls for a 20-degree compensation. Do you remember that when you took a bearing on Billfish Mountain, you had to add the declination in order to get a true bearing? But this was a case of taking a bearing from the map and transferring it to the field. On the Canadian lake, however, you are doing just the opposite—taking a bearing from the field and transferring it to the map. So the reverse becomes true regarding declination. Instead of adding 20 degrees, you must subtract, so that your bearing is not 195 degrees, but 175 degrees.

Now, do not change the position of the housing on the base plate. Locate one corner of the plate (with the direction-of-travel arrow pointing roughly in your direction) at the top of Hill 1 on the map. While holding the corner of the base plate on the hill, rotate the entire compass slowly until the compass needle (and the orienting arrow under it) are parallel to one of the north-south meridians on the map or to its north-south margin. Draw a line along the straight edge of the base plate. Your location is somewhere along this line.

Repeat the process with a bearing on Hill 2. You obtain a reading of 325 degrees. But, remember, you must deduct 20 degrees for declination so that your true bearing is 305 degrees. With one corner of the base plate atop Hill 2, again rotate the entire compass until the needle is parallel to a north-south meridian or the map's margin. Draw a line as before. If you have taken accurate readings, the two lines will cross precisely over the island on which you took shelter. (This assumes that you have not forgotten to deduct the declination factor; otherwise your cross bearings will miss your location, possibly by a matter of miles.)

You can simplify the triangulation process by drawing in the magnetic-north lines on all of your maps, as suggested on page 271. Take your first bearing, on Hill 1—195 degrees. With magnetic-north lines drawn in, you will not have to deduct for declination. Place one corner of the base plate on Hill 1, and without changing the housing's position, rotate the entire compass slowly until the compass needle points along one of your magnetic-north lines, or is closely parallel to one. Now draw the line along the edge of the base plate. With this system, you can forget about declination and the need to add or subtract it.

Triangulation needn't be confined to lake and river routes. The principle is also applicable to mountain travel. Here, however, you'll probably need to climb to a

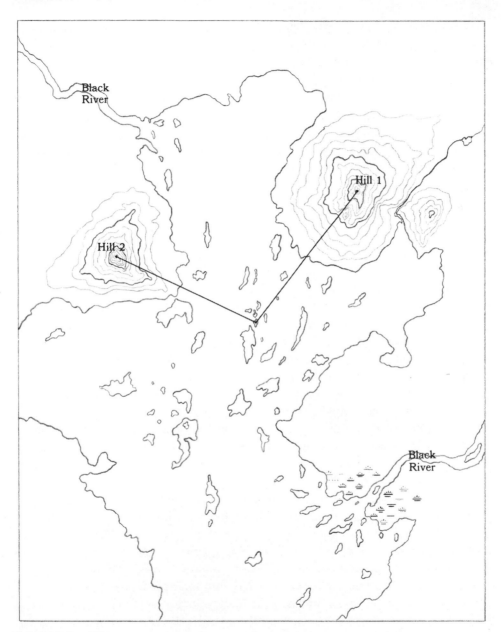

Triangulation Map

prominent knoll in order to obtain a clear view in at least two directions. Since this is often impossible along a heavily wooded mountain trail, consider adding a pocket altimeter/barometer to your outfit. It probably won't be much larger than your orienteering compass and it will weigh well under four ounces. An altimeter/barometer will not only help you to predict weather (See Chapter 1) but also to pinpoint your position with remarkable accuracy.

Assume that you're bushwhacking up the side of a mountain and that you simply hike uphill, knowing that eventually you will reach the summit. Not good woodsmanship, but it's done. After a while you begin to suspect that you may be straying from the most direct route. You pause and look out over the pitch you've just climbed; off in the distance on another peak, you notice a forest-fire lookout tower. You unfold your map and examine it for a fire-tower symbol—a tiny triangle. There it is, clearly indicated; there is no other tower anywhere. You note on the map that the tower is at 2,400 feet above sea level. Now, check your altimeter/barometer. It reads 2,300 feet. Continue uphill until the instrument reads 2,400 feet, the same elevation as the fire tower.

The next process is identical to that used when you took sights on Hill 1 and 2 to locate your position on the lake. This time, however, you'll need only one sighting. With your direction-of-travel arrow pointed roughly at yourself and aligned with the fire tower, rotate the compass housing (but not the base plate) until the orienting arrow in the housing is directly overlaid by your compass needle when it settles solidly toward magnetic north. Note the bearing where the azimuth scale intersects the point of the direction-of-travel arrow—145 degrees. Now place one corner of the base plate on the location of the fire tower and rotate the entire unit slowly until your compass needle points along one of the magnetic-north lines you've drawn on your map. Without moving the compass from the map, draw a pencil line along the side of the base plate. You can now remove the compass. Your position? It's precisely at the point where your penciled line crosses the 2,400-foot contour line on which you're standing.

It should be noted that such observations are most accurate when the line of sight (to the fire tower, for example) crosses a contour line as near to a right angle as possible. Any position line that crosses at a very sharp, or very obtuse, angle is likely to be less accurate.

An altimeter/barometer can also give you pinpointed "progress reports." For instance, you're hiking a mountain trail for the first time and you wonder how much farther it is to a shelter under the brow of the peak. You check your altimeter/barometer. It reads 2,300 feet. You then examine the map. Your position is where the trail crosses the 2,300-foot contour line. An altimeter can perform the same function even when you're bushwhacking up the slope of a mountain. You know your position approximately but not precisely. You come to a tumbling mountain stream. You note on the map that there's only one such brook in your vicinity. The altimeter reads 1,940 feet. Your position, then, is precisely where the 1,940-foot contour line crosses the stream.

All in all, an altimeter is well worth carrying in mountain country, whether you're a backpacker, fisherman or hunter, or a skier. It adds a third dimension—the vertical. For the utmost accuracy it's wise to set your altimeter often, at least at every interval of a few hundred feet, or whenever you reach a known elevation. On Geological Survey quadrangles, contour lines, mountains and hilltops, ponds and lakes, and, of course, bench marks, have their elevations clearly indicated.

It's a good plan, too, to be sure that your altimeter/barometer is set for the correct elevation at the end of each day so that barometric fluctuations can be read accurately.

SOME SPECIAL CANOE-TRAVEL PROBLEMS

There's little likelihood of your getting "lost" while canoe tripping down a major river. So long as you continue with the current, you'll ultimately arrive at your destination, barring problems en route. But rivers, especially in the wilderness, often have a deceptive sameness about their banks. Coasting along, borne by the current, enjoying occasional encounters with wildlife, you can easily lose your "position." What is your precise location? How many miles have you covered on a given day? Will you arrive at your destination in ten days as planned? There's even the possibility that you may overshoot your take-out point—especially if it's not distinctly marked.

It's crucial to know your position along any waterway at all times. Keep your map unfurled to the appropriate section and encased in a waterproof plastic case. Note each landmark as you pass it, then study the map so that you are ready for the next one.

This may seem like superfluous caution, but it isn't. Suppose, for instance, that you encounter a series of islands, perhaps a dozen or so, not an unusual occurrence on major waterways. Most of them you can pass on either side. The map indicates plenty of water. However, two of these islands—let's say No. 4 and No. 7—have indistinct passages on one side of each. If you slip through among the islands without noting which is which, you have a good chance of passing by Island No. 4 on the wrong side. It could be a bottleneck—too little water for navigation—and you may have to backtrack, losing time and expending unnecessary energy. And if you're really "lost" among the islands, you might even repeat the error at Island No. 7. Careful map watching avoids such predicaments.

Along some rivers, decent campsites are not always plentiful. The banks may be too steep, or extensive marshes may border the only campsites along your route, some of them as much as fifteen miles apart, due to rough terrain or long stretches of swamp. You've cruised happily all day, watching the scenery slip by, but have paid little attention to your position on the river. Suddenly it's late afternoon and the promised campsite is nowhere in view. Have you passed it, and should you put about and push back upstream to find it? Or should you gamble that it's still some distance downstream? If it's not, are you ready for at least ten more miles of paddling to reach the next one—after dark and dog tired? The alternative may be a "siwash" camp and a night of misery.

Even careful map watching may not prevent you from missing landmarks. For instance, you've been noting the feeder streams that enter the river, each one indicating your position. However, it may be that one or more of those streams is not marked on the map. Observing landmarks is good technique, but use your compass, too.

Let's say that you can see a long ridge off to one side. At one end of the ridge, the terrain drops off sharply, almost in a cliff. This should be easy to find on your map. Use the same process by which you located yourself (page 274) by sighting on the fire tower. There's no need for true triangulation here. A single sighting will do it. Let's assume you obtain a bearing of 110 degrees. You've marked your maps with magnetic-north lines, so transferring that bearing to your map and drawing the line along the base plate of your compass is a simple matter. Your precise position is the point where that line crosses the river. If there are prominent features along your route, it's a good practice to take frequent sightings; they will corroborate your marking of various landmarks such as feeder streams, sharp turns, rips and rapids.

Traversing a large lake is another matter. It may put your navigating skills to the test.

According to the scale on the map of Lake Rousseau (cited here as a fictitious example) the lake is roughly thirty-six miles long. However, its shoreline, like that of so many wilderness lakes, is irregular, its shape resembling a splotch of blue ink thrown onto the map. You enter the lake from the river in the southeast corner of the map and you're headed for the outlet in the northeast quadrant. It's clear that you'll find no easy direct route. The region is typical of the northern bush country, relatively flat, with no prominent reference points in evidence. And the distances are great—this will not be a leisurely afternoon paddle.

As you enter the lake, pull ashore and study your map. The first leg of your crossing is obvious. You must pass between Wanigan and Teepee islands. But as you look in their direction, some twelve miles away, you'll face similar visual conditions. But your map tells you there's a passage between the two.

At this point, you use the same procedure as you did when you took a bearing on Billfish Pond (see page 266).

Draw a pencil line from the outlet (Point A) to Teepee Island (Point B)—your proposed route. Now orient the map, aligning it under your orienteering compass so that the needle overlays one of the magnetic-north lines that you have drawn in before leaving home. Next place the edge of the base plate along your penciled route. Then, without disturbing the base plate, rotate the housing until the orienting arrow points to magnetic north under the needle. Your bearing is at the point where the direction-of-travel arrow intersects the azimuth scale—350 degrees. It's still early in the day, barely midmorning, so you strike out across the lake, your compass on the floor of the canoe, tied by a lanyard to the thwart or gunwale in case of a spill. Although the wind is not strong, there is a light chop that causes your canoe to bob a little. However, with a liquid-filled compass, needle "jiggle" is minimized and with careful reading every ten minutes or so, you'll probably be able to hold your course.

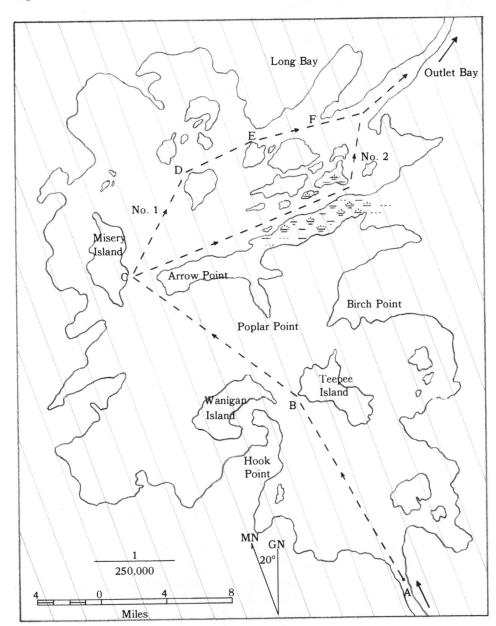

Lake Rousseau

You finally arrive at Teepee Island, find an attractive campsite and camp for the night. Early the next morning the weather looks good. You're ready for the second leg. Repeat yesterday's procedure with the map and compass. You'll come up with a bearing of 340 degrees for another twelve miles to Misery Island (Point C).

When you get to Misery Island, you will face a decision that your compass cannot make for you. It may be possible to avoid a large expanse of open water by following the north shore of Arrow Point (Route No. 2 on the map). This is not only sheltered water but you probably won't need to bother with precise navigation. Your course will lie along a fairly straight shoreline for some fifteen miles. However, some nine to ten miles beyond Point C there is a huge marsh extending into a cluster of islands—it is difficult to tell how far. You may find yourself pushing through mile after mile of marsh grass or, with luck, it may be clear sailing, the marsh on one side, the islands on the other. If the marsh does interfere with travel, you could probably cut in a northerly direction, winding among the islands until you reach clear water again. But that cluster is ten miles long, five miles wide, and the map probably shows only the larger islands. It may be more of a labyrinth than you think.

You decide against the marsh route. It may be a poor decision, but you'll never know. At least, you feel surer with the open-water route. So from Point C, Misery Island, you take a bearing on Point D, the tip of an unnamed island—60 degrees. At Point D you aim your direction-of-travel arrow at Point E for an 85-degree azimuth.

From Point E to the outlet, it's seven miles. But once again, when you arrive here, all you can discern is a dark ten-mile-long shoreline with no evidence of bays. The outlet bay is barely a half-mile wide. Your compass bearing has to be on the nose. Your map shows three bays. Enter the wrong one and you'll probably paddle five miles in, and five needless miles back again. Trial and error has no place in wilderness canoe travel. It was just such a situation that led Dillon Wallace and Leonidas Hubbard into the wrong bay in Labrador and to the tragic ending of their expedition. So you're careful with your compass sighting and come up with a bearing of 110 degrees. In a few hours, you'll be paddling into Outlet Bay. You know this is the right one. A mile or so into the bay you begin to feel the current helping you along. You've just completed a difficult lake traverse.

Not all lake traverses are this complicated. On the other hand, some are far more complex with intricate, narrow winding passages to be navigated, the wrong one often leading to a dead end, miles off course. This is all the more reason that practicing with a compass and map, even when you're on familiar water, will ease the chore of future lake crossings.

What is true of lake travel is true of woods and mountain travel as well. Only when using a map and a compass becomes second nature for you, can you truly enjoy to the hilt tripping afoot or by canoe.

Appendixes

APPENDIX I

Additional Reading

Obviously, no manual can possibly cover every aspect of life in the outdoors today, and this one is no exception. Because it is largely oriented toward equipment, technique is touched on only incidentally, usually as it affects the choice of gear. Fortunately, outdoor literature is replete with definitive works. In fact, an all-encompassing library must comprise several hundred volumes. The following titles form the nucleus of such a library.

The books, marked with an asterisk (*) are out of print. However, these are not usually difficult to locate. Check your local library or enlist the aid of a used-book dealer. If they do not have the title you're seeking, they can probably locate it for you.

Chapter One—Into the Backcountry: You and the Weather

Canadian Atmospheric Environment Services, "Temperatures and Precipitation 1941–1970." Reference table of average and extreme temperatures/precipitations listed for all regions of Canada. Obtainable by writing the Canadian Atmospheric Environment Services, 4905 Dufferin Street, Downsview, Ontario, Canada M3H 5T4.

Lee, Albert, *Weather Wisdom*. Doubleday, 1976. Devoted almost entirely to the reading and understanding of natural weather signs.

Leopold, Aldo, *A Sand County Almanac*. Oxford University Press, 1979. Seasonal sketches and reflections on the spiritual value of wilderness, and the wilderness ethic.

Ludlum, David, *The Country Journal New England Weather Book*. Houghton Mifflin, 1976. An almanac of weather records and weather history. Includes a section on basic meteorology.

Reifsnyder, William, *Weathering the Wilderness.* Sierra Club, 1980. Detailed treatment of meteorology including helpful information on the climate of particular regions of the country and on weather hazards.

Rutstrum, Calvin, *The Wilderness Life.* Macmillan, 1975. A collection of wilderness reflections by a seasoned outdoorsman and guide.

Sager, Raymond M. and E. F., *The Sager Weathercaster.* Weather Publications, 1969. A book/instrument that translates wind and barometric readings into a weather forecast. To be used in conjunction with a barometer.

U. S. Department of Commerce, "Monthly Averages of Temperature and Precipitation for State Climatic Divisions 1941–1970." Reference table of local temperature and precipitation norms and extremes by region. Also informative discussion of general topography, climate and unusual weather patterns. Obtainable through the U. S. Department of Commerce, National Climatic Center, Federal Building, Asheville, NC 28801.

Watts, Allan, *Instant Weather Forecasting.* Dodd, Mead, 1968. Designed to help the outdoorsman predict weather based on natural weather signs—clouds, wind, etc. Especially useful information on the timing of expected changes. Twenty-four color illustrations show the major sky appearances and the weather they portend.

Chapter Two—Clothing: Comfort Through Thick and Thin

Dasheff, William and Laura Dearborn, *Good Garb.* Dell Publishing Co., 1980. Source book for functional clothing. Alphabetical listing of manufacturers and retailers and their garments. Illustrated.

Klapper, Marvin, *Fabric Almanac.* Fairchild, 1971. Reference book for fiber and fabric information. Includes comprehensive glossary of common terms.

Pizzuto, Joseph J., *Fabric Science.* Fairchild Publications, 1974. A technical but informative reference book on fiber characteristics and fabric construction.

Chapter Three—Boots and Shoes: Your Best Foot Forward

Cohn, Walter E., *Modern Footwear Materials and Processes.* Fairchild, 1969. Technical reference guide to all aspects of footwear manufacturing.

Donaldson, Gerald, *The Walking Book.* Holt, Rinehart and Winston, 1980. Coverage of all aspects of footwear construction, design and fit.

Manning, Harvey, *Backpacking: One Step at a Time.* Vintage, 1980. Contains a good chapter on how to select a pair of hiking boots.

Chapter Four—Sleeping Bags: Slumber on the Trail

Kemsley, William, *Backpacking Equipment Buyer's Guide.* Collier Books, 1977. Contains several selections on down and polyester sleeping-bag construction and design. Comparative weight and warmth information. Section on cleaning sleeping bags.

Chapter Five—Shelter: Tents for All Seasons

Hatton, E. M., *The Tent Book*. Houghton Mifflin Co., 1979. Worldwide history of the tent with extensive section on modern tent materials and styles.

Chapter Six—Packing Gear: Afoot and Afloat

"Internal Frame Packs," *Backpacker,* October 1979/November 1979, Issue 35. Brief review of pack features including an evaluation of some current models.

Kemsley, William, *Backpacking Equipment Buyer's Guide*. Collier Books, 1977. External frame pack construction and design. Covers frame styles and features. Review of some of the more popular external frame models.

Manning, Harvey, *Backpacking: One Step at a Time*. Vintage, 1980. Advice for backpackers on how to select an external frame pack.

"Packs for Cross-Country Skiers," *Backpacker,* December 1978/January 1979, Issue 30. Review of internal frame pack features.

Rugge, John and James West Davidson, *The Complete Wilderness Paddler*. Alfred Knopf, 1977. Short section on packs and waterproofing techniques for wilderness canoe tripping.

Chapter Seven—Pots, Pans and Stoves: Dining Under the Sky

Angier, Bradford, *Field Guide to Edible Wild Plants*. Stackpole. More than one hundred edible plants, fruits, nuts and berries. Descriptions of their appearance and where to find them. Illustrated.

Barker, Harriet, *Supermarket Backpacker*. Great Lakes Living Press, 1977. For those who want to plan lightweight camping fare using supermarket ingredients.

Bunnelle, Hass, *Food for Knapsackers*. Sierra Club Books, 1971. Diet planning for backpackers. List of suppliers.

Ewald, Ellen B., *Recipes for a Small Planet*. Ballantine 1973. Nutrition and menu planning. Natural foods recipes.

*Riviere, Bill, *Family Camper's Cookbook*. Holt, Rinehart and Winston, 1965. Campware and cooking technique for family campers. Includes recipes.

Chapter Eight—Woods Tools: On Warming Yourself Twice

Kephart, Horace, *Camping and Woodcraft*. Macmillan, 1917. Chapter on basic axemanship, splitting techniques, wood types and wood seasoning. Outdated in parts but largely relevant.

*Mason, Bernard, *Woodsmanship*. A. S. Barnes and Co., 1954. Classic guide to traditional loggers' tools and techniques.

Vivian, John, *How to Select, Cut and Season Good Firewood*. Colonial Printing Co., 1977. Working up firewood for home or backwoods camp.

Warner, Ken, *The Practical Book of Knives*. Winchester Press, 1976. Complete coverage of knife design, construction and care for the collector and outdoorsman. Illustrated.

Chapter Nine—Winter Travel: Cross-Country on Skis and Snowshoes

Caldwell, John, *Cross Country Skiing Today*. Stephen Greene Press, 1977. Sections on cross-country technique and equipment for both beginners and experienced skiers.

Gilette, Ned, *Cross-Country Skiing*. The Mountaineers, 1979. Treatment of cross-country ski equipment and technique with special emphasis on wilderness touring and mountaineering.

Osgood, William and Leslie Hurley, *The Snowshoe Book*. Stephen Greene Press, 1975. Brief history of snowshoeing. Much of the book is devoted to choosing snowshoes and to snowshoeing technique.

Prater, Gene, *Snowshoeing*. The Mountaineers, 1974. Snowshoeing equipment and technique. Sections on snowshoe repairs, winter mountaineering and safety.

Roberts, Harry, *Movin' On*. Stonewall Press, 1977. Winter camping equipment and technique.

Chapter Ten—Canoes: Pole, Paddle and Portage

Beletz, Al, Syl and Frank, *Canoe Poling*. A. C. MacKenzie Press, 1974. Covers pole types and techniques. Many photos.

Davidson, James West and John Rugge, *The Complete Wilderness Paddler*. Alfred Knopf, 1977. The story of a journey down the Moisie River in Labrador, the book also gives a thorough description of trip planning, canoeing equipment and navigation techniques.

McPhee, John, *The Survival of the Bark Canoe*. Farrar, Straus and Giroux, 1975. Using a trip down the Allagash River in Maine as its basis, the book covers contemporary canoe characteristics and other related subjects.

Riviere, Bill, *Pole, Paddle and Portage*. Little, Brown, 1969. Covers canoe design, paddling and poling technique. Section on canoeable rivers and waterways.

Urban, John T., *The A.M.C. Whitewater Handbook for Canoe and Kayak*. Appalachian Mountain Clubs, 1976. Booklet on all aspects of white-water paddling.

*Wallace, Dillon, *Packing and Portaging*. Macmillan Co., 1912. The equipment discussed may be out of date, but the information about wilderness canoe travel is as sound as ever.

Wood, Peter, *Running the Rivers of North America,* Barre Publishing, 1978. Basic canoeing, kayaking and rafting technique for river running. Includes descriptions of the major rivers in North America.

Chapter Eleven—Map and Compass: North Is That Way . . .

Kjellstrom, Bjorn, *Be Expert with Map and Compass*. Charles Scribner's Sons, 1976. Guide to map and compass work with an emphasis on orienteering.

Rutstrum, Calvin, *The Wilderness Route Finder.* Collier Books, 1967. Map and compass navigation for the wilderness traveler. Includes section on celestial navigation, finding your way without a compass and what to do if you become lost.

General Works on the Outdoors

*Bean, Leon L., *Hunting—Fishing and Camping.* Dingley Press, 1942. How to hunt, dress fish and game, cook outdoors, navigate and set up a backwoods camp.

Danielsen, John A., *Winter Hiking and Camping.* Adirondack Mountain Club, 1979. Equipment and technique for winter travel. Chapter on physiology, survival and mountain rescue. Geared for mountaineers but applicable to all cold-weather camping.

Fletcher, Colin, *The New Complete Walker.* Alfred Knopf, 1974. Modern backpacking equipment and technique based on the author's extensive experience.

Hart, John, *Walking Softly in the Wilderness.* Sierra Club, 1977. A guide to lightweight camping equipment with an emphasis on minimal environmental impact.

Hillcourt, William, *The Official Boy Scout Handbook.* Boy Scouts of America, 1979. Introduction to camping equipment and basic technique.

Kemsley, William, *Backpacking Equipment Buyer's Guide.* Collier Books, 1977. Lightweight camping equipment from bags, packs, tents and footwear to snowshoes and stoves. General reference information and reviews of specific models.

Kephart, Horace, *Camping and Woodcraft.* Macmillan, 1917. Several different editions. The classic in its field. Much of the material on technique still valid.

Landi, Val, *The Bantam Great Outdoors Guide to the U.S.A. and Canada.* Bantam, 1978. Outdoor recreation sourcebook for camping-trip planning. Information on where to go, how to get there, where to camp, etc. Lists of outdoor instruction schools, outfitters, guides.

Manning, Harvey, *Backpacking: One Step at a Time.* Vintage Books, 1980. Guide to all types of lightweight carrying gear, hiking boots, sleeping bags and kitchen equipment.

Perry, John and Jane G., *The Random House Guide to National Areas of the Eastern United States.* Random House, 1980. Outdoor recreational source book; organized by state. Lists parks, trails, rivers, bicycle trails, touring centers, ski areas, places for hunting and fishing.

Thomas, Lynn, *The Backpacking Woman.* Anchor/Doubleday, 1980. Backpacking, from a woman's point of view.

Roberts, Harry, *Movin' Out.* Stonewall Press, 1975. Backpacking in the East; guide to equipment for those new to the outdoors.

Van Lear, Denise, ed., *The Best About Backpacking.* Sierra Club, 1974. Fifteen chapters on backpacking equipment. A compilation of chapters written by nine well-known outdoor writers.

Other Outdoor Subjects

Fishing

Brooks, Joe, *Salt Water Game Fishing*. Harper and Row, 1968. Tackle and technique for fishing everything from marlin, tuna, tarpon and shark to barracuda.

Fly Fisherman Magazine, *Fishing with the Fly Rod,* Ziff Davis, 1978. Guide to casting, reading water, fly tying and fishing tackle. Chapters by Joan and Lee Wulff, Carl Richards, John Merwin, Ernest Schweibert and others.

*Haig-Brown, Roderick, *A Primer of Fly-Fishing.* William Morrow, 1964. Equipment and technique by one of the authorities in the field.

McClane, Albert J., *McClane's New Standard Fishing Encyclopedia and International Angling Guide, Revised Edition.* Holt, Rinehart and Winston, 1974. Treatment of all types of fishing.

Wulff, Lee, *Fishing with Lee Wulff.* Alfred Knopf, 1972. Tackle, technique and tactics for fresh and salt water fishing.

Hunting

*Connett, Eugene, ed., *Duck Hunting Along the Atlantic Flyway.* Bonanza Books, 1947. A classic for duck hunters.

Evans, George Bird, *The Upland Shooting Life.* Alfred Knopf, 1971. Equipment, dog training, where to hunt, general technique for the upland bird hunter.

O'Connor, Jack, *The Art of Hunting Big Game in North America.* Alfred Knopf, 1967. Hunting technique for all types of big game.

Tapply, H. G., *The Sportsman's Notebook.* Holt, Rinehart and Winston, 1951. Information for hunters and fishermen. Tapply is author of *Field & Stream* feature "Tap's Tips."

Mountaineering

Chouinard, Yvon, *Climbing Ice.* Sierra Club, 1978. History of ice and snow climbing. Comprehensive sections on climbing technique, crampon use and rope work. Also sections on avalanche travel, general safety and mountaineering equipment.

Ferber, Peggy, ed., *Mountaineering: The Freedom of the Hills.* The Mountaineers, 1974. Treatment of equipment, rock, snow and ice technique, safety and weather.

Smith, Howard E., Jr., *The Complete Beginner's Guide to Mountain Climbing.* Doubleday, 1977. Basic equipment, planning and technique for climbers, including sections on rope technique, ice climbing and general safety.

Bicycling

Sloane, Eugene A., *The Complete Book of Bicycling.* Simon and Schuster, 1974. Guide for cyclists that includes such subjects as choosing a bike, bike touring, bike accessories, and maintenance and repair.

First Aid and Survival

The American Medical Association. *The American Medical Association's Handbook of First Aid and Emergency Care.* Random House, 1980. A fully illustrated first-aid manual for laymen.

The American Red Cross. *Standard First Aid and Personal Safety, Second Edition.* Doubleday, 1979. A first-aid manual for laymen.

Angier, Bradford. *How to Stay Alive in the Woods.* Collier, 1956. How to find food, water and shelter. Plus sections on navigation and survival techniques.

Darvill, Fred Jr., M.D., *Mountaineering Medicine—A Wilderness Medical Guide.* Skagit Mountain Rescue, 1980. Pocket-size first-aid guide for wilderness travelers.

Lathrop, Theodore G., M.D., *Hypothermia: Killer of the Unprepared.* The Mazamas, 1972. The causes and treatment of hypothermia written for laymen by a physician active in mountaineering.

Olsen, Larry Dean, *Outdoor Survival Skills,* Brigham Young University Press, 1973. Sections on finding shelter, food and water in survival situations. Illustrated.

Washburn, Bradford, *Frostbite.* Boston Museum of Science, 1972. The author, a noted mountaineer, describes frostbite and how to treat it.

Wilkerson, James A., M.D., *Medicine for Mountaineering.* The Mountaineers, 1979. Diagnosis and treatment of disease and injury that a mountain climber is likely to encounter. Lists of suggested medical supplies for mountaineers and backwoodsmen.

Fitness

Bailey, Covert, *Fit or Fat.* Houghton Mifflin, 1980. Emphasis on aerobic exercise and physical exercise rather than diet.

Cooper, Kenneth, M.D., *The New Aerobics.* Bantam Books, 1970. Programs for maintaining and developing your body.

Outdoor Photography

Pfeiffer, C. Boyd, *Field Guide to Outdoor Photography.* Stackpole (Harrisburg, Pa.), 1977. Introduction to outdoor photographic equipment and technique. Sections on picture composition, lighting and film exposure.

Periodicals

Adventure Travel
One Park Avenue
New York, NY 10016

Audubon
950 Third Avenue
New York, NY 10022

American Rifleman
1600 Rhode Island Ave., NW
Washington, DC 20036

Backpacker
One Park Avenue
New York, NY 10016

Canoe
131 East Murray Street
Fort Wayne, IN 46803

Ducks Unlimited
P.O. Box 234
South Lyme, CT 06376

Field & Stream
1515 Broadway
New York, NY 10036

Fly Fisherman
P.O. Box 2705
Boulder, CO 80322

Grays Sporting Journal
1330 Beacon St.
Brookline, MA 02146

Nordic World
P.O. Box 366
Mountain View, CA 94040

Outdoor Life
380 Madison Avenue
New York, NY 10017

Outside
3401 W. Division Street
Chicago, IL 60651

Rod and Reel
P.O. Box 1309
Manchester Center, VT 05255

Sports Afield
250 W. 55 Street
New York, NY 10019

APPENDIX II

Equipment Checklists

The following comprises a master checklist of apparel and equipment; you can devise your own list from it, adapted to your specific needs. Bear in mind that the more extensive your trip and/or the larger your party, the more important the use of such a checklist becomes. Once you're in the backcountry, it's almost impossible to replenish supplies or obtain equipment. For convenience, the footwear and apparel section of the list has been divided into two parts, one for warm weather, the other for cold. Obviously, some overlap is to be expected. Also, if you plan to be out for more than a single night you'll need to adjust the amounts.

    I. APPAREL AND FOOTWEAR
        A. *Warm Weather*
            Cotton t-shirt or fishnet shirt
            Cotton briefs
            Polypropylene underwear (optional)
            Innersocks
            Wool socks (two pairs or more)
            Shorts (optional)
            Long pants—cotton or cotton blend
            Long-sleeve cotton shirt
            Lightweight long-sleeve wool shirt or sweater
            Raingear—jacket and pants
            Nylon shell (optional)
            Visored cap or rain hat
            Leather or leather top/rubber bottom footwear
            Moccasins or sneakers (in pack)

        B. *Cold Weather*
            Fishnet, polypropylene or two-layer underwear
            Inner socks
            Wool socks (two pairs or more)
            Lightweight long-sleeve wool shirt
            Wool trousers
            Second pair of wool trousers or knickers (optional)
            Insulated vest or wool sweater
            Wind resistant shell with hood
            Down- or polyester-insulated jacket (optional)
            Raingear—jacket and pants
            Windpants (optional)
            Wool cap or balaclava
            Wool or insulated gloves/mittens
            Insulated leather, leather top/rubber bottom or rubber footwear

Insulated booties (optional)
Overmitts (optional)
Gaiters (optional)

II. OTHER PERSONAL GEAR

Belt or suspenders
Bandana
Eyeglasses (extra)
Sunglasses

Toothbrush/toothpaste
Soap
Toilet paper
Lip balm
Sunscreen
Insect repellent
Small towel or washcloth (optional)

First-aid kit (see Appendix III)

Watch
Compass
Map(s)
Matches (in waterproof case)
Knife
Flashlight
Extra batteries, bulb (optional)
Pad and pencil (optional)

Licenses/permits (if necessary)

III. BEDDING, SHELTER AND PACKS

Sleeping bag
Liner bag (optional)
Ground pad or air mattress
Air mattress repair kit (if applicable)
Tent or bivouac sack
Extra stakes, line
Tent poles

Tarp (optional)
Pack (waterproof if necessary)
Internal or external pack frame
Pack-frame repair parts (tape, clevis pins, etc.)
Rain cover (optional)
Day pack (optional)

IV. KITCHEN

Stove with fuel
Extra fuel
Fuel spout (optional)
Spare generator (if applicable)
Matches
Eye dropper or priming paste
   (optional)
Cookset
Griddle (optional)
Pot holder
Reflector oven (optional)
Nails (optional)
Spoon, fork, cup, plates
Ladle or dipper (optional)
Water bottle
Water bucket(s)
Can opener
Cook spoon

Chef's knife (optional)
Salt, pepper, sugar
Spices (optional)
Folding pack saw (optional)
Axe (optional)
Food
Beverage mix, tea, coffee, etc.
Paper towels (optional)
Aluminum foil or plastic wrap
Trash bag(s)
Spatula
Grate (optional)
Dish scrubber
Water purification tablets (if necessary)
Nylon dining fly (optional)
Fifty feet of extra rope
Lantern (optional)

V. TRANSPORTATION

Canoe
Life jacket(s)
Spare paddle(s)
Portage yoke (optional)
Painter lines
Bailer or sponge
Canoe repair kit
Kneepads (optional)
Outboard motor
Motor bracket (where applicable)
Engine gas, oil, (if applicable)
Tool kit, spare parts (if applicable)
Wetsuit, wetsuit booties and gloves
    (optional)
(or)
Snowshoes
Repair kit (extra lacing, silver duct
    tape)
Poles (optional)
Snowshoe crampons (optional)
(or)
Skis
Waxing kit (if applicable)
Poles

Extra basket (optional)
Ski boots
Extra tip (wood skis)
(or)
Bicycle
Extra tire or flat-repair kit
Accessory pump
Tools and spare parts
(or)
Off-road vehicle
Extra oil and gas
Spare tire
Auxiliary pump (optional)
Heavy-duty jack
Thirty to fifty foot tow chain
Jumper cables
Come-a-long
Auto compass
Flashlight
Shovel
Fire extinguisher (optional)
Tool set
Axe

VI. MISCELLANEOUS

Extra shoelaces
Sewing kit
Fishing gear (optional)
Hunting gear (optional)
Binoculars (optional)
Camera, film, extra lenses (optional)
Book or other reading (optional)
Playing cards or cribbage board (optional)
Gorp
Rescue blanket (optional)

APPENDIX III

First Aid

For any sort of a trip into the backcountry, or even for a short day hike close to a highway, a first-aid kit is mandatory. The items suggested below for inclusion in such a kit are adequate for two persons on a two- or three-day trek. For more extensive trips, or for a larger party, a more complete kit is required, and most first-aid manuals will suggest what you should carry. It is generally preferable to assemble one all-inclusive kit, rather than to depend on an assortment of individual kits. This central kit should be packed in a waterproof bag or pack and be clearly labeled so that any member of the party can locate it quickly.

- Any medication for pre-existing diseases or disorders
- Aspirin (5 gram tablets)   18 or more
- Band-aids® (1″ size)   12 or more
- Sterile Gauze Pads (2″ x 2″ size)   2 or more
- Sterile Gauze Pads (4″ x 4″ size)   2 or more
- Adhesive Tape (1″ wide)   1 small roll
- Moleskin (4″ x 4″)   1 or 2 squares
- Antibiotic Ointment   Small tube
- Tweezers   1 pair
- Needle (1½–2″ long)   1
- Butterfly Bandages   3 or more
- First-Aid manual (booklet size)
- Razor blade   1
- Iodine, alcohol or antiseptic   1 ounce
- Ace bandage with safety pin (optional)
- Snake-bit kit (optional)
- Sunscreen lotion (containing PABA)

APPENDIX IV

Outdoor Organizations

Even if you're not a "joiner," membership in an outdoor organization is worthwhile. Such groups, many with local chapters affiliated with a national or parent club, publish bulletins, full-fledged periodicals and even detailed regional guides. Some conduct training sessions in a variety of subjects: canoeing, ski touring, even fly tying. Others run group trips on which experts act as guides and advisers. Still other groups will help you plan a personal trip. Whatever your interest—backpacking, ski touring, canoeing, fishing, hunting, mountain climbing, archery, orienteering—there's a group specializing in it, with members eager to share their expertise.

Adirondack Mountain Club
Gabriels, NY 12939

American Canoe Association
P.O. Box 248
Lorton, VA 22079

American Hiking Society
1255 Portland Place
Boulder, CO 80302

American Orienteering Service
Box 345
La Porte, IN 46350

American Whitewater Affiliation
Box 1584
San Bruno, CA 94066

Appalachian Mountain Club
5 Joy Street
Boston, MA 02108

Appalachian Trail Conference
Box 236
Harper's Ferry, WV 25425

Bass Anglers Sportsman Society
P.O. Box 17116
Montgomery, AL 36141

Boy Scouts of America
P.O. Box 61030
Dallas/Fort Worth Airport TX 75261

Ducks Unlimited
P.O. Box 234
South Lyme, CT 06376

Federation of Fly Fishermen
519 Main Street
El Segundo, CA 90245

Federation of Western Outdoor Clubs
4534½ University Way, N.E.
Seattle, WA 98105

Girl Scouts of America
830 Third Ave.
New York, NY 10022

Green Mountain Club
108 Merchants Row
Rutland, VT 05701

International Atlantic Fishing Federation
100 Park Avenue
New York, NY 10017

Isaac Walton League
1800 N. Kent Street
Suite 806
Arlington, VA 22209

National Audubon Society
950 Third Ave.
New York, NY 10022

National Campers and Hikers Association
7172 Transit Road
Buffalo, NY 14221

National Hiking & Ski Touring Association
Box 7421
Colorado Springs, CO 80933

National Rifle Association
1600 Rhode Island Ave., NW
Washington, DC 20036

National Wildlife Federation
1412 16th St., NW
Washington, DC 20036

Ruffed Grouse Society
994 Broadhead Road, Suite 304
Corapolis, PA 15108

Safari Club International
361 Charles Street
Reading, MA 01867

Sierra Club
530 Bush Street
San Francisco, CA 94108

Trout Unlimited
P.O. Box 361
Denver, CO 80201

United States Canoe Association
9021 F. North 91st St.
Milwaukee, WI 53224

The Wilderness Society
1901 Pennsylvania Ave., NW
Washington, DC 20006

APPENDIX V

Sources for Trip Planning

Maps

Outfitters in both the United States and Canada usually stock topographic maps as well as guidebooks that cover their immediate areas. Local, regional and national outdoor organizations are also excellent sources. If, however, you cannot obtain maps from any of these, write to one of the agencies listed below for an index map from which you can order specific quadrangles.

United States

Topographic maps of areas east of the Mississippi:
    U. S. Geological Survey
    Map Distribution Center
    1200 Eads Street
    Arlington, VA 22202
Topographic maps of areas west of the Mississippi:
    U. S. Geological Survey
    Map Distribution Center
    Federal Center, Building 41
    Denver, CO 80225
Nautical maps of inland waterways and coastal areas:
    U. S. National Ocean Survey
    Distribution Division
    Riverdale, MD 20804

Canada

Canadian Map Office
Department of Energy, Mines and Resources
614 Booth Street
Ottawa, Ontario K1A 0E9

Weather

The National Weather Service and National Park Service both furnish valuable information on the climate and weather patterns of any area you plan to visit in the United States. For more detailed reference tables on precipitation and temperature, write to one of the following agencies. Be sure to specify your area of interest.

United States	Canada
U. S. Department of Commerce	Canadian Atmospheric Environment Services
National Climatic Center	4905 Dufferin Street
Federal Building	Downsview, Ontario M3H 5T4
Asheville, NC 28801	

Index

About the Author

BILL RIVIERE has spent his lifetime exactly where he wants to be—in the out-doors. He has worked as a lumberjack, served with the U.S. Border Patrol, and is a former Maine Guide. He has fished and canoed from Okefenokee Swamp to British Columbia, and has demonstrated American outdoor equipment in the Soviet Union. His many books include *The Camper's Bible, Pole, Paddle and Portage* and *Backcountry Camping.* A long-time columnist for the Boston *Globe,* Riviere is a member of the Outdoor Writer's Association of America. He lives with his wife in North Berwick, Maine.

1922 MAINE HUNTING COAT

In use

Showing large back pocket

Showing four small pockets for Drinking Cup, Compass, Whistle and Watch

SO MANY shooting accidents occur in the big game country that everyone should take some precautions.

The Maine Safety Hunting Coat is so colored that it not only gives you this protection, but does not frighten big game.

It is an all wool, smooth finished, medium weight, unlined and made extra long. Comes in two colors, as shown below, also in Plain Dark Green. The Black and Brown plaid and Green has belt that is bright red on one side.

The arrangement of pockets is ideal. A separate pocket is provided for each article needed, thus avoiding all noise of rattling or breaking.

The most convenient pocket is directly in the back with opening on the right outside seam. This pocket is very large and is intended for carrying lunch, game or any thing bulky. There are two outside pockets for gloves, a match pocket and a 2½x5 camera or pipe pocket, all with button flaps. There are four pockets, as shown in cut, for compass, drinking cup, whistle, and watch.

These things, once placed in your coat, are always with you when you need them and are so distributed that they are no bother whatever.

Designed, made and sold by one who has hunted Maine deer for the past twenty-four years.

Price: Coat without belt $15.00, with belt $16.50. Complete suit, either pattern, $23.00.

Delivered free anywhere in the United States.

Send for free samples of cloth.

The following pictures show the two patterns of plaid cloth used in our Hunting Coats, Hunting Pants and Hunting Shirts.

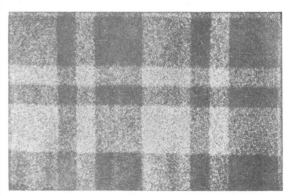

Cut of red and black plaid. One-fourth actual size. Makes a handsome coat for ladies.
Suit $23.00. Either Pattern

New Lace Bottom Hunting Pants showing our pattern of black and brown with green over-plaid.
Price, Pants $8.75, Coat $15.00

SEPT. 1, 1922